A Very Simple Secret

A VERY SIMPLE SECRET

MY PARENTS, THEIR MISSION TO CHANGE THE WORLD, AND ME

Judi Conner

Troubador Publishing Ltd
Unit E2 Airfield Business Park,
Harrison Road, Market Harborough,
Leicestershire LE16 7UL
Tel: 0116 279 2299
Email: books@troubador.co.uk
Web: www.troubador.co.uk

ISBN 978 1 80514 162 4

British Library Cataloguing in Publication Data.
A catalogue record for this book is available from the British Library.

Printed and bound by CPI Group (UK) Ltd, Croydon, CR0 4YY
Typeset in 11pt Minion Pro by Troubador Publishing Ltd, Leicester, UK

For Chérie, Bill and the global family who gave their all,
and for the children who were loved and left

THE POLAR BEAR SONG

*The polar bear breezed in from the North, from the
land of the frozen sea,
With his eyes so bright and his fur so white!
What could his secret be?
Tell us, polar old boy, what can your secret be?*

From the 1950s musical *The Bungle in the Jungle*
music by George Fraser

CONTENTS

PROLOGUE

WEST LONDON 2000

'I'm putting it all together. The history. But there are big gaps. Do you know where I was in the 1950s and '60s?'

The unexpected, sweeping question threw me. It came from my petite 83-year-old mother, seated beside me in the passenger seat of the car I'd just parked. Her eager expression switched to dismay when she saw me freeze.

'What on earth's the matter?' she asked, placing a hand gently on mine. 'Did I say something wrong?'

For a moment I couldn't find words. She'd touched a deep chord that had caught me off-guard. I wanted to stay composed, reassure her and take her safely inside to her flat. But a switch had been flicked and I couldn't stop tears welling up.

Her question was one I couldn't answer. If my mother hadn't been in the early stages of dementia she would have understood. But she was confused, newly-widowed and alone, and I felt protective. I'd learnt to spare her feelings, sometimes avoiding the truth. Yet this time I had to put it plainly.

'There's nothing wrong, this just caught me out. Of course I'll help you with the dates.' I tried to smile, and went on carefully. 'The thing is, those years you're talking about, the 1950s, the early '60s… they were my childhood. They're forgotten years for me too. I don't actually know where you were. You and Daddy were always on the move. We weren't together much. Sometimes we barely knew each other.' There was a pause as she took this in. I added, 'Your question made me sad because I felt abandoned, and I didn't really understand.'

My mother looked forlorn. 'Oh dear,' she sighed with feeling. 'I'm SO sorry.' She searched my eyes, perhaps for signs that I believed her. 'Truly, I'm SO, SO sorry,' she repeated. 'You must have been just a child. On your own.' Now she was dabbing her own eyes with a tissue. Her heartfelt response warmed me. We sat for a few companionable, healing moments, holding hands, gazing through the windscreen into the car park.

Then someone walked out of the apartment block ahead, and the front door slammed noisily behind them. It broke the mood. I checked my face in the visor mirror and returned to the present. 'It's OK. It was ages ago!' I said with forced cheerfulness. 'We're together now! Let's go in, and I'll help you with those dates later.' She looked at me blankly.

Minutes later my mother was settled in her flat. She was always relieved to return to familiar surroundings, and she'd gravitate towards her writing desk, piled with history books, notebooks and Post-its reminding her when to eat or take her pills. She'd quickly forgotten our conversation, and the hospital visit before that.

But her question had planted itself firmly in my mind and was generating others. Where *were* my parents in the 1950s? Where was I? And why did questions about them silence me as if I were hiding a secret? It was too late now for my mother to fill in the gaps in her past, although her attempts to do that, leafing through books and noting dates, kept her happily occupied. One day I'd put the pieces together myself, I decided. I'd work through photo albums, letters and contemporary accounts and find answers. I'd go back to the 1930s when my parents' journey together began, to understand their unusual life choices from their own point of view. Had they ever lived ordinary lives?

With reluctance I realised my own childhood memories also needed unlocking. Those first twelve years of my life, from 1952 to 1964, were missing years for me too. Mine was a separate, parallel story, one I'd preferred to forget. But my mother's moment of awareness in the car when she acknowledged my pain had brought us closer. For the first time I wanted to discover her history, even if it meant facing my own. Even if, sadly, it was too late to share either account with her. I'd narrate the two stories as they unfolded from both sides, leaving others to reach their own conclusions.

Handing my mother a mug of tea that day, I saw her eyes turn to the window to follow a plane descending over the Chiswick rooftops towards Heathrow. 'Of course, most of my family is in Egypt,' she informed me brightly. 'One day soon I'm getting on a plane like that to see them all, and there'll be quite a celebration!'

1

Two Worlds

Bexhill-on-Sea, Sussex, October 1963

I wake with a heavy heart. I try to settle back into the comfort of sleep but a deep foreboding nags at me until I realise: it's my birthday. I stifle the urge to groan aloud for fear of waking my roommates. Yes, it's my eleventh birthday, a date I wish, hopelessly, could be written out of the calendar. Or at least shifted to the school holidays.

In a few minutes Matron will burst through the door, and the silent dormitory will break into the school version of a dawn chorus. High-pitched voices will chirrup and chatter, mixed with deeper ones chanting instructions. I'll be pounced on by friends only too pleased to vary the routine by starting a pillow fight.

The ritual play-battering, generally against the rules, is tolerated on someone's Special Day. At least at this school I won't be given the bruising 'bumps'. At my prep school they allowed us the birthday privilege of being tossed up and down in a blanket like a giant pancake. I lie in bed wondering why we ever put up with it, and realise the discomfort is better than standing out as a 'coward'.

My thoughts are interrupted by Matron's raucous arrival as she urges us out of bed with cries of 'Wakey wakey!' Known affectionately as 'Fifi', she's a straightforward, stocky, kindly woman with a severe pudding basin haircut. I try not to cringe as she declares with a flourish, 'And it's Happy Birthday to a certain someone today! Who can that be?'

Bracing myself, I put on my plucky, bring-it-on face, and bounce to my feet, ready for action. I have good friends in the dorm of six, and play along well. I fend off the volley of pillows flying at me, thrashing back with mock enthusiasm. A chorus of 'Happy birthday to you' starts up in a discordant screech, and I look suitably pained by the usual lyrics: 'You look like a monkey, and you stink like one too!' It's only week five of the autumn term, and we're all new first-years. I have to show them I know the form.

While secretly shrinking from phoney boarding school heartiness, this isn't the part of the day I'm dreading. That will come later, when my other world makes itself felt, and puts me at risk of being found out. This bit's easier. I'll just fling back the mock insults and banter. Stay determinedly cheerful and carefree at all times.

I throw myself into the bustle of getting up, as we queue for chilly toilet cubicles, elbow a space at the washbasins, and hurry back to the dorm in our thick cotton vests and pants. Everyone hurries into their Viyella shirts, gym slips and ties more quickly on a birthday. There's a frisson of raised expectation. Who knows what shared treats and mild rule-bending might be possible? Most days I quite enjoy being launched into the day by Fifi's urgent commands and the rush and tumble. I don't have to think too much. But today my stomach's knotted as we down our porridge and eggs, brush our teeth, make the beds and pack our satchels for class.

Then life starts moving in slow motion. On normal days we'd already be heading out across the blustery clifftop to the main school building, but today we first-years are allowed to linger awhile in the Junior House Common Room. Because it's time to open my presents from home.

It's the moment I dreaded. However tedious double maths may be, I'd rather be heading to the classroom. I don't want to be reminded of presents or home, or to be exposed to questions about either. And as luck would have it, I'm not the only Birthday Girl today. Alone, I might have been able to speed through this bit, cover up with a few jokes and excuses, and quickly escape. But it's also Linda's birthday. Not only will this drag out the proceedings, it will also invite comparisons and draw more unwanted attention.

I'd heard Linda's own pillow fight antics from a neighbouring dorm without giving it much thought. But now the day's become a shared event, making it worse than ever. Linda's parents will do things in the expected way. Her presents will make her special. It's a contest I can't win, and exposure I can't avoid.

Here goes. My dorm friends push me cheerfully into

the Common Room, and we join a jostle of girls already gathered around Linda. Fifi and a young under-matron have pushed together tables in the middle of the room to make space for her heap of brown paper parcels. There are whoops of 'Golly, that's nice!', 'Hey, can I have a go later?', 'How fab!'. Over bobbing heads I glimpse a tennis racket and a stuffed rabbit passing between hands as more parcels are ripped open.

'Come on, let's see what the postman brought YOU!' urges Fifi, directing me to a smaller table bearing two shoebox-shaped packages and three envelopes. I'm determined not to show embarrassment at being a sideshow. My happy swagger switches to an attempt at casual indifference as I reach for the birthday cards, one from my parents, one from my brother, one from Granny and Grandad. 'Go on, open up!' my friend Libs urges, handing me the parcels to unwrap. The gifts are in fact just what I've asked for, and secretly I'm delighted. But here they seem childish. Each tissue-lined box contains a wooden string puppet. One of them looks like a country boy from a fairytale in his lederhosen and jaunty feathered hat. The other puppet is a cute black and white dog. Handled properly, the strings can make them dance, wave, nod and even move their mouths and eyes. I've seen puppets like these on television and in shops, and have imagined putting on shows with them. These will need a bit of work as their strings are tangled. But they could be the start of a collection.

I keep my delight to myself. With their strings knotted, the puppets hang limply and look a mess. Worse still,

Fifi and her colleague are trying to compensate for my paucity of presents with exaggerated enthusiasm. 'What wonderful puppets!' they exclaim. 'I've never seen such good ones!' 'Well, they're Pelham Puppets, which are SO well made!' 'Yes, they're lovely,' agrees Libs. 'We'll have to do a show later!' I do like Libs. She gets things. A couple of girls move over from Linda's table to glance at my gifts before returning to the main spectacle.

I look at my cards, which I'll study and relish on my own. I knew they'd all remember. For my family, that's the most important thing about birthdays when you're far away: remembering. It shows you care. They don't go in for multiple presents, and I wouldn't want them, so I don't mind. What I *do* mind is that everything my family does is always so darned *different* from everybody else.

The matrons look at their watches, and help me pack away the puppets. 'By the time you're back after class we'll have those strings sorted out,' Fifi assures me. I try to look grateful yet not too concerned. The ordeal's almost over. Nobody's asked me about home, or where my parents are, or what they do. Phew!

Libs and I take a look at Linda's table, where her gifts are now stacked, and she's sizing up the toy rabbit. 'I'm much too old for this! What were they thinking?' she laughs, amid protesting cries of 'Ooh I'll look after it!' Linda sits the rabbit beside her star item: a compact portable record player. It looks like a mini suitcase, with a speaker in the lid. A girl cries, 'Yes, yes! It *can* play both EPs and LPs!' and mock hysteria spreads at the thought of real pop music in the Common Room, not just crackly radio programmes. Someone's waving a bag of sweets in one hand, *The Beatles Hits* EP in the other.

'Get cracking, girls!' Fifi's calls are sounding insistent now, and the room clears. We grab our coats and bags and I gratefully melt back into the pack. Crossing the playing field, an icy gale is blowing, and I welcome the chance to let down my guard. The eye-watering blast of sea air easily disguises a few tears of self-pity and relief, and I have a discreet sob behind my upturned collar. Why is life so hard? Why can't I be normal? What happens when I'm found out?

*

São Paulo, Brazil, October 1962

Six thousand miles from England, a British couple pause from their busy schedule to consider a letter they've just received. They look like typical European ex-pats with their well-tanned fair skin and smart summer casuals. One of them, Chérie, re-examines the creased airmail sheet in her hand, not quite able to believe its contents. Her husband Bill puts a calming arm round her shoulder. 'Let's not jump to rash conclusions,' he urges. 'It's all quite unclear, and we've no idea what's actually happened. We'd have heard from your parents if anything was seriously wrong. Just keep your mind and heart on the bigger picture.'

'But you're right, we've no idea at all!' Chérie persists. 'It doesn't make sense. We left behind a confident, well-behaved little girl. She writes us perfectly happy letters. Something doesn't add up.'

'Yep, it almost sounds like the Head has the wrong pupil,' Bill agrees. 'We'll find out more. And seek guidance on it. The Almighty's never let us down yet.' But Chérie remains lost in thought. Perhaps there have been signs and they just haven't noticed them. And how could they have noticed? It's deeply disturbing to realise how distant she is from her children, and how uninformed she may be.

'Bigger picture!' Bill reminds her cheerfully, reaching for a folder and the lightweight jacket that he spends more time carrying than wearing in this subtropical heat. 'We must get to the meeting now though. The traffic's terrible. We'll talk about it later.'

2

London 1938

When Chérie and Bill's paths first crossed, some twenty years earlier, nothing had been further from either of their minds than romance, marriage or raising a family. They had both joined a community in which such conventions were generally considered an impediment, and for the time being they'd effectively renounced all three.

Bill was 23 and Chérie 21, and they were working together in offices in Hays Mews, in the heart of Mayfair. He was publishing books and magazines, she was a secretary, but these were far from standard 9–5 office jobs. They were part of a large, youthful workforce known as the Oxford Group, which lived and worked together, putting in long hours. Later they would both admit to mutual sparks of interest all along, but they could never quite pinpoint the moment they first met.

On her first day, Chérie attended the daily London team meeting in 45 Berkeley Square, which adjoined and fronted the offices at 4 Hays Mews. She was excited to be here at the heart of the Group's British headquarters, and she found a seat at the back of the packed room, ready to be an attentive observer. But the meeting had barely begun before Chérie heard her name called.

'Let's give a big welcome to Chérisy Oram, who's recently arrived from Egypt to join our secretarial team!' said a hearty young Oxbridge type leading the meeting. 'She's an accomplished linguist, we gather! Now where's Chérisy? Please come on up and tell us why you're here!' Chérie's stomach lurched, but she stepped forward, realising this was an inevitable part of her induction. She knew everyone had their own story of how they'd joined the Oxford Group and was expected to make it known.

She'd been getting used to answering questions. Some friends and relatives had asked her bluntly, 'Why on earth are you doing this?' adding, 'Those Buchmanites are pure poison!' … 'They're a cult of religious maniacs.' … 'And they're not even paying you! That's not on for someone with your skills!' Here in this room it wouldn't be so hard to explain herself. She was among converts. Yet she hadn't imagined herself addressing so many people – maybe a hundred – on day one. She wished she'd taken a quick look in a mirror to check her hair and her stocking seams, and she regretted not preparing something sensible to say.

'Well, yes. Thank you,' Chérie launched in, having squeezed her way to the front of the meeting. 'Yes, I was living in Egypt – in Alexandria – where my father was with the Army. I was having a wonderful time, studying Italian to add to my French and German. In fact, I'd just spent a year in Berlin and Wuppertal improving my German, and things were getting difficult there, as you can imagine. But Alex is a beautiful, cosmopolitan city, and life away from Europe seemed carefree and exciting.'

Chérie tried to get to the point. 'I was busy with my course and my friends. There were beach parties and dances, and all I wanted was to have a lot of fun... find a good job using my languages... and eventually a good husband.' She stopped abruptly, blushing a little. Perhaps she shouldn't say that. But there were supportive chuckles around the room and she moved on.

'Then my parents' friends joined the Oxford Group in Alex, and that caused quite a stir, as he ran Barclays Bank in Egypt. I wasn't at all interested. I'd heard the Group made people change to puritanical ways. But my parents started investigating, and I noticed a few things at home. They weren't arguing so much, and they seemed more considerate and trusting of each other, and even of me! I ended up going to a meeting out of curiosity, and was surprised to find young people there, including Egyptians, Italians and French. So I realised it wasn't just for old British codgers like my parents!' Laughter in the room emboldened Chérie further.

'I still didn't see it was for me at first. But I began thinking. Parties were fun at the time, but I'd been in a few tangles...' Her freckled cheeks pinked again as she chose her words with care, not wanting to be too graphic. She tried to blank out the image of an obsessive Italian naval officer and the love affair that went horribly wrong. The desperate, lonely search through the backstreets of

Alex to find an abortionist. The fear her father would find out. Her evasion of the persistent boyfriend whom she'd never really loved. The dread of a good life being diverted forever. It had turned out she wasn't pregnant after all, but the shock had stayed with her, reducing the allure of both the naval officer and her party-girl reputation. She'd found herself wanting to be as happy, innocent and purposeful as the energetic young Oxford Groupers she'd met.

Chérie brushed over the detail. 'I was walking out with a young man,' she said demurely, 'but I kept it from my parents. And I smoked and drank to fit in, not because I wanted to. Someone in the Group persuaded me to try out a "quiet time", tune into God's "guidance" and examine my life in the light of the "four absolute moral standards".' As a result Chérie had made a few changes, even ditching the cigarettes and sundowners, and found she felt different. 'My priorities shifted, and I became more interested in helping other people.'

Finally Chérie told her audience how the Oxford Group had made her think about the forces at work in the world, and the realities around her in Egypt. 'I'd never really noticed the tensions rising in Alexandria,' she admitted. 'Fascism was being promoted at my Italian college – and I'd heard people say the Italians were encouraging Arab nationalism for their own purposes. But even living in Egypt, I hadn't thought much about the Egyptians, and what they wanted for their own country. I started looking at the world differently, and I wanted to help change things for the better. When my course finished I decided to return to Britain and do a secretarial training so I could help out here.'

She wished she'd put it better, but warm applause accompanied Chérie back to her seat. 'Well that's terrific!' the young chair enthused as the clapping subsided. 'We certainly need you, and together we'll definitely change things for the better! Now. Let's hear from the Press Team. What's new from you fellows?'

Afterwards people clustered round Chérie and hands reached in to shake hers. 'Well done, Chérie! Good to meet you. I'm Roly.' 'Glad you'll keep those secretaries on their toes. I'm Kit. You couldn't type me a letter in German today, could you?!' 'I'm Margot, welcome.' 'Edward.' 'Francis. *Ahlan Wa Sahlan!*'

It was a little overwhelming, but thrilling too, to be among these open-hearted, upbeat young people. Chérie felt immediately accepted, and over the next months she found herself extending the same warm welcome to others coming through the London centre. Some were people she hadn't mixed with before, including factory workers, farmers and politicians. 'Every soul is a royal soul,' someone once said in a meeting, and Chérie liked that thought, considering it the essence of Christianity lived in practice.

She also enjoyed the friendly banter among the young men and women. The talk was businesslike and respectful, while allowing for occasional teasing and fun. By contrast, conversations with friends in Berlin and Alexandria had often been laden with flirtatious innuendo as people sized each other up for possible relationships. Chérie found the straight-laced yet genial culture of Hays Mews more comfortable. One male contemporary, Morris Martin, later described it as 'an early glimmer of feminism, or at least of treating women as equals, as friends, instead of sex objects or sources of temptation'.

Yet this didn't stop Chérie feeling drawn like a magnet to one particular member of the book team. Over communal meal tables and evenings stuffing envelopes, she'd come to realise that she and Bill shared similar backgrounds. Both had Irish family connections in County Cork, both had undergone governess and boarding education, and both had a father who was, or had been, a British Army colonel.

At first Bill had seemed a little quiet. She noticed he wasn't among the high-profile young men leading meetings, rallies and campaigns, or reporting back on their conversations in Parliament and Fleet Street. But he had a dapper dress sense and an endearing way of switching from serious talk to a mischievous aside, which made her melt at the knees.

'Did you hear what those two got up to yesterday?' another secretary asked her once, when Bill and Peter, a photographer friend, had just passed through their office. 'They staged a drunken exit from the Coach and Horses over the road! In fact, they hadn't even had an orange juice, but they staggered out of the pub door, arm in arm, singing *Show me the way to go home* as if they were completely corked! Apparently they'd seen Stephen and Roly coming up the road, and they did it deliberately – all because they thought those chaps were getting a bit over-earnest and needed some joshing!' The story was told with a hint of disapproval, but it made Chérie smile. It's easy to conform here, she thought to herself. This showed some spirit and she liked Bill's maverick style.

In time, Chérie found out more about Bill. Once she heard him telling visitors how he'd first heard of the Oxford Group in his last year at school. His mother had walked into the wrong Oxford college looking for a horticultural meeting, and had come across a Group house party going on. It was one of many held through the 1930s all over the country to recruit new followers. Bill's mother had been so struck by the cheerful, motivated young people running the event that she determined to get her own teenagers involved.

On dishwashing duty one night, Chérie found herself scrubbing plates and polishing cutlery with Bill and a few others. When a natural opening arose in their casual chat, Chérie asked Bill about his first impressions of the Group. 'Oh, I was frightened to death at the first meeting I was dragged along to!' Bill responded without hesitation. 'I was still at school, and the four standards shocked me! It put me off for a while. But my sister Erica and cousin Agnes were keen. So they sat at the front of that meeting, while my younger brother and I sat at the back, terrified the girls might get up and "share" something embarrassing! I left full of criticism, and if you'd told me then that I'd be working with those cranks after Cambridge I'd have laughed at you!'

'That was rather the same for me in Alexandria,' Chérie smiled, as she and other colleagues pitched in with their own 'first impressions' tales.

It wasn't until he'd been halfway through university that Bill found himself wanting to know more about the Oxford Group. Life at Cambridge had suited him well at first. He enjoyed studying history, listening to the lectures of G. M. Trevelyan, Arnold Toynbee and John Maynard Keynes by day, and discussing politics into the night. Life was unpressured, sociable, and his rooms at Corpus Christi College were in the heart of the city. Bill loved the cheery, Woosteresque exchanges batted to and fro as he passed friends in the courts or King's Parade. 'Baxter!' 'Conner, no less! Quick pint?' 'Can't, old bean. Tutor.' 'After rugger? Eagle at six?' 'Top-hole!'

Before long he'd upgraded from owning a motorbike to a car, a 1927 Alvis 12/50. It was his pride and joy, and a huge social asset. 'You've no idea the effect of that old bus going down King's Parade with the colleges up each side,' Bill would recall. 'You'd change down and scatter the mob with a noise like a Zeppelin. It was tremendous for the ego.'

Then it had all started to feel a bit empty. He began noticing distinct philosophical camps around him, which made him wonder about his own beliefs. The Oxford Group had a strong following among undergraduates, and he cautiously agreed to let one of them call on him in his college rooms. This visitor asked Bill one day, straight out, 'What are you living for? Everyone's guided by something, all the time! What about you?!' He'd challenged Bill to try out the idea of being 'guided by God', a proposition Bill thought very distasteful yet couldn't get out of his mind.

Initially Bill had gravitated towards the sports

hearties, joining the college rugby club. But this was the turbulent mid-1930s, and he found most of his companions apparently unbothered about the political and economic crises deepening by the day. In 1934, the year he went up to Cambridge, three million people were unemployed, hunger marches on London had taken place, and the capitalist system appeared to be failing. Bill was interested in possible solutions, and groups as varied as Marxists, evangelicals and fascists were speaking out about rebuilding the world and changing the course of history in their lifetime. Far from feeling powerless in the face of global crisis, many undergraduates in the 1930s saw themselves as players who could impact the future, stop wars, shake governments. Bill became fascinated by the ferment of ideas around him, and the idea of fighting for a cause.

A growing number of undergraduates, despairing at the state of the capitalist West, had become interested in the Russian model of a new society. The Cambridge Union had recently voted through a motion that 'this house sees more hope in Moscow than Detroit', Detroit being considered the heartbeat of capitalism. The poet Cecil Day-Lewis wrote in his autobiography that it was hard to convey 'how much hope there was in the air then, how radiant for some of us was the illusion that man could, under communism, put the world to rights'.

For many this remained an ideal to live and die for. Among the best-known Cambridge communists of the 1930s, centred at Trinity College, were Anthony Blunt, Guy Burgess, Donald Maclean and Kim Philby, soon to be recruited as Soviet spies. These men had graduated before Bill arrived at Cambridge, but among his contemporaries in their circle was the poet John Cornford, who died fighting fascism in the Spanish Civil War alongside other British communists. Cornford's poems reflect his passionate belief that '*We are the future. The last fight let us face*'.

At the opposite end of the political spectrum was Oswald Mosley's British Union of Fascists (BUF) or 'blackshirts', founded in 1933 in an attempt to emulate the successes of Hitler, Mussolini and Franco. The BUF's exploitation of the nation's problems to whip up populism and anti-semitism had no appeal for Bill or many other Cambridge undergraduates. But Moseley's huge rallies and the fierce backlash they provoked from the Left underlined the ambitions of two extreme ideologies, intent on winning the war of ideas.

And now, joining in the fray was the controversial, self-proclaimed 'third way': the Oxford Group. Bill could see why the Group had a bad press, with its worthy talk of absolute moral standards and listening to God, but he decided to explore it further. He discovered that they'd started as a small Christian revivalist campaign in the 1920s. They aimed to live the teaching of Jesus in the simple ascetic ways of the first-century pre-Church Christians, to impact society for the better. The Oxford Group's founder and leader, Dr Frank Buchman, was an American Lutheran pastor. His words came over as an outspoken visionary, a prophet even, but in photos Bill thought he looked ordinary and unassuming in plain suits and wire-framed glasses, not the archetypal charismatic American leader at all. When Bill eventually met Buchman, this impression was confirmed. The man was a kind, gentle-mannered listener, yet sharply perceptive and direct in his speech. Bill particularly admired his global understanding, and his belief that any one person could help change the world.

Prior to Buchman's targeting of British universities for recruits in the 1930s, he'd travelled the world developing his idea that practical Christianity could transform society. Buchman raised a few eyebrows in the Church by simplifying the theological language he'd grown up with and studied. He never dismissed anyone's desire for particular rituals, churches or religions. But above all he believed the world needed spiritual revolutionaries who'd unite across their differences to tackle corruption, discord and poverty. His vision was a 'hate-free, greed-free, fear-free world under God'.

The task, Buchman argued, was urgent because totalitarian ideologies on the rise around the world would stifle faith, freedom and human respect. Buchman saw both communism and fascism as dangerous, materialist ideologies that fed on people's fears, self-interest or apathy, and ultimately led to war and dictatorship. Democracy, he believed, could only flourish when people lived by shared moral values and followed a higher authority: God, conscience, inner voice, or however that may be understood.

At the heart of the work was the idea of 'life-changing'. Anyone could start by changing themselves, then they could change others, and change the world. The process started with a person acknowledging the places in their own life that needed an overhaul. This was achieved by using a checklist of four 'absolute' moral standards: absolute honesty, absolute purity, absolute unselfishness and absolute love, considered to be a distillation of Christ's Sermon on the Mount. Where personal changes needed to be made, they should be shared with a friend for support, and restitution applied wherever possible.

A 'changed' person should dedicate themself to following the guidance of their inner voice, or God. In practical terms, this was achieved by having 'quiet times', listening to that inner voice, pen and paper in hand, ready to write any thoughts down. If they were open to it, a person would be guided in the choices they made and in the direction of their lives. The practice became known as 'having guidance', and thoughts had to be shared and checked with teammates. The new path taken was to be not simply a private journey, but one pursued in fellowship with others, and passed on widely.

Nowadays the approach is familiar to those following the 12-Step or Alcoholics Anonymous (AA) programmes, and this is no coincidence. Around the time Chérie and Bill were trying out the ideas in the mid-1930s, a couple of Oxford Group members in the United States were adapting the same tenets to create the AA strategy. More recently the use of AA's 12 steps has been widely extended to treat addictions to drugs, sex, food and gambling. Chérie and Bill would have been interested to see how closely these programmes reflect Buchman's original template for turning one's life around. Seeking a higher power, acknowledging mistakes, making amends, helping others, are all there.

In a spirit of enquiry Bill finally decided, within the privacy of his college rooms at Cambridge, to give the idea of a life audit a go. Later he wrote of this pivotal moment: 'I thought about the question of what guided me. My car was high on the list, also my future career, marriage and money. I got hold of a notebook and pencil and tried to make my mind available for some form of inspiration.

'To my great surprise', he continued, 'I soon got a very clear thought. I thought that the main thing guiding my life was what people thought about me, how to be popular, how to be in with everybody. That led fairly soon to a thought about alcohol. I didn't like the stuff much, but one had to drink to "keep in". So I made the decision I'd no longer be run by what people thought. I would stop drinking.

'That was fine for about two days, and then at dinner one night the rugby captain came in. He'd had a drink or two already and he called out, "Drinks on me tonight!". A waiter came round and I said, "I'm not drinking." All hell broke loose. Tumblers banged on the table and one fellow shouted, "If Bill doesn't drink, nobody drinks!" All very embarrassing! But I didn't lose friends through that decision, in fact the exact opposite. I don't think they all understood what I was after, but many of them supported it'.

Tougher decisions were to come. Turning down his regular evenings at The Eagle was a struggle. From his rooms in Corpus Christi he could see his friends socialising in the pub courtyard below. It wasn't just the drink he was giving up but the girls he met there. After an all-male school and now at an all-male college, he enjoyed these encounters.

'I thought, "Am I chucking up everything that's interesting in life and going after a spectre?" For two hours a tremendous turmoil went on inside me. I don't know why, but it ended in a remarkable way, because I prayed that night, and made a decision that as far as I was concerned, I was not going into the market for sex from that time onwards. The extraordinary thing was that I very soon found myself getting much more interested in other people. I began to experience what I think psychologists call sublimation. Many creative people in history have found the sex drive doesn't have to preoccupy your mind. It had obsessed mine for long periods. But it could be part of a great creative development in one's life'.

Bill had left Cambridge in 1937 and joined dozens of other young volunteers working with the Oxford Group. The impending threat of war in Europe gave them an added sense of urgency. At Hays Mews Bill helped publish and circulate worldwide the Oxford Group's books, with titles like *For Sinners Only* by A. J. Russell, *When Man Listens* by Cecil Rose, *The Philosophy of Courage* by Philip Leon and *Life Began Yesterday* by Stephen Foot. These all explained and promoted the Oxford Group. There were also pamphlets, and a million and a half copies of *The Rising Tide,* a pictorial magazine that was being translated into nine languages when Bill joined the publishing team.

This was a formative time in the growth of the Oxford Group. In 1938, the Group became an incorporated charity. Up to this point Frank Buchman had enjoyed minimal red tape and structure in his work, but the rising scale of donations and expenses now required formalised records. At the same time supporters across the country had donated to the purchase of a 99-year-lease on 45 Berkeley Square, with 4 Hays Mews behind it, to be a London centre with offices, accommodation and entertaining space. In previous years Dr Buchman had worked from a suite at the nearby Brown's Hotel, rented at a bargain rate. But more space was needed now that the Group had stepped up its outreach and its volunteer numbers were rising.

Buchman himself travelled constantly, keeping pace with other centres of activity not just in North America and Europe but across the world. When in London he kept in close contact with all his full-timers, but made it plain the work depended on each of the workers themselves. There was no formal hierarchy. No contracts. No pay, although living expenses were covered by donations. Buchman led on strategy and was the central point of authority, but he expected everyone to share responsibility, keep him informed of their activities, and live on 'faith and prayer'. Teamwork and problem-solving were achieved through frequent quiet times to find consensus. 'Go for *what's* right, not *who's* right,' he urged them.

Apart from the insistence on moral standards there were few formal rules. Communal life was new to everyone, and nobody could claim to be an expert, although many brought with them valuable professional skills. Uniting the team was the firm belief that history was at a crucial turning point – and a better world could be built if they gave everything they had.

As pioneer workers at the London headquarters, Chérie and Bill witnessed another development in June 1938, when the Oxford Group entered a new global phase and acquired a different name. Amidst increasing international tension, Frank Buchman wrote at the time, 'I am trying to find an approach that will give the message more intelligently to an age that needs it but is desperately afraid of it'. His biographer Garth Lean, who was then on the Group's press team, writes, 'He was looking for a thought that was simple enough for millions to grasp and realistic enough for national leaders to put forward. He also wanted to shake those who, having found a rich personal experience of faith through the Oxford Group, were hugging it to themselves, and to persuade them to enter the struggle to answer the problems of the wider world'.

Finally, Buchman was inspired by a Swedish friend, who, responding to the European nations re-arming for possible war, was calling on Sweden to re-arm itself morally and become a reconciling force. Buchman seized on the idea. He saw 'moral and spiritual re-armament' as the perfect vision of how to respond to world crises, and the only way for democracies to stay strong in the face of a totalitarian threat.

A few days later Buchman had been due to address a meeting of 3,000 people in East Ham Town Hall in London, hosted by several local mayors. Buchman took the opportunity to launch the new campaign for moral re-armament. 'The world's condition cannot but cause disquiet and anxiety,' he told the gathering. 'The crisis is fundamentally a moral one... Hostility piles up between nation and nation, labour and capital, class and class... The remedy may lie in a return to those simple home truths that some of us learned at our mother's knee... honesty, purity, unselfishness, love... We can, we must and we will generate a moral and spiritual force that is powerful enough to remake the world.'

Bill in his book team and Chérie in the secretarial pool were now promoting Moral Re-Armament, or MRA, rather than the Oxford Group. Buchman developed his theme at the first MRA assembly in Sweden a couple of months later, challenging his audiences to go beyond religious revival, into the realms of revolution and renaissance. For some supporters this was a step too far. They didn't like Buchman's dismissal of 'goose-fleshy Christians with their armchair Christianity' and they parted company. But Chérie and Bill and many others embraced the wider vision with even more enthusiasm. Over the next years their terminology became less explicitly Christian as the work spread across non-European cultures and beliefs and reached out to agnostics and atheists, but with the same central message: change lives, remake the world.

Against this backdrop the Hays Mews team focused firmly on their goal rather than their personal lives. But when Chérie confided in girlfriends about her feelings for Bill, she found she wasn't the only woman drawn to one of the young men, and some 'special friendships' were common knowledge. The understanding was that this was natural, but that such feelings must be surrendered and God's guidance awaited. In view of a possible war their work came first, and affairs of the heart were collectively pushed to the backburner.

Chérie was still able, as time went on, to find out more about Bill and his family, which he mentioned very little. She'd noticed people sometimes treating him protectively, and he didn't often push himself forward in meetings, despite his confidence and wealth of ideas. She was curious, sensing on occasions a shadow hiding the cheery, mischievous façade that had first caught her attention.

Her observation turned out to be right. 'Don't put Bill on the spot too much,' someone quietly advised Chérie after seeing her question him on a seemingly trivial matter. 'We need to give him space. He went through a dreadful time recently, although he'd never let on.' Seeing Chérie's concern, the friend opened up further. 'Well… perhaps you should know since you work together,' she added. 'But please remember, it's not common knowledge.'

Chérie then learnt the part of Bill's story that he kept well concealed. She was already aware of his early childhood in Ireland, where his father, Colonel William Conner, had been a Protestant landowner and magistrate in County Cork. Although his Irish bloodline went back to ancient times, the retired British Army colonel's loyalties lay firmly with Britain, and he was a prime target for the Irish Republican Army in their fight for independence. In 1921 the family had fled for their lives as neighbouring country houses were burnt down around them. Homeless for a year, they'd finally resettled in Malvern, Worcestershire.

While this much was public knowledge, secrecy surrounded the fact that Bill's much-loved mother Maye, herself an Oxford Grouper, had died under tragic circumstances in 1936 while Bill was at Cambridge. Maye had never fully recovered from the family's expulsion from Ireland, and suffered bouts of depression that became more frequent and intense following her husband death a few years later. During one spiral of despair Maye had locked herself in her bedroom, overdosed on her medicine and hanged herself. And it was Bill, with his younger brother Arthur, who'd discovered their mother's body, after climbing a ladder and breaking in through her bedroom window.

Maye's sisters and her Oxford Group friends had rallied round Maye's children, whose distress was exacerbated by the fact that suicide was then a criminal offence, and a sin according to the Church. Bereaved families in these cases were often shunned, and the taboo around suicide made it hard, in an already inhibited age, to grieve openly. The tragedy was additionally hushed up for fear of sensational press headlines linking it to the Oxford Group. So Maye's death was kept quiet, and even within the Group itself few people knew about it, or of Bill's ordeal.

Chérie's heart went out to Bill when she heard this. The heartbreak of losing his mother like this seemed to explain so much: his reticence, his ability to compartmentalise, his bursts of caustic humour. The trauma must also have impacted Bill's time at Cambridge, she thought, not least his change of heart about the Oxford Group soon after it happened. Presumably he'd found support in this tight-knit, caring fellowship, and his new spiritual path helped ease his grief and guilt. Perhaps the all-encompassing commitment had come as a timely distraction. Or was it something of a parting gift to Maye, who'd longed for her four children to champion the Oxford Group with her? Musing on these possibilities, Chérie kept the revelation to herself. But she hoped one day she could reach out to help him. Far from putting her off, she was even more fascinated by this young man.

Sometimes Chérie sensed Bill's guard slipping a little. Occasional shared glances and asides seemed to indicate a hint of an understanding between them. And even Bill admitted much later that he'd once left a copy of Shakespeare's *Sonnets* on his desk so that Chérie might appreciate his sensitive side. But any brief displays of feathers were not to be followed up for several years now, because suddenly the world was at war, and the close community at Hays Mews was about to scatter in all directions.

3

Country House

Sussex 1957

Mummy and Daddy were on a mission. What it was I didn't know or care when I was four years old. I just knew it was urgent and important because they were always busy. They wrote in notebooks, made phone calls, went off to meetings and talked over long grown-up meals.

The mission, sometimes called 'the battle', had to come first, and it never stopped. It took Mummy and Daddy away to other countries, and sometimes they sent postcards or brought me back a present. When I saw them again I knew they wouldn't stay long. They'd be off again soon.

My first inkling that others might consider my life unusual didn't come until I was six years old. At that point a trivial incident at school made me aware we were 'different' and that made me anxious. But up until then, like most very young children, I took life as it came and enjoyed myself. I had no idea it was strange to live apart from my parents and my brother, and to have no family home. Mummy and Daddy always came back eventually. It felt normal to move from place to place, living with friends. It felt normal to only rarely see my brother Patrick, who was five years older than me. I wasn't quite sure where he was, but assumed he was 'away at school' like most older children.

Snippets of early recollections, endorsed or inspired by battered black-and-white photographs, place me in London parks, a room with a rocking horse and books, a small paddling pool on a roof terrace, sometimes with Patrick. After that my memories are more plentiful, opening out into complete cameo scenes. In these I'm living in the countryside, in a world of picnics, ponies, pigs, dressing-up clothes, stone ginger beer bottles and story books. Where the sun was always shining.

It was 1957, and I was living with the Pelham Burn family in a large house called Elenge Plat, deep in the Sussex countryside. It was a happy, carefree time, immersed in adventures with Amelia, the youngest of seven siblings.

Amelia had a breezy, confident air and a radiant smile. She was more than a year older than me but we got on famously. There were no fights that I recall, nor any apparent resentment by Amelia of my cuckoo-ish presence in her family nest. We generally made our own entertainment, but we were never far from the protective eyes of Mary, Amelia's 21-year-old sister who was my carer, or their mother Pamela, who was In Charge of Everyone. Aunt

Pamela was serenely unflappable, combining effortless elegance with a warm heart and a gentle tinkly laugh.

But it was Mary who was the significant adult in my life: cheerful, creative, dependable Mary. She had wavy light-brown hair and wore neat blouses and cardigans with skirts and sensible shoes. I saw her as roughly the same age as her own mother, or my mother, so it seemed most unlikely to me that she was really Amelia's sister, but I took their word for it.

'Mary looks after me,' I'd say with conviction if someone asked me the whereabouts of my parents, and if that didn't satisfy the enquirer it always satisfied me. I didn't know the word 'carer', and I knew Mary wasn't a nanny or nurse like the ones Christopher Robin had, because they wore uniforms and weren't part of the family. Most grown-ups I had to call 'Aunt' or 'Uncle', but Mary was simply 'Mary' and the distinction didn't bother me. The important thing was to know who, at any given time, looked after me, and for now it was Mary. I never thought of Aunt Pamela, or her husband Uncle Ian, or Mary as replacement parents. But I did feel happily one of their family, and I loved them and all the sons and daughters who came with them.

Having a constantly-available best friend like Amelia was the key reason I felt so much at home. And the fact that she seemed to know the ropes was a special bonus. With her extra age and experience, I relied on her for a knowledgeable steer and lots of fun. I took her advice on everything, and never regretted the consequences.

'Now, drink up that chocolate milk, you'll need much more than that,' Amelia instructed me one hot summer afternoon. We'd been running around outside in bare feet, stripped to our shorts, then rolling in the long grass to cool off. Chatting away on the random topic of vomiting, I had rashly confided that I didn't know what it felt like to throw up. I couldn't remember ever doing such a thing. Amelia immediately thought of a quick remedy to fill this gap in my life experience. She didn't want to inflict pain or discomfort, I know. But there was a logical way to experiment.

She mixed up a large jug of chocolate milk, probably helped by someone in the kitchen, and I sat in the garden, eagerly drinking mug after mug of the delicious stuff. Easy! Next, I climbed into the rope hammock slung between two silver birch trees by the paddock, and Amelia began to swing me vigorously. 'Are you sick yet?!' she called after every push. 'NO!!!' I yelled back as I swung faster and higher. It was hilarious until the queasiness set in. And then it happened! Being sick really wasn't so bad, I thought, as Amelia brought the hammock to a quick standstill. I felt so much better getting rid of all that chocolate milk, and the experiment was a success. We were both delighted.

As we lay giggling and messy on the grass, Mary appeared and threw a bucketful of cold water over my bare chest to clean me up. She was undoubtedly cross, and Amelia was probably told off, but I don't recall any harsh words spoken. The adults generally stayed calm, while making it very clear that there were consequences for overstepping the mark. Slapping was the usual punishment for misbehaviour, and Mary occasionally delivered a brief smack on the leg, but this was neither painful nor something to dread. In fact, Amelia and I sometimes consciously weighed up the risks of a dubious activity, and prepared to face a slap or telling-off if it seemed worth it.

One day we'd watched Mary tidy up a first aid box, and we imagined the delights of taking apart its contents and using the bandages and plasters to transform ourselves into hospital patients. Mary could read our thoughts. 'This is not a toy, it's for real emergencies ONLY,' she said firmly. 'Leave it on the shelf and don't touch it or you'll get a smack!'

As soon as Mary had left the room, Amelia and I looked at each other and knew what had to be done. We reached for the box and pulled out the rolls of dressings, a tin of Elastoplast, packs of lint and cotton wool, tiny coloured bottles and tubes of cream. We fingered, squeezed and sniffed them all, and tested the shiny scissors, tweezers and safety pins. Everything smelt fresh, like new soap. Then we set to work. Amelia was the nurse, while I was the patient. Bandages were unrolled, plasters cut up, and soon my arms and legs were well patched and swathed in dressings.

We were rarely furtive in our activities, and the incident ended predictably. Mary found us admiring our handiwork amid the debris of her first aid box, and she looked exasperated. Slaps followed speedily, but we had no doubts at all that the experiment, however brief, had been infinitely worth it.

People constantly came and went at Elenge Plat: family members, visitors and the cheerful Mrs Mantle, who came in on weekdays to cook, and whose bristly chin fascinated me. 'Mrs Mantle, you've got a beard!' I told her once, loudly, and Amelia, half amused and half horrified, shushed me up firmly. I wouldn't say it again because Amelia knew these things. But I couldn't imagine why it was wrong.

Amelia's father Ian was a kindly, slightly reserved ex-army major who ran a pig farm with the help of a farm manager. If he wasn't in his office, Uncle Ian could be seen either heading out of the kitchen door in his farm jacket, boots and cap, or out of the front door in a suit and hat if he was 'off to town'. We mainly saw him over meals, taken in the kitchen or at the long oak dining table. Every day he'd read *The Times* and the *Daily Worker* newspaper. I could read the big headlines, but the dense, pictureless columns of small print looked too boring to even attempt.

Periodically Amelia's and Mary's other brothers and sisters would appear. Libby and Henry were the oldest, and they did whatever grown-ups go away to do, while Vicky, Sarah and Johnnie came home from boarding school for their holidays. Occasionally my own brother turned up too. Patrick would play with Johnnie, Sarah and Vicky, who were closer to his age, but I loved having him in the house for a while. Amid the bustle, Coral, the miniature dachshund, would trot across the wooden floors behind Aunt Pamela as if tied to her ankles. Returning family were greeted with Coral's delighted yelps and 'excitement puddles' in the hall.

When the sounds of footsteps, doors and crunching gravel on the drive indicated particular busyness, there were always quiet places to retreat to. Amelia and I played in all corners of the house and gardens. Our main indoor play space was Amelia's bedroom, which had one door through to her parents' room and another opening onto the long corridor, which ran, as we sometimes did, the whole length of the first floor. My own bedroom was on the second floor, in a row of small rooms with gabled windows in the roof. This floor was approached by a narrow back staircase rising from the kitchen area. My cosy room next door to Mary's was the scene of our soothing bedtime story and prayers routine.

Another favourite place was the drawing room. This was used when the household was large or visitors came for tea, and it had a carpet and upholstered seats. A large wooden box on a side table contained rows of slim shiny discs, each silky-smooth to the touch. I was told they were used in adult card games, but they seemed more like exquisite jewels. They were for stroking and examining, far too beautiful to play with.

In term-times Amelia and I went to school, but unlike her siblings we travelled there and back each day and slept at home. Mary or Aunt Pamela would drive us to a bus stop every morning, and wave us off to St Christopher's School in Horsham. One day we were chatting so hard we missed the school stop. The driver must have been new, as it was only on his return to the depot that he found us still at the rear of the bus and drove us safely back for our classes.

In the school holidays we weren't always left to our own devices, and Mary was good at keeping us occupied. We had walks to pick wild flowers in the woods, and learnt to be 'ballboys' on a neighbour's tennis court. There were occasional outings to point-to-points or the seaside. Sometimes we were walked along a country road to a tiny shop selling ginger beer in stoneware bottles. Best of all were the picnics. Whatever the weather, there were always picnics, whether in woodland, a field or on a stony beach. The location was less important to me than the adventure of creating a camp with coats, blankets and hampers, and the ritual of unwrapping countless packages to reveal their treasures: sandwiches, hard-boiled eggs, and cake.

Most afternoons Aunt Pamela would serve tea for everyone from a tray rattling with delicate cups and saucers. Her tea had a delicious smoky perfume, and Amelia and I would dunk sugar cubes into it, and munch buttered French bread slices sprinkled with 'hundreds and thousands', demerara sugar or, in summer, fairy-sized wild strawberries.

Even better than teatime was the reading aloud from story books, which took place after lunch if we weren't at school. In summer we'd often lounge on blankets on the sunny terrace steps. Other family members or visitors might join us, and Coral the dachshund would lick any salty bare arms and legs she could find as we sat or lay around listening. I'd scarcely notice her, losing myself in the absorbing worlds of these stories.

In larger groups we'd read big books with long words, like Kenneth Grahame's *Wind in the Willows* or Rudyard Kipling's *Just So Stories*. If it was just us two younger girls we had shorter, simpler books. I loved stories about animals who wore clothes, or favourite toys who came alive and went on adventures. Little Grey Rabbit, Hare and Squirrel, created by Alison Uttley, felt like personal friends, as did Ivy L Wallace's *Animal Shelf* toys, a stuffed zebra, puppy, giraffe and fez-wearing monkey who lived in a boy's bedroom. The Beatrix Potter tales *The Pie and the Patty-pan* and *Mrs Tiggywinkle* also felt real to me, despite their scary hint of danger and deceit. A. A. Milne's poems were fun, and the adventures of Ant and Bee. The Ameliaranne Stiggins books were another top choice, featuring a plucky girl I imagined to be just like *my* Amelia, who helped her impoverished washerwoman mother look after her five brothers and sisters. Other favourites were *Little Black Sambo* about an Indian Tamil boy, and the stories of *Babar the Elephant* in Africa. Now discredited for promoting racial stereotypes and colonial superiority, these were thought, in the 1950s, to be introducing children to the wider world.

Being read to by Henry, Amelia's tall, lanky oldest brother, who also told his own quirky stories, was particularly blissful. He was the cleverest, funniest person I could imagine and I believed every word he said. At breakfast one morning I announced dramatically, 'Henry was born in the olden days!' 'Oh, really?' someone responded politely. The family always took a four-year-old seriously, or at least played along well. 'It's true!' I went on with a flourish. 'He TOLD me so!' And the power of the statement hung in the air, unquestioned, while everyone pretended to be hugely impressed.

As far as I was concerned, all grown-ups knew what they were doing, and of course I neither questioned nor expected to understand them. Words flew around above my head: 'fighting', 'battle', 'the work', 'God', 'guidance', 'miracles' – words that came as easily to Mary, Aunt Pamela and Uncle Ian as they did to Mummy and Daddy. I had no idea that the world was being put together again after the upheavals of a global war, and that for all these people in my universe the fight went on. I was happy and oblivious to any life beyond this place. 'Mummy and Daddy have important work to do for now,' I'd be reminded from time to time, 'but they'll be back soon.'

4

Britain, Middle East 1939–45

Chérie stood up to stretch her back and survey the long rows of cabbages ahead of her. It was a sunny afternoon in June 1942. At the far end of the field her friends Elisabeth, Mary and Margot were bent over their work, while Heather steered a laden wheelbarrow towards the truck taking their produce to market next morning. My turn for a hot bath tonight, Chérie thought cheerfully. There should be time for a soak before high tea and an evening at the typewriter.

Stooping again over the crops with her knife, she enjoyed the sun's warmth on her back. As a child she'd disliked her freckles. But now as an outdoor working girl – a land girl, no less – she prized her weather-beaten skin. She felt fortunate to be playing her part in the war effort in the rolling Cheshire countryside among good friends. Market gardening hadn't quite the *cachet* of fighting on the front, but she felt as much a part of the battle as Bill and the other young men. Chérie wished Bill could see her now in her shirtsleeves and jodhpurs, with a streak of her brown curls bleached by the sun. Perhaps one day he'd see photos. *If* this war ever ends. *If* he returns. She stopped the train of thought abruptly. *Stay positive. Focus on the task at hand.*

While Chérie picked cabbages in Cheshire, Corporal Bill was seated in a lounge of Shepheard's Hotel in Cairo, enjoying the breeze from a ceiling fan. After a morning of guard duty and lectures he'd slipped into the city to meet his friends Tom Shillington and Geoffrey Currell over tea. It was almost like old times in Cambridge or London, but now they all sported severe army haircuts and sat straight-backed in their uniforms. The three had met at university through the Oxford Group. Now Geoff was at Cairo's General Headquarters supervising records and casualty details for the Royal Sussex, and Tom was back from a first stint in the desert with the Royal Tank Regiment. Bill had just joined the 8th Kings Royal Irish Hussars and expected to see action soon.

'Well, who'd have thought it?' Tom laughed as a pianist and singer started up in the next room. 'Thousands of miles from Mayfair, and they're playing our tune – or should we say *your* tune, Bill?!' They all smiled at the strains of *A Nightingale Sang in Berkeley Square*, and Tom and Geoff sang along nostalgically, while Bill ignored the pointed teasing. 'This place is too British by far,' he said, steering the topic away from himself. He was familiar with Tom's chummy attempts to further his romantic interest in Chérie, but they had no place here. There was a war on. 'Better "too British" than have *Gute Nacht Mutter* sung at Shepheard's if Rommel makes it this far,' Geoff chipped in.

'Anyway, let's get down to business. I can't stay long.' A tray of tea and sandwiches sat before them and there was news and guidance to share.

For the MRA team, the war of ideas and World War Two had merged into a single battle when the hostilities had begun three years earlier. Until the last minute they'd hoped their work might bring people together to avert conflict. But once war was declared, the task became defeating the forces of materialism and oppression.

Bill had been at Hays Mews on Sunday 3rd September 1939 when Prime Minister Neville Chamberlain announced on the radio that Britain was at war. After the broadcast Bill had walked out into the London streets to take it all in. It wasn't a surprise. Germany had invaded Poland two days earlier, blackout precautions were already in place, and most people had assumed war was inevitable. But it was still a dramatic turning point, and Bill hoped to be in uniform as soon as possible.

As he headed towards Piccadilly, the mournful wail of air raid sirens started up almost immediately. 'I remember walking casually, if not entirely slowly, to the nearest shelter,' he wrote later, 'wondering if this heralded the arrival of some monstrous form of new warfare, with new weaponry of destruction. But in fact nothing happened, and the all-clear sirens went off moments later'. Bill wasn't alone in fearing the worst. British politician Harold Macmillan recalled how he and his contemporaries 'thought of air warfare in 1938 rather as people think of nuclear warfare today'.

Over the next days, Bill determined to follow his

brother and father and many Oxford Group colleagues into the army. He'd been in the Officers' Training Corps at school and hoped to be considered officer material. But his plan was dutifully postponed when he realised the MRA team in London needed to keep up its numbers. Frank Buchman had cabled them from America, reminding them that their work was also an essential part of the war effort, and at the start of the war the Oxford Group was among selected charities, NGOs and churches exempt from military service. So for the time being Bill joined the 29 others in MRA's London team who, although eligible for conscription, continued their work. The remaining staff, including Chérie, continued to live and work at Hays Mews, converting the cellars beneath their offices into dormitories for use during air attacks. Bill and his friend Tom Shillington took on additional air raid warden duties around the Berkeley Square neighbourhood.

As it turned out, that first year was to be the quietest period of the war, while the pace of work at Hays Mews accelerated. In the book department, Bill and his colleagues produced literature to encourage people fighting on all fronts: at home, in the forces, in factories and on farms. One of their pamphlets was *Come Wind, Come Weather* by the author Daphne du Maurier. Published in August 1940, it was a collection of stories about people inspired by MRA, and called for the country to join them in 'arming with faith and fortitude to face the future'.

Chérie and the other secretaries kept communications flowing with colleagues around the world, including those now in the forces. Meanwhile a national campaign was launched across British cities, sponsored by 360 mayors and provosts, to raise morale and promote a united front. The press team worked hard to publicise the campaigns, while also trying to counter MRA's critics. Rumours had spread that Frank Buchman was pro-Nazi and his workers conscientious objectors, too unpatriotic or afraid to fight.

The false claims rankled intensely with Bill and his friends. They also led to a new face being seen around Hays Mews, that of the *Daily Express* journalist Peter Howard, who decided to investigate the Oxford Group for himself. Howard was known for his biting political commentaries, but Frank Buchman had trained the team to be bold, and the household let this firebrand live with them for a few weeks. In time Howard's initial scepticism about the Group changed into appreciation. 'The members treated me exactly as though I were a member of their fellowship', he wrote. 'Even if you disliked these people, you could not, if you surveyed the scene with an open mind, distrust them. Sincere goodwill one to another – and indeed to everyone – radiated every room and person in the dwelling. There was a stimulating air about the place'.

Having expected to find cranks, Howard found the place abuzz with 'ordinary, everyday people from every corner of life'. He described meeting 'businessmen, secretaries, Tommies, as well as Army officers, Naval officers and Naval ratings, a trade unionist organiser or so, agents of political parties, fitters, riggers and pilot officers, several MPs, a couple of journalists apart from myself, and some clerks and other rather dim City workers who came in at the end of the day's work and joined straight away in the life of the community'.

Eventually Peter Howard concluded that the popular criticisms of the Oxford Group were groundless. However, this was not the line the *Daily Express* editor wanted to take, and he refused to print Howard's report. Instead, Howard wrote a book, *Innocent Men*, about his findings and his own consequent espousal of the Group's ideas. When the *Express* refused to let him publish the book while on its staff, Howard resigned from the paper. He spent the rest of his life writing books, plays and speeches promoting MRA, and he became the movement's leader when Buchman died.

Howard's arrival on the scene was a huge asset to Bill's books team. *Innocent Men*, published in 1941, was quickly followed the same year by *Fighters Ever*, a 'pungent, hard-hitting constructive review of where Britain stands today and how to create the new spirit needed for total victory'. Howard argues in this that physical weapons are 'not enough by themselves. Morale, spirit, devotion and sacrifice are needed to win'.

The young team at Hays Mews worked long hours, meeting frequently to share news from round the world, have quiet times and make plans. Amid the constraints of deadlines and curfews they also made time to relax with sing-songs, recitals, book groups and birthday celebrations. Sometimes they listened to music or a comedy on the radio. The popular song about a nightingale in Berkeley Square invariably amused them by referencing their address, and always made Chérie's heart beat a little faster.

Every day they'd listen to the BBC radio news, although it was under strict wartime censorship. Chérie strained to hear any reports from Cairo, where her parents were now posted at the army's Middle East Headquarters. Her brother Tom, aged 12, had been flown back to England, and Chérie had met his plane and delivered him to his school, Eastbourne College, shortly before it was evacuated to the relative safety of the Oxfordshire countryside. Meanwhile her older brother Richard was completing his army training at Sandhurst, and would soon be off to... who knew where?

By mid-May 1940 the threat of bombing raids and invasion felt more real, as Germany moved with horrifying speed into Scandinavia, Holland and Belgium, and finally invaded France. Yet until the bombs started falling, many aspects of Hays Mews life had continued almost as normal. One Saturday in late May was a case in point, a day Chérie always treasured as a precious and slightly surreal memory, given the wartime context.

There'd been a run of summery weather, and one of her colleagues had suggested a picnic by the river at Richmond in Surrey. Rumours abounded that the defence of France wasn't going well. Why else had the following day been designated a national day of prayer, with King George attending a special service at Westminster Abbey? But BBC reports gave nothing else away, and in the absence of definite news, the friends seized the moment for an excursion.

At Richmond the party spread blankets on the banks of the Thames to sunbathe or read. Some, including

Chérie, had come prepared for a dip, and they plunged bravely into the cold water. 'Not much on the provisions front,' someone remarked, peering into a carrier bag. 'Are we rationing our rations?' 'Oh – we'll eat well, I think!' said Bill, who lay stretched out in the sun. 'The helpers packing books with us yesterday gave us some dough – didn't you hear? They said we deserved a break!' Getting to his feet, he drew a few notes, coins and coupons from his trouser pocket, to whistles of appreciation around him. Bill thought nostalgically of the improvised picnics of his teens in the Malvern Hills, meeting friends and pooling their resources. 'The High Street's just up there,' he said, 'I'll go and see what I can find.'

Chérie returned from her swim, and found herself the only volunteer to accompany Bill to the shops. Still in her damp bathing costume, she wrapped herself in her towel and went off with Bill in search of a grocer's store. It was for her a Hollywood moment, when fate was surely bringing them together. Bill was the man for her. There was no one else she'd rather be alongside, whether fetching groceries or remaking the world. That evening she described the experience to two girlfriends, and surrendered her heart's desire to God, praying that in some future time of peace she and Bill might be together. And if Bill wasn't yet entertaining such thoughts, he did later admit to admiring Chérie's carefree approach to high-street shopping.

For the picnic party as a whole, the abiding memory of that afternoon was the sudden throng of boats appearing on the Thames – pleasure craft, yachts, launches, fishing vessels, barges – all bustling downstream towards the city.

At first the flotilla was just a mild diversion as the friends enjoyed their sandwiches. Then they realised there were scores, if not hundreds, of boats. 'Remember that radio announcement?' someone said. 'Boat owners had to report to the Admiralty. Perhaps it's that.' 'Yes, but that meant big vessels, surely?' another argued. 'This lot can't be used in combat! Most of them wouldn't stand a chance!'

Over the next days the full drama of the Dunkirk retreat and the heroic role of those small boats emerged through media reports. Sure enough, the vessels passing Richmond had been part of the fleet raised to rescue hundreds of thousands of British and French troops from France, after they'd been driven back to the Channel by the advancing German army. But despite the successes of the evacuation, the retreat itself was labelled 'a colossal military disaster' by Prime Minister Churchill. He went on to famously appeal to the nation: '*We shall fight on the beaches, we shall fight on the landing grounds, we shall fight in the fields and in the streets, we shall fight in the hills. We shall never surrender.*' A German invasion of Britain now seemed imminent.

This turning point in the War led to major changes at Hays Mews, and to Chérie and Bill moving off in different directions. Shortly after Dunkirk, a single woman in her fifties called Irene Prestwich generously offered her large country house and estate for use as a wartime base for MRA. The proposal coincided with the start of the London bombing raids by Germany, and it was rapidly accepted. Before long, much of the Hays Mews operation had moved to Tirley Garth, near the village of Tarporley in Cheshire.

'Within a week desks, beds and furniture began to arrive at Tirley', Irene Prestwich recalls in her memoir, 'and we were making our first attempt to transform the home into a training centre for Moral Re-Armament.' Chérie was among the 40 full-time workers who travelled there from London in September 1940. Some of them continued their London work, running the city campaigns, or producing newsletters, press releases and training materials. Others adapted to new roles that were needed to run this large community and to help meet Britain's wartime food requirements.

Around the Tirley estate large areas of lawn, shrubbery and meadow were ploughed up to grow vegetables. Some of the produce fed the substantial household and its visitors, but most was sold in the Chester and Liverpool markets for distribution in north-west England. Chérie joined six others who became land girls, growing and delivering crops by day and helping with office and domestic tasks in the evenings.

Others in the MRA network came to manage the house and cook meals, and Irene Prestwich admits the arrival of fifteen 'older women' to rearrange her home was 'not always easy!'. She describes how 'an exact and often painful discipline started at Tirley: punctuality, perfect standards of work, early morning quiet times, obedience to guidance – the training, in short, of a force who could bring a moral and spiritual breakthrough to a country in mortal peril'. She adds with pride that of the 'scores of servicemen who came to Tirley on their leave, some said the discipline here was tougher than in the services!'.

Other visitors were civilians, seeking to help improve the country's morale in these dark days. Regular press articles were sent out, books and songs were written, and a play called *Giant Otherfellow* was produced, illustrating the power of personal change and listening to God.

Even in the countryside air attacks were a constant threat. German raids on Liverpool, twenty miles away, had begun in August 1940 and continued until 1942, killing around 4,000 people. It was a city death toll second only to London's 40,000. Night and day, Tirley householders took turns to spot planes from the porch, and the women slept in the cellar. The buildings were blacked-out by night and were never seriously damaged, but Chérie and her friends would hear the menacing roar of German planes flying over, and after one raid in November 1940 they found 36 incendiary bombs outside the house, including some on the terrace and one on the roof.

Back in London Bill had helped pack up the offices and load trucks with equipment for Tirley, but he'd remained behind as one of the core staff looking after the headquarters. The Blitz had started, and with bombs falling on the city round the clock Bill and Tom were busily occupied with air-raid duties. One house in Berkeley Square was destroyed and another hit, but No. 45 stayed intact during eight months of air assaults. Being under fire only strengthened the two men's resolve to fight on the front lines, and since the army was calling for further reinforcements they now decided to enlist together. On the same day in July 1941, Bill and Tom joined the Royal Armoured Corps and headed off to two different camps for intensive training.

Around this time objections had been raised in parliament and by the media to the Oxford Group's official status as 'work of national importance', which spared its staff from military service. The issue was debated in Parliament in August 1941, and Labour Minister Ernest Bevin decided in favour of conscription for the young and able-bodied males in the Group. In fact, by this point Bill and Tom were already a month into their army training, and only 11 British male full-timers were still civilians. The work of the Oxford Group continued its momentum, relying on staff who were exempt for health or age reasons, or those employed locally who could help in their time off.

Bill was pleased to be joining the army at last, although Bovington Training Camp in Dorset took some adjustment. The obligatory shaved head, scratchy uniform and slavish obedience to shouty sergeant majors were disconcerting, but his Oxford Group training helped him embrace the discipline and see the point of it. 'The main marvel of those first weeks', he writes in a war memoir, 'was the speed with which every sense of an individual having any rights or liberties or indeed reason for existence other than to react to the requirements of the army machine were entirely removed. One could say one became the complete totalitarian man in an incredibly short period of time'.

There followed a hellish six weeks spent in the lower hold of a troopship, eating, sleeping and living almost cheek-by-jowl with hundreds of other soldiers. Their destination was unknown, although by the time they'd stopped off at Freetown and Durban they realised they were heading either for the Middle East or Asia, via South Africa. The Axis forces had blocked the Mediterranean and access to the Suez Canal, so this had become the standard route to the East.

The long journey was a claustrophobic nightmare for the naturally squeamish and fastidious Bill, who liked his own space. He describes being 'squashed in there, stripped to the waist, encased with sweating humanity', subjected to 'appalling, uncouth, uncomfortable and sordid conditions'. He wished he could compare notes with Tom, who he guessed may be on another ship in the convoy. But Bill was good at blocking off personal feelings to focus on his goals. His Oxford Group training and faith in God's guidance helped keep his mind on a bigger vision. He believed he was called to be here, and he was certain that by surrendering his concerns in prayer and observing his quiet times he would cope.

In fact, Bill came to find his companions' incessant banter, hyperbole and swearing a 'saving grace'. At night he'd lie in his hammock listening to the men's worldly chatter with amusement. It took his mind off the confined space and threat of attack. Once, the ship behind them hit a mine and they were rocked violently. Close to the Equator a man died of heatstroke. Bill watched as the body, wrapped in the man's hammock, was dropped over the back of the ship with little ceremony. He told himself to get used to it. There would be worse sights in a tank battle.

On 4th June 1942 the ships reached the southern end of the Suez Canal. There Bill describes himself as 'one of a horde of sweaty soldiers pouring like cattle off the *RMS Mauretania* at Egypt's Port Tewfik. I stood, stunned by the oven-like heat, and blinked at the exotic scenes, sounds and smells, the desperate poverty, the barren desert and the lush villages. I wondered what horrendous thing lay ahead. The last thing I had in mind was the reason we were there, namely the urgent need to deny Hitler the oilfields of the Middle East. For whoever held these would ultimately win the war.'

The troops boarded a train to Cairo, where trucks delivered them to the old Turkish Abassieh Garrison on the outskirts of the city. Bill recalls the colonies of biting bugs in the ancient plaster walls, which swarmed over them at night. 'We were innocents abroad,' he said. 'Later I learnt to sleep on the verandah on a folded blanket surrounded by a little wall of DDT'.

The newcomers were thrown into guard duties and courses in gunnery, wireless and mechanics. They were also updated on the North African Campaign, which wasn't going well. The Germans and Italians had swept across Tunisia and Libya, and were now heading towards Egypt. The men learnt they were part of reinforcements sent from Britain, South Africa, Australia and New Zealand to push back the enemy advance.

One morning Bill was among those told to drive 100 newly-landed American jeeps from the Canal to units in the Western Desert. They were expected to travel in convoy, but while waiting for instructions at the Canal depot, Bill fell asleep in the hot sun. He awoke to find the rest of the group already refuelled and leaving. 'Which way did the other jeeps go?' Bill asked a guard at the gate, once he'd filled his own petrol tank. The man pointed firmly down the road, and Bill drove off, covering many miles before realising it was the wrong way. 'It was a hectic day', he recalled, 'roaring across the roads and through the villages of the Nile Delta, trying to get some sort of information in Arabic, of which at that time I knew not one word'.

With profound relief, he eventually caught up with the other jeeps near Alexandria. The convoy continued west along the desert road, only to run into 'the most horrifying columns of trucks, vehicles, tank transporters, every sort of mobile equipment, sometimes four columns abreast, heading eastwards' back towards Alexandria. They pressed on, handed over their jeeps, and were instructed to pick any transport they liked from a huge collection of parked cars and trucks, and drive back to Cairo. They later discovered that the traffic queue they joined on their return was the humiliating Allied retreat from Libya, known as the 'Gazala Gallop'. Days later the Libyan port of Tobruk was recaptured by the Axis forces in one of the worst Allied defeats of the war.

On more typical days at Abassieh Bill would go into Cairo in his time off. He described the city as 'an absolute wonderland' despite its proximity to the battlefront. At the heart of Cairo was Britain's General Headquarters (GHQ) for the Middle East, and the streets seethed with the 200,000–300,000 members of the British and Commonwealth armed forces stationed in camps around the capital. In Cairo they found shops, restaurants and distractions, including the Gezira Club, run like a British country club with its swimming pool, tennis courts, bars and tearooms.

The Egyptian population of Cairo was much smaller than today, and generally lived a parallel existence. Bill recalls with shame that 'one only met the shopkeepers and shoeshine boys, and was quite unaware of the professional classes of Egyptians, cultivated and university-educated, who would be jostled off the pavement by some boorish louts from the British Army. No doubt the presence of the European forces was very much resented by many Egyptians, but one wasn't aware of this because those we met were only too delighted to take one's pay off one, whether for a postcard or a precious stone allegedly from a pharaoh's tomb in Upper Egypt'.

Years later, when Bill was working with MRA in the region, one of his closest Egyptian friends would be Dr Abdul Mogni Said, a socialist politician, twice interned by the British, who took part in the 1952 revolution against King Farouk. But in 1942 Bill knew few Egyptians, and little about Islam or Egyptian nationalism. 'When I was at school', he writes, 'you learned about the crusaders being attacked by the "infidels". The first Moslem I ever met socially was a young doctor in Egypt, Abdu Sallam, when I was there with the army. I learned so much from Abdu over the years, and felt very challenged and humbled by his obedience and selflessness. He followed his guidance from Allah to give up a good job in order to work with the poor. Later he became a very effective Minister of Health under both Presidents Nasser and Sadat'.

Bill met Dr Abdu Sallam and other Egyptian friends

– Moslem, Jewish and Christian – through the MRA network in Cairo. But initially his contacts were mainly colleagues from London. Bill had barely arrived when Geoffrey Currell tracked him down at Abassieh, having seen Bill's name on a list of arrivals at GHQ. 'This was a tremendous boost', writes Bill, 'and we stuck together for the weeks that followed'. A regular meeting place for Group members in Cairo was the apartment of Garnet Lloyd, who ran the leading department store, Robert Hughes, on Qasr El-Nile Street. 'Without this flat I don't know how we'd have all managed', Bill writes of the hub where both long-term and transitory MRA team members could meet and stay in touch with their friends world-wide.

'Trooper Shillington, I presume!' Bill exclaimed happily, spotting Tom at Lloyd's flat one day. 'Well I never…!' It was the first time they'd met in Egypt. 'And guess what?' Tom told Bill at once. 'I hope you're free for lunch on Sunday, because we're both invited out! By Chérie Oram's parents, no less! The Colonel and his wife. Roy's on the Medical Advisory Staff at GHQ, and Dulcie runs the military canteen in Ezbekieh Gardens. I met them the other day, and they said Chérie had mentioned us both in a letter!' Bill's eyes narrowed suspiciously, and Tom hastily added. 'Oh don't flatter yourself, you fool! Chérie just told them we were two friends from the Hays Mews team who might appreciate some home cooking. Nothing special!' Bill visibly relaxed.

Re-engaging with his MRA colleagues in Cairo was energising for Bill, and reinforced his sense that his personal and his national commitment were one and the same. Later he'd describe the 'tremendous strength and zest and tingle it added to life to go into the army and the war with the knowledge of belonging to an ideological force of men and women, many of whom were joining their own armed forces all over the world during this great conflict'. With so many dedicated people, he thought, they'd surely not only win the war, but also produce a new civilisation once the war was over.

Team members in Cairo met regularly in small cells that changed as people came and went. When Tom and Geoffrey moved from Abassieh others arrived, including Matt Manson, a gunnery instructor, Harry Rook, a military curate, and Robin Mowat from the Education Corps. And while some at the Garrison might head to clubs, bars or brothels in their free time, these men would gather to share their thoughts and pray. 'We were committed to a way of life based on MRA's moral standards', Bill wrote, 'and we strove to find some time every day before reveille, where possible, to be quiet, to maintain a life of the spirit and keep perspective.' Keeping in touch took ingenuity since wartime security prevented people revealing their location, and reunions were often unexpected. A naval officer friend who'd docked in Alexandria surprised Bill at 1 am one night at the Garrison, having had to wake Bill's commanding officer to gain access.

The determination of these men was partly fuelled by their understanding of other ideologies at work around them. The threats posed by Nazi Germany and fascist Italy were now clear, but the activities of the Russians and their supporters were much less obvious. Bill and his friends suspected that some of their university contemporaries who'd become communists were now working for Russia from within the British establishment. But it was hard to know anything for sure. The scale of misinformation and espionage carried out for years within the British Foreign Office and Intelligence services by agents of Soviet Russia, most notably by the 'Cambridge Spies', only became widely known decades later when government documents were released and Russian defectors presented direct evidence. At the time it wasn't common knowledge.

From the vantage point of the 1990s, Bill cites in his wartime memoir two British officials in Cairo during the war who'd helped change the course of history in Russia's favour. They worked for British Intelligence on Balkan affairs. One was Basil Davidson, later a distinguished journalist and historian, who then ran the Special Operations Executive (SOE) Yugoslav Section in Cairo. The other was Davidson's second-in-command James Klugmann, a close friend of the Russian spy Donald Maclean. At the start of the war Klugmann had been recruited to MI5, despite his membership of the British Communist Party at Cambridge in the thirties. In the 1990s he was revealed to have been a KGB agent and instrumental in recruiting the 'Cambridge Five' spies.

Davidson and Klugmann briefed SOE agents in Yugoslavia and helped shape Allied policy in the Balkans. When the Axis forces invaded Yugoslavia in 1941, Britain had initially supported a royalist resistance group as allies against the enemy. But by mid-1943 Churchill had been persuaded to switch to supporting the communist guerrillas led by Tito, who subsequently became the authoritarian President of Yugoslavia for almost thirty years.

For both committed communists like Klugmann and committed MRA workers like Bill, ideology was not just a student whim, it was a life purpose and a means of transforming society. The MRA team identified entirely with the scale of the communists' vision and commitment, while always considering their own to be the greater cause. Frank Buchman often quoted William Penn, the Quaker founder of his home state Pennsylvania, who'd said 'Men must choose to be governed by God, or they condemn themselves to be ruled by tyrants'. Buchman and his team considered Hitler, Mussolini and Stalin to be power-hungry materialist despots who dismissed spirituality, morality and civil freedom. The advance of enemy armies across Europe, and Britain's vulnerability, left no doubt in Bill's and his friends' minds that they had to stop them succeeding, however they could.

A couple of months after arriving in Cairo, Bill was invited to join the 8th Kings Royal Irish Hussars as a tank commander. The regiment's numbers had recently been decimated during tenacious fighting in North Africa, hence its need to regroup and recruit. Bill was proud to be in a regular regiment with a distinguished cavalry history, and part of the 7th Armoured Division under General Harding.

The 'A' Squadron that Bill joined provided the forward screen for the regiment, and almost immediately it took up a task on the southern end of the Alamein Line, across which lay the German and Italian forces. By day they held their position on an escarpment looking across to the enemy, about two miles away at the far end of a broad valley. At night they'd move the tanks back and 'leaguer' in a defensive formation behind the front line, while the infantry carried out patrols.

Bill describes those early weeks waiting for action, as 'in general exceedingly enjoyable'. For one thing, he loved the desert. 'It's quite hard to explain. The desert itself was so vast, clean, sometimes awesome. At night it had its own peculiar feel: jet-dark sky, with bright stars, and pleasantly cool'. He also loved the simplicity of this life. 'One lived with the other members of one's tank crew: gunner, wireless operator and driver. The tank was one's home. You slept beside it, ready to move at a moment's notice if a surprise attack should arise in the night'. Each tank carried its own supplies of food, mostly canned, with tea and biscuits.

On the downside was the scorching daytime heat, the desert sores resulting from even a small scratch, and Bill's disgust at the 'myriads of millions of flies, breeding no doubt on the corpse-strewn minefields that scattered the desert. If you brewed a mug of tea it was impossible to drink the stuff without drinking drowned flies, even with your hand firmly over the top of the mug'.

In the weeks waiting for the order to advance there was 'enough of the unexpected, and possibly hazardous, to prevent life becoming boring'. One challenge was desert navigation, 'an art I never mastered well. Upon it depended whether one made contact with the second echelon of transport, bringing up rations, ammunition and petrol. If we didn't succeed in meeting them at the right map reference after dark we went without food or fuel for the next day'.

Once, Bill was ordered to rescue a 25-pounder field gun and its quad vehicle that had sunk into soft sand. By the time Bill's tank had pulled it out and towed the gun back to its base, night had fallen. As he tried to navigate his crew back in darkness to their own leaguer, Bill realised their vehicle probably sounded like a whole armoured division on the move. Then he spotted vehicles ahead that could have been either German or British. To Bill's immense relief they turned out to be a unit of Scots Greys. But his tank's unexpected appearance in the dark, when German attacks were expected, made them unpopular, both here and also with their own unit when they finally made it back.

When the British attack began, it was only on the second day that the true reality of fighting sunk in for Bill. 'Up to then I had been thrilled to be part of the war,' he writes. 'It fitted in with my picture of myself. But on this second day we came under fire from some highly effective German 88mm anti-tank guns, and the tanks around me began to go up. A tank is a horrific sight when it really gets hit. It carries about 150 gallons of petrol and the whole fighting chamber is full of high explosive shells. After a direct hit people don't normally come out alive'.

The attack had started on 23rd October 1942, day one of what was to be the decisive Battle of El Alamein. Earlier that day Bill noticed that 'there was a good deal less chatter and badinage. We knew we were opposite the 21st Panzer Division, and everyone wondered what the whole thing would be like'. The quartermaster went around gathering up personal belongings: letters, addresses, cap badges, anything that might be found on your body, revealing the identity of one's unit to the enemy. 'So where will our next issue come from – you, or St Peter?' someone joked desperately, as they all handed in their regimental badges depicting an angel with an Irish harp. 'Where we're going, we won't need these winged fellas – we'll get the real thing!' quipped another.

It was almost a relief when the order finally came that night to advance in a line towards the enemy. Picking their way through vast minefields laid by both German and British, a massive artillery barrage crashed overhead and the sky lit up with fire as the fighting began. 'That night ended with the four tanks in the line in front of me all knocked out. They set up a terrific illumination all around and we were silhouetted completely', Bill writes. The blazing light made them highly visible to the enemy, and Bill's unit was ordered back. Things hadn't gone to plan and they hadn't advanced as far as intended.

The following afternoon the order came to go in to 'mop up' the guns that had blocked the advance the night before. As a tank commander, Bill would wedge himself in the turret of his tank, equipped with binoculars, maps, guns and ammunition, and two microphones: 'A-mic' was to confirm receipt of Control's orders or information, and 'B-mic' was for the tank intercom, to direct the driver and the gunner, who often operated blind at night, or under fire.

Bill lost track of time as he listened for and issued the staccato, coded orders of intercom speech over the radios.

Bill to Sherwood the driver: 'If you can hear me, Sherry, rev up!'

Control to Bill (through headphones): 'Edward Nuts advance in sub-unit column. One front protection. Over.'

Bill to driver: 'Advance Sherry, right of these slit trenches.'

Bill to Control: '1B OK. Off.'

'With a roar like ten Bentleys we jerked forward out of the wadi', Bill writes, 'towards Jerry's positions. Soon the air seemed filled with the squealing swish of shells. I grabbed my tin hat and told Sherwood the driver to drop his flap. For some very lengthy minutes we continued ahead to get the number and positions of the guns. Then over the air the order came to take up hull-down (semi-concealed) positions, while behind us the 25-pounders of the artillery tried to dislodge the opposition'.

At this point German 88mm anti-tank guns and 105mm shells started pounding the British tanks, causing some to explode. 'All at once I found myself paralysed with fear', Bill recalls, 'totally unable to think'. He knew his crew depended on him for information and reassurance. A wireless operator had once told Bill how relieved crews felt when they peered up and saw their commander's head still intact in the turret, a thought Bill found hard to dispel. 'Under shell-fire one looks at death and sees it swoop on one's friends', Bill writes. 'The first near-miss brings with it the strong temptation to lose nerve and send up panic prayers for a quick end or a blackout until waking in hospital'.

But instead of losing hope, Bill's Oxford Group training kicked in. God's love and calling were real to him, and he found he could surrender his terror. 'The unforgettable thing', he reflects later, 'was the way in which all fear and tension totally disappeared as one took a grip of oneself and handed back one's life to God. I often read Psalm 91:

> *He is my refuge and my fortress: my God; in him will I trust...*
>
> *Thou shalt not be afraid of the terror by night; nor of the arrow that flieth by day;*
>
> *Nor for the pestilence that walketh in darkness; nor for the destruction that wasteth at noonday. A thousand shall fall at thy side, and ten thousand at thy right hand; but it shall not come nigh thee.*

'This gave me more confidence than the armour-plating around me. I found myself relaxing immediately, and able to carry on coolly and more or less efficiently, to a surprising extent. It surprised my crew too, I think'.

With a new clarity, which was 'nothing less than a miracle to me', Bill suddenly thought of a practical way to respond to the ceaseless bombardment. 'I remembered from gun practice that you'd aim behind the target before the direct hit. The safest place to be is where the last shell fell. So whenever a gun was targeting us, I would have Sherwood shunt us back and up on the right stick or on the left for a few yards, just in time to see the shell hit the spot where we'd just been. We moved around like this, and in the next 45 minutes we survived, despite one or two minor hits. Eventually we came back, having lost 15 tanks in this short period. That personal liberation from fear altered the war as far as I was concerned, and it remained one of the big experiences of my life'.

Those first four days at El Alamein were 'a terrible slugging match. 39,000 people were killed, and the chaos was unbelievable'. Bill had no idea whether strategic progress had been made. A tank commander had no overview, he simply followed orders and hoped their actions amounted to something positive.

In a letter written in his tank turret during lulls in the fighting, Bill told his London friends about his miraculous liberation from fear. 'God in his love is supervising', he writes, 'even when the APs screech by and the HEs crack around one. Possibly my crew owe their lives to the fact that my mind wasn't at all "taut" when we got a hot reception the other day'. He also wrote that 'the Scofield' was his 'last remaining literature' in the tank. This referred to a black pocket Bible, edited by American scholar Cyrus Scofield. The front page is inscribed *To Bill, from his friends July 1941,* the month Bill joined the army, and it's signed by 55 Oxford Group colleagues, including Chérie. Bill didn't speak much about his Christian faith specifically, preferring to use faith language that was inclusive of all beliefs, but he read the Bible daily. This small, battered volume, its pages covered in his pencil notes and underlines, remained with him for life.

Ten days into the battle they were moving forward. Bill's diary notes an advance north at first, towards the Mediterranean, then west, then south in a pursuit role, to cut off Rommel's retreating forces. They passed battle debris from the heaviest fighting. 'German Mark III and IV tanks were still blazing with a dull red flare', he writes, 'and dense diesel smoke like tramp steamers dotted an ocean of sand and scrub. Newly-abandoned gun positions were on all sides, there was scattered kit of every sort, and the still unsearched dead lay contorted and impersonal in one's path. The scenes reminded one of all the poems and histories written about battle and wars'.

Bill's squadron was then given a reconnaissance role, and they were sent out, troop by troop, to investigate unidentified vehicles and moving objects ahead. Often they ran into the rear guard of the enemy and were shelled. Where possible they rounded up and disarmed Germans and Italians, before troops behind took them off as prisoners.

As they continued west, Bill describes seeing 'the whole desert, from horizon to horizon, one mass of armoured fighting vehicles, as we swept across the broad stony wadis. These days we often had no time to brew up a mug of chai, and we lived on biscuits and bully that we could eat on the move. We were unshaven and yellow-faced from the churned-up sand. This was a glorious freedom. They were sunny days, every shred of bullshit was forgotten and everything was allowed that made for our fighting fitness. Three hours of sleep, less 20 minutes on guard, seemed plenty'.

Days later, when the weather broke, Bill's notes are less cheerful. 'November 6–7th: a nightmare battle with the elements. Cloudbursts soaked us, greatcoats were saturated, the wireless sets got wet and failed. Tracks sank in and the tanks bellied. We dug and sloshed knee-deep and the tank became mud-plastered inside and out… I must have towed 30 vehicles out of the bog one day. The night of the 6th was one of the most unpleasant I've ever had. Our clothing was shocking, there was water in the tank, the turret leaked. All night we sat cramped and icy-cold in the black, oily interior. Tea with a good lacing of rum just before darkness was the one welcome thing'.

As the weather improved so did morale and movement, and they soon crossed the Egyptian border into Libya. The land was still covered in mines, and enemy fire always possible, but 'the chase to Sollum and up Halfaya Pass, then on to the final blow-up just short of Dherna, was exhilarating', culminating in the pursuit of some retreating Italian tanks. 'It was like some massive great mechanised Quorn or Pytchley Hunt as we clattered along through the dark after them', Bill writes, 'and getting the Italians' intercom all over ours was a tremendous confirmation we were right on their trail'.

Three of the 8th Hussars' tanks, including Bill's, survived to enter the Libyan port city of Benghazi on 21st November 1942. But Bill himself never witnessed that moment of triumph. A week earlier he'd been on the coast road, near Tobruk. Leading their column of tanks was Sergeant Major Kirkham, on the lookout for German positions, while Bill followed second, identifying mines along the way. They were getting up speed to follow fresh German track marks when a mine appeared in the middle of the road. Bill decided that the mine was so obvious and easy to avoid that he'd point it out with arm gestures to those following, without stopping to mark it. To Bill's disbelief, the tank behind drove straight over the mine and was blown off the road. The crew was unhurt, but the tank was out of action. Its commander insisted on taking charge of Bill's tank and crew, leaving his own crew, with Bill, on the side of the road. The four men watched as their column moved off, realising that for them the advance was finished.

For two days they waited by the deserted road, expecting the main body of the army to follow along shortly. Then, realising it may still be days behind them, they changed tack, and set about finding some transport. Searching the battle wreckage scattered around them, they managed to find and repair an abandoned Vichy French truck. From other stranded vehicles they collected petrol, spare parts, food and even paint, with which they daubed an RAF roundel on their truck to deflect friendly fire. Fully equipped, they set off in search of the oncoming army.

'In fact we had a marvellous week or so entirely on our own', says Bill, 'swanning around, spending nights on the beach'. The break was all the more pleasurable when they discovered, by chance, that the campaign they'd been part of had not just succeeded, it was being celebrated worldwide. One night in the desert Bill heard the sound of a radio somewhere in the darkness, and he went to investigate. He came across some Signallers with a No. 19 wireless set in the back of their vehicle. They were picking up the BBC, so Bill and his other news-starved friends gathered round to listen.

'To our absolute incredulity', Bill writes, 'we heard reports of a colossal battle and victory in the desert, and that bells were chiming in church towers all over Britain for the first time since the war started. Churchill had even ordered aircraft to go up and spell out in smoke trails the names of the regiments that had taken part in this "famous victory of El Alamein"! One could hardly credit it! The incredible confusion and shambles and to-ing and fro-ing of the last weeks had amounted to an event that would go down in history!'. It was the first clear-cut, irreversible defeat of the Axis forces: a turning point of the Second World War.

When the crew finally reached their regimental headquarters in Tobruk, the course of Bill's war took another unexpected turn. On arrival he suddenly developed a fever and burning throat, and was diagnosed with diptheria. Instead of rejoining the 8th Hussars he was shipped to Alexandria, and spent the next weeks at Helmia Army Hospital in Cairo, followed by further weeks of convalescence in hospitals at Sarafand and Nathanya in Palestine. The lengthy sick leave was to mark a watershed in Bill's army service, between active service and a new phase as a captain in the Army Education Corps. After a rigorous officers' training in Palestine, he took up posts in Cairo and then Cyprus, delivering courses to the troops. It was 1945 before he returned to 'a fogbound Britain' for a final year's posting before resuming civilian life.

During his weeks in hospital, Bill reflected deeply on the futility of war. He pictured the faces of the desert Bedouin when his crew had searched their tents for

German prisoners. 'A burnt-out German dive bomber lay nearby. Guns were firing and as the tanks roared off we waved a "Saida" at these camel men. They seemed to look back at us as if to say, "So this is 'civilisation', is it…?"'. Bill also thought of a night, travelling back to Tobruk, when he'd sat out alone 'under a great dome of a sky with its bright stars. I remember thinking we might now get back home, and if I did get back I must find something dealing with the root causes of what's wrong in the world, because clearly war isn't going to do it'.

The letter from Bill to his London friends in the midst of battle had already indicated he'd fight on with them, whatever the outcome of the war. It also showed he knew this wasn't an easy option. 'A day or two before the push', he'd written, 'I had a miraculous four days' leave, and found the joys of civilian food and a bed after eight months on the deck gave me a longing for an easier life. However, I was soon out of that, for my guidance was "Will I live hard always?", and "We are an expeditionary force with a life-long goal"'.

The toughest part of the war for Bill was the final clincher in his choice to work for MRA. In hospital Bill had heard that twelve days into the Battle of El Alamein, not far from his own unit, his close friend Tom Shillington had been killed in the tank he'd been commanding. He was 29, two years older than Bill. 'I later met the sergeant who had buried Tom beside his tank', Bill writes. 'He told me Tom had been fatally hit while trying to get his wounded driver out of his seat to safety'. Other friends killed in battle included Geoffrey Currell. Never one to display his grief,

Bill writes that their deaths were, 'inevitably bound up in their readiness to sacrifice everything for a great aim and purpose, following God's call to them at that particular moment of history'. Bill knew he could have died too, and having survived he owed it to them to keep on fighting.

5

Town House

London 1958

It was only when I moved from Sussex to London and started school there that I began to get an inkling that my home and my life were not entirely typical, possibly even a bit peculiar. But it took a while for the penny to drop.

43 Charles Street in Mayfair was, like Elenge Plat, a large house with good potential for young explorers. This one had six floors including the basement. The high-ceilinged reception rooms on the ground and first floors had formal, shiny furniture, and the smell of wood polish greeted you when you came in the front door. There were chandeliers and paintings in gold frames, and fireplaces so deep I could have hidden in them if I'd been allowed. But I soon gathered that these were not playrooms.

Life here was more regimented than it had been with the PBs. Many different people lived here, not just one particular family, and there were no-go areas. I quickly learnt to venture with care, avoid getting in the way of grown-up business, and never enter bedrooms unless they were Mummy and Daddy's or my own. There was a courtyard area outside, but I couldn't go there or leave the house without an adult.

In this house there was no Amelia, or any other child my age, to run off and play with. Patrick was at boarding school in Worcestershire and a rare visitor, often spending his holidays with our cousins near his school. Mary PB was also missing here, although she reappeared on occasions. But the pleasure of rejoining Mummy and Daddy helped make up for all this, even if they still went away sometimes and we were rarely alone as a family apart from in our bedrooms. My parents' room and my own small single were close together on the same floor, and if my brother came he stayed somewhere else in the maze of corridors and staircases winding up the building.

I soon found out that we didn't just live with the others in 43 Charles Street, but we also had 'family' in neighbouring houses, where my parents would come and go as easily as they did in our own. We were in some way part of Numbers 40, 41 and 44 on our side of the street, and 12A across the road. Sometimes we even packed and went to stay in one of the other houses, but mainly we were in 43.

Round the corner from our street, in Berkeley Square, was the biggest of all our houses. Like all these buildings it was usually referred to by its house number, in this case '45', but sometimes people called it 'Frank's London home', or 'Clive of India's house'. All the houses were filled with the same kinds of people who lived at 43, and even if they didn't know me much they were friendly and chatted as if they did. They'd say, 'Don't you have lovely freckles!', or 'What fine dimples!', or 'You look so like your mother!', which I didn't mind at that age. Even the men in smart suits who talked together in serious huddles were kind and smiley away from their huddles.

We'd go to the other homes if one of my parents had to see someone, fetch something, go for a meal, or drop me off to be looked after by somebody. Often I'd sit quietly at the back of a grown-ups' meeting, reading or making a Fuzzy Felt picture. At the Charles Street houses we mainly used the front entrances, not the back doors leading into the cobbled mews behind. But at 45 we'd enter by the rear entrance, which had another name on that side: 4 Hays Mews. This door opened onto a low-ceilinged, twisty corridor, passing offices and mysterious rooms, until it reached the main house fronting onto Berkeley Square. One office door was generally ajar, revealing a telephone switchboard operated by two women wearing headsets. Lights flashed on a panel in front of them, and they'd pull and push long cords in and out of holes, while speaking into their mouthpieces. When they were busy their hands danced all over the board, and they seemed to be chanting a nonsense song. It was mesmerising.

'Grosvenor 3443. Can I help you?' they'd say.

'Certainly. Putting you through!'

'I'm very sorry, he's out at the moment. May I take a message?'

'Mr McPherson on the line, urgently wanting Mel. Is Mel with you by any chance?'

'Sorry to keep you!'

'Grosvenor 3443.'

'Putting you through!'

'Operator! Yes, of course Roly, hold on one moment.'

In time I learnt that, via these lines, people dialling our phone number could reach anyone in our houses and offices. And grown-ups could chat to friends in the other houses, or make calls elsewhere. The operators were like magicians, knowing everyone's names and where they might be found. They were perpetually cheerful, and during breaks in calls they'd chat to me until another light blinked. One told me there was a phone in every room of our buildings, although my bedroom didn't have one.

It was clear from the linking of our houses and the way people knew each other that we all belonged together. We were 'the family'. The others here, who I knew were not '*real* family' like Mummy and Daddy, came in many shapes, sizes and ages. Most were adults, and the few children in the other houses were all older than me.

Although the adults were mostly smiley they could also look very solemn indeed, especially at meetings or in discussion. On the rare occasions someone looked a bit sad, they might be taken somewhere quiet for a chat. Sometimes I'd be told that So-and-So needed 'special care' and we should be 'extra thoughtful' for them, but their problem was rarely explained. I decided it was best to look happy, otherwise someone might think something was wrong and we'd have to talk about it.

Some visitors to the house weren't quite part of the family and might be less friendly, but we had to make them feel welcome and special whatever they were like. I learnt not to comment on habits that were different from ours. Daddy told me that Patrick had once, when very young, asked a visiting relative, 'What do I smell?' when he was overwhelmed by their alcoholic breath. This was always held up, with amusement, as a model of what *not* to say to visitors in this teetotal household.

Number 43 was home, no question, but it wasn't like homes in my school reading books. Children like Janet and John had their parents to themselves. Their house was a small peaceful place, where Mother cooked and Father read and smoked a pipe after work. My place was much bigger, with no pipe smoking that I ever saw, and endless visitors. I knew important things were happening here, grown-up things.

Occasionally there were visiting children with whom I'd have to play and share my toys. I liked the company, and was used to sharing. Two of them were princesses, I was told, and I must be specially caring for them. I was pleased the girls seemed much like other children I'd met, and even though one of them took a shine to my doll Bella and renamed her 'Beauty', I knew the doll would be mine again later.

Sometimes my parents went away, and they'd often bring back a present. One treasured gift was a box set of tiny books from America, each with a story about a baby wild animal and its parents. I spent ages losing myself in the world of the baby hippo stuck in the baked mud of a drying creek, or the baby gorilla who dropped a coconut onto his sleeping father's head. The picture of Daddy Gorilla beating his chest in fury and fright was scary. I'd never seen my Daddy get angry like that.

Young women stood in for my parents when they were away, just as Mary PB had in Sussex. They always seemed to know what was going on, so routines continued, whoever was in charge. Family meals for the whole household took place in the dining room, and sometimes I ate in the basement kitchen or a side room. My toys and books were kept upstairs, not in the drawing room with its smart sofas and chairs. This room was mainly for formal gatherings or tea parties, where I might be asked to pass round the biscuits. But I enjoyed playing in my parents' bedroom, and spent happy times there alone with Mummy and Daddy.

My room was cosily small, with a single bed, and just enough space for a narrow chest of drawers and a chair. On the wall hung my cherished Molly Brett picture of teddy bears picnicking in a bluebell wood. I'd lie on the bed tirelessly examining every detail of the teddies, some in dresses, or waistcoats and trousers, toasting bread and boiling a kettle on an open fire. Looking on was an owl, a woodpecker, a squirrel, a robin, and even a caterpillar climbing out of a mug. Yet more teddies are arriving on a gypsy caravan pulled by a donkey. To me the scene perfectly depicted my favourite song *The Teddy Bear's Picnic* and offered me a private peek *beneath the trees where nobody sees*.

Another prized possession, hanging above the bed,

was a Swiss cuckoo clock brought back from another of my parents' trips. It was carved in dark wood, and a tiny white cuckoo sprang out of a door sounding a 'Coo!' every quarter of an hour. I loved it, but the coo and the pendulum's loud tick kept me awake at night, so the clock was stopped. That didn't matter. The clock, the teddy bear picture and a few soft toys made the room truly mine. Sometimes I'd pretend my bed was a boat on a wild, raging sea, and, huddled on board with my toys, I'd feel quite safe.

My parents' nearby room was much bigger than mine, with an adjoining bathroom. It had twin beds, a fireplace, a desk, an armchair and a sofa, on which my mother sometimes lay, holding an intriguing contraption to her face that hissed out steam. She said it helped cure the headaches that often bothered her in cold weather.

In the privacy of our rooms, Mummy and Daddy were affectionate and fun. Downstairs everyone looked smart: Mummy in a dress and high heels, with gloves and hats for outdoors; Daddy in a suit and tie; myself in a frock or skirt and blouse. But up here on the second floor, shoes and ties were discarded, and we could relax. I enjoyed books, games and the BBC Home Service radio's *Listen With Mother* or *Children's Hour*. Sometimes we'd switch to music on the BBC Light Programme and hear *Music While You Work*, *Housewives' Choice* or *Children's Favourites*.

When Mummy and Daddy had to write letters or make phone calls, I could still be in their room if I was quiet. First thing every morning when I crept in, they'd be sitting up in bed holding cups of tea, while thinking and writing in notebooks. This was their Quiet Time, when they listened to thoughts from God for an hour, and I would play or read until it was time to talk and get dressed. At first I used to snuggle right into Mummy's bed with her, until one day she said, 'No, you're a bit old for this now.' But I could still sit beside her on the eiderdown. Downstairs it wasn't done to hug or kiss, and I was once lightly corrected after flinging my arms round a nice man called Uncle Tom. Upstairs there weren't so many rules, and it was usually fine to cuddle my parents.

My father was the most different of us all when he was upstairs. He could be fiercely earnest talking with grown-ups, and I knew not to intrude on those conversations. But in private he was funny and twinkly and teasing. He had a portable Roberts radio, a modern delight that you could switch on immediately, unlike the chunky wooden wirelesses that took a while to warm up. Sometimes Daddy listened to boring men using long words on the Home Service, and I'd pick up a book to read instead. But when he'd finished he'd turn the dial and find some cheery music that we'd sing along to. Sometimes he even danced with Mummy round the room, and we'd all laugh. There were songs with silly words, like: *There's a bird on a branch, there's a branch on a tree, there's a tree in a meadow where you said you love me.* Another one went: *Would you like to swing on a star, carry moonbeams home in a jar?* And the best one was about *seven little girls, sitting in the back seat, kissing and a'huggin with Fred.* I'm not sure if Mummy told me not to sing these downstairs, or whether I instinctively knew they were private songs, between us and the radio.

Most of all I loved storybooks, whether read aloud together or silently to myself. We borrowed many of them from the local library, and I knew Mummy liked them too, as she often said children's books were for all ages. I still liked stories about animals who dressed or talked like humans. Noddy and Big Ears stories were alright too, but the characters in Little Grey Rabbit or Pooh Bear books seemed more real to me.

Then I discovered Milly Molly Mandy, a little girl living with her parents, aunts, uncles and grandparents in a country cottage, and I read all her adventures. Other favourites were the Mary Plain and Stuart Little books, which took animal stories to a new level. Mary was no toy teddy but came from the Bern bear pit in Switzerland, while Stuart was a two-inch boy who'd been born in New York looking exactly like a mouse. Little orphaned Heidi was special too, running free in the Swiss mountains, with only her surly grandpa in charge. One day Mummy started reading me *Little House on the Prairie*, a true story about two young American sisters who trekked off with their parents in a covered wagon to find a home. *What bliss!* I thought. For all the dangers they faced, that family's life together in a horse-drawn cart – and later in a log cabin – seemed the ultimate dream. All these books created convincing worlds I felt a part of, and nothing was better than closing the bedroom door and immersing myself in them. The characters were my best friends, who stayed with me long after a story ended.

Occasionally I was given a comic to read. *TV Comic* was full of cartoon stories based on characters like Noddy and Muffin the Mule. In one issue I crayoned in a picture of a circus for a colouring competition. 'Why not add a little colour to that?' Mummy suggested, noticing my picture was almost entirely black. We rubbed out a few areas so I could add some bright splashes. She must then have posted off the picture, as I won a prize for this modest effort: two tickets to Bertram Mills Circus.

It was exciting and a little overwhelming to sit at the front of a packed circus audience in Olympia a few weeks later, and meet the terrifying Coco the Clown, a well-known 1950s celebrity. In his oversized suit and shoes, Coco flapped across the sawdust ring to shake my hand. I stared at his red lips, white eyes and red bobble nose and smiled politely, but I didn't like him much, even when he made his hair stand on end. And yet meeting the real Coco the Clown and watching the glittery, noisy show with its elephants, lions and acrobats was like stepping into a magical story book. I felt very special, and had plenty to report to enquiring grown-ups back at 43.

There must have been a big box TV somewhere in the Charles Street houses, as I sometimes watched *The Flowerpot Men*, *Sooty and Sweep* or *Andy Pandy* on a screen. But television was a new medium in the 1950s, not yet found in all households. I may also have seen these classic children's programmes on visits to Granny and Grandad's quiet flat in Croydon.

Another place we sometimes visited was Whitbourne Hall, where we'd see Patrick. This was the home of my Aunt Erica and Uncle Edward, who were a 'real' aunt and uncle, like Milly Molly Mandy's were. I liked it there as Aunt Erica made a fuss of me, but the house was even bigger than 43 Charles Street. The ceilings and doors would have allowed a giant to pass through, and footsteps and voices echoed around the building. It took ages to walk to a bathroom or climb the white marble stairs at bedtime.

Whitbourne was full of big boys of Patrick's age and even older, who played cricket in the hall using the brass gong for wickets. When the house went quiet it usually meant they were fishing or camping, or swimming at the Deep End of the Pool, as they called the lake outside. For my part I trailed after a big spaniel called Rags, or was taken rowing or paddling in the Shallow End. Aunt Erica gave me 'jobs' to do, like handing round toffees at a fishing competition, or striking the hall gong before meals. We never stayed long. A day always came when Patrick had to return to school, and we'd head back to London.

At 43 you never knew who'd come through the front door next. Different languages were spoken, and some guests wore bright saris or African robes, with bare feet in sandals, even in winter. I couldn't take my eyes off a Canadian man called Chief Walking Buffalo, who wore a traditional headdress made of buffalo mane and horns, with a fringed leather jacket. Some of his companions had feathered headdresses like the Native American Indians in Patrick's comics who fought cowboys, but these were obviously friends. One day I opened the front door to a beautiful black woman whose smile dazzled me as she bent down and offered me an elegant white-gloved hand to shake. 'She's a very big star,' somebody whispered to me as she was welcomed and ushered away by some grown-ups, and the term 'star' seemed to suit her even though I didn't fully understand it. 'She's Muriel Smith,' my informant went on. 'A brilliant actress and singer from America.' Another time, when Patrick was in the house, an important friend from Cyprus kept coming for meals, and my 11-year-old brother beat him at chess. Our parents worried the man might be put out, because 'the British have treated him very badly', but he didn't seem to mind about losing.

I'd just turned seven when I was buttoned into my grey gaberdine coat and hurried across the park to Victoria Station with others from Charles Street. 'We're going to greet a distinguished German leader who's arriving by train,' I was told. Crowds of people turned up, and it was actually the Prime Minister Harold Macmillan who escorted the man from the train, not us. But we all cheered as they walked past. Some in the crowd shouted at them rudely, but one of our cleaning ladies who'd come with us started singing, '*For he's a jolly good fellow*!'. We all joined in, drowning the jeers.

The special train passenger was Konrad Adenauer, the German Chancellor. 'It's important he's received warmly in London,' someone explained to me, 'because our countries have been at war but now we need to work together for peace. Some people don't want him in London, but he's doing important work and we must make him feel welcome.' *Feel welcome*. It was a phrase often used when we had visitors in the house.

Germany was also frequently mentioned in Charles Street, along with other faraway places like France, Russia,

Japan, Cyprus and America. With all this talk, and all these guests, I knew I was part of something important and good. But I had very little grasp of what that 'something' was.

Gradually I became more familiar with some of the recurring words and topics in the household. People had a *quiet time* if there was a problem. A *7.30* was an early morning meeting before breakfast, and *morning meetings* were after breakfast, and these events generally took place over at 45. Occasionally I sat in a meeting reading a book, and when the whole room had a quiet time together I had to be extra quiet, as everyone stopped talking. Some of them closed their eyes, or scribbled notes. After a while, people started to share the thoughts they'd had while they'd been quiet, and I'd be able to fidget and turn my pages again.

Sometimes the grown-ups called quiet times *having guidance*, and they'd say things like, 'What's your guidance on this?' or 'Let's have guidance about that.' It was a stern word, which generally meant something serious was going on. If something was 'guidance' it had to be obeyed. It was used to decide things like when to make a particular journey, or how to help someone, or what next steps to take.

Guidance and quiet times could also be called *listening to God*. Grown-ups might say, 'God told me to do that', and I knew Mummy and Daddy had to do what God told them. Last thing at night, I said prayers with them or whoever put me to bed, and then we prayed to Jesus, not God. I knew more about Jesus. He was born in a stable at

Christmas to show he loved everyone, and to show us how to love others.

Another word that often came up was *battle* or *fight*. It seemed we were involved in war. We were all part of a world family that was fighting this war, but I couldn't picture that family or the conflict. I simply knew there were many people like us, all connected. Somewhere deep in the heart of it was someone called *Frank*, another popular topic in conversations. I hadn't seen him myself, but there were photos of him in the Charles Street houses, and the grown-ups obviously knew him well, liked him and took his opinions seriously. I had no doubt that this 'Uncle Frank' would one day walk through the front door and I'd recognise him from the round metal-frame glasses and pointy nose I'd seen in pictures.

Vital as these concerns were to the adults, they became even more of a background blur to me once I started at Glendower Prep School for girls in Kensington. Suddenly there was a new daily regime to keep me occupied, and I was happy to be back at school, even though this one was more formal than St Christopher's in Sussex.

Miss Macdonald was my no-nonsense form teacher at Glendower. She had dark wavy hair and arching eyebrows and she'd peer at us severely over her glasses. I didn't warm to her, but in the fifties pupils didn't expect teachers to be friendly. I barely thought of her after leaving, apart from one small incident that troubled me for years. In just a few words and gestures it was Miss MacDonald who first made me realise that my family didn't match other people's 'normal'.

Before this happened I'd rather enjoyed the new London school and the routines it imposed. Each morning I'd walk, sometimes skip, through Mayfair to Green Park beside a handful of older girls from the Charles Street homes, all of us wearing our purple uniform. Of these girls I particularly liked walking with Anne, who was closest in age to me and had freckles and a cheeky grin, but I rarely saw any of them beyond that journey to and from school. The route took us along Lansdowne Row, past a pet shop that usually displayed adorable puppies in its window. They'd jump up against the glass when we passed, and I yearned to at least touch one. But we were always hurried on by a grown-up worried we'd miss our 14 bus from Green Park.

Glendower School was, and still is, housed in a white stucco building on a corner of Queen's Gate, close to South Kensington tube. Every morning the plump headmistress greeted each of us with a handshake at the front door. At morning break we drank milk from third-pint glass bottles with straws. In summer this was fine, but in winter the crate was left by the radiators and the warm milk tasted like sick.

After lunch we had to lie on our blankets on the floorboards, for a rest. Few of us slept, but a teacher walked around us so we didn't dare get up. One day I saw right up a teacher's skirt, and the complexity of her undergarments – under-slip, stockings, suspenders – added to my growing concern that adult life might be unfathomable.

Most afternoons we walked together like a giant purple centipede up Queen's Gate for a quick turn in Hyde Park before trudging back to school. Kicking our way through thick mounds of leaves on the pavement was a pleasant distraction in the autumn, but in other seasons the walk felt long and dull. On a good day we'd return to a ballet class, and we'd spring around the floor dreaming we were Margot Fonteyn.

In Miss MacDonald's classroom the lines of small wooden desks were well-spaced to discourage distracting conversations. It didn't occur to me that school had a social side, apart from a few birthday parties to which the whole class was invited. These were usually held in someone's house, and we'd have games or an entertainer. In my best dress with smocking front and full skirt, topped with a fluffy angora bolero, I blended in with all the other little girls in similar outfits. Once a birthday party was laid on for me in the drawing room of 43 Charles Street. I forget the details, but my classmates came, and there would certainly have been a good tea, a cake with candles, and games.

Apart from this there were no visits from school pals or invitations to play at their homes. Perhaps casual socialising was less common among young children in those days, or maybe it was discouraged in our busy adult household. Perhaps none of my friends lived near Mayfair. Whatever the reason, I never expected to make friends at school, and it wasn't a problem. The friends I revelled in were the ones in my books, like Milly Molly Mandy and Mary Plain.

Once my parents made a rare visit to the school for a Sports Day, held in a local garden square, or possibly a corner of Kensington Gardens. For the rest of his life, my father delighted in reliving the event that marked, for him, the discovery that his six-year-old daughter had no clue about sport. 'We searched for her in vain among the winners sprinting towards the finish,' he'd say, 'and finally we spotted her, skipping along, way behind the others, waving to the crowd!' I always hated the story, partly as it grew in the telling, and partly for its self-fulfilling assumption that sport wasn't my forte. Most jarring of all was his complete failure to recognise a small girl's overwhelming excitement at seeing her parents attend her school event for the first time.

Soon after this came the galling episode that made me suddenly self-conscious about my parents and the life we led. We were sitting at our desks one morning when Miss MacDonald opened a new topic: occupations. 'Now girls,' she began, 'today we're going to think about the different things people do when they grow up and go to work. I'm a teacher, for instance, so I work in a school. In the countryside someone might be a farmer.' So far so good. This sounded interesting.

'So, girls,' she continued, 'I'm going to go around the class and ask you all what jobs your fathers do. Your mothers all work very hard being your mummies. They may not go out to work if they have a home to look after. But what do your fathers do?' She paused while we thought about it. 'Molly, let's start with you. What does Daddy do?' I listened attentively to the various responses as they came, one by one. A doctor. A banker. A shop manager. A lawyer. It reminded me of that chant *Tinker, Tailor, Soldier,*

Sailor… Each contribution was rewarded with a quick word of approval. 'Yes.' 'Good.'

Suddenly it dawned on me that I had no idea what to say. My turn was coming and I didn't know the answer. I knew all the grown-ups in our houses, even the mummies, were busy doing 'the work'. They were 'remaking the world', and 'changing people'. But what did that mean, and how did you say that in one word or two?

'Judith?' Miss MacDonald was now waiting, and I was flummoxed, desperately wanting to get it right. In the nick of time I thought of something people often said about Daddy.

'My father was in charge of a tank in the war,' I declared with relief at finding an answer. But to my surprise it didn't go down well. Instead of nodding approval, Miss MacDonald looked confused, frowning a little. 'Well… all right,' she said slowly. 'That was a very good thing to have done, commanding a tank in the war. Very brave too. But that was over ten years ago. Before you were born. What does he do now, dear?'

'I'm not sure,' I mumbled, ashamed to be caught out on something the others found so easy. 'But you *must* know what your father does!' the teacher persevered. 'Well, not really,' I insisted. 'I don't know the word.' My collar felt itchy, my face was hot, and I wished the bell would go for lunch. I usually did well in class. How had I got it so wrong? The teacher moved on to the next girl, and I was glad to be out of the spotlight.

I'd felt a similar discomfort a few weeks before, when I'd tried to tell the class about some visitors at our house.

I'd been convinced everyone would like to know about the men from Canada who'd worn feather headdresses, tasselled sleeves and long hair, like Indians in *The Lone Ranger*. I knew Chief Walking Buffalo wasn't play-acting from the way the grown-ups talked with him normally. He was one of the family, and he'd been here to meet real people like the Queen and the Prime Minister. It was all true. But Miss MacDonald had shushed me and changed the subject. I'd winced at the unfairness, realising she hadn't believed me, and so my schoolfriends probably didn't either.

Back at 43 that night, the unanswered question about Daddy's job weighed on me. 'When someone asks "what's your father do?", what do we say?' I asked over supper. 'Don't worry about it,' someone, possibly one of my parents, reassured me. 'We'll give you one of our new booklets to give your teacher tomorrow. Just say to her "My father works for Moral Re-Armament, and here's something to read about it".'

The grey and white booklet I was given was small and thin, and had *Ideology and Co-existence* written on the cover. The text inside was dense, the letters tiny, and there were no pictures. The chapter headings used more words I didn't understand, like *communism* and *strategy*. The opening line read, '*We are at war. World War III has begun.*' It was clearly for adults, and I assumed it would please Miss MacDonald and answer her question.

Slipped into a crisp white envelope, the booklet travelled with me to school next day in my leather satchel. I was looking forward to clearing things up so that all would be well. In the classroom, I went straight up to Miss MacDonald at her big desk by the blackboard. 'My father works for Moral Re-Armament, and here's a book about it,' I blurted out. I don't think I had ever tried getting my mouth round the laborious words 'moral re-armament' before this, although I'd often heard them. Using 'MRA' for short was much simpler, but I'd been told to say the whole thing.

Miss MacDonald opened the envelope flap with raised eyebrows and cast a quick glance at the cover of the pamphlet inside. I watched her face anxiously, but nothing much happened at all, beyond her closing the flap again and placing the package in the drawer of her desk. 'Thank you. That's very nice. Very helpful,' she said flatly. 'Now, settle at your desks everybody, please,' she called out loudly, getting to her feet. 'Sit up nicely, girls, and we'll get started!' Deflated, I slunk back to my seat. I still hadn't got it right. Clearly it was best not to talk about home things at school. Or school things at home, for that matter. They didn't understand each other. I wouldn't do it again.

The matter was never followed up, at school or at home, but the memory lingered uncomfortably in my mind. I'd wanted to do well at school, but there was something the teacher wasn't happy with. It was confusing for a six-year-old, about to turn seven, who just wanted to fit in and be liked. The episode may well have contributed to the fact that, around this time, I started to become increasingly fearful about school life and its future challenges. I watched the older schoolgirls and realised that as I went up through the next forms, expectations of us younger ones would rise. I wondered how I would ever discover all the rules and knowledge that came so naturally to the big girls.

The school bell became a particular fixation. It was a loud hand bell, rung by one of the senior pupils. We'd catch glimpses of them swinging it noisily as they passed up and down the intricate stairways and corridors of the converted Kensington houses accommodating the school. The clanging marked the end of a class, the start of break, lunch or going home time. Its delivery was clearly a crucial job, witnessed by the entire school community, and privately I became wracked with anxiety. What if I were made a bell monitor sometime soon? How would I know the right time to ring the bell? How would I find the route through the school? What if I made a mistake? The weight of worry was almost unbearable at times. There seemed to be a myriad of things older children and adults knew automatically, and I felt panic-stricken at the thought of all the things I might be told to do but wasn't prepared for.

It didn't occur to me to talk about my fears with anyone and seek reassurance. I had no habit of confiding in my parents or carers, and maybe I couldn't find the right words. However, one day a measure of relief arrived in the form of a simple poem a woman happened to read out at a family meal. The lines were apparently written by a young American girl the woman had met, and I secretly remembered one couplet and cherished the words:

If you have a kind of worry, you need not worry at all

As you know you're in God's pocket, where you cannot have a fall.

The idea I could simply trust that things would be taken care of by God was like healing balm to me, even if it was incomprehensible. Maybe school and adult life, however complex, would somehow be OK after all.

Unfortunately the verse went on to elaborate some conditions, along the lines of:

Unless you're bad and fall right out... then things will look rocky again.

But then it all came right, as the poem said you could always climb back into the pocket again. I pictured a baby kangaroo asleep in its mother's pouch. Or the side pocket of Daddy's suit. Good old God would just take you back into that warm, safe place, even if you'd been bad! Although God was a familiar word in the house, it had until now always sounded grim, conveying a powerful, menacing spirit that laid down rules. Now this simple poem offered some comfort, suggesting that God might actually be loving and protective. The words stuck in my head, becoming a kind of mantra, and my fears faded somewhat when I imagined myself in that pocket *where you need not worry at all.*

Within a few months of memorising the rhyme, everything changed. Suddenly I was told I'd be moving schools again. I could scarcely believe I would never have to be bell monitor and learn the senior rituals after all my worrying. What a relief! What luck! Or had I been rescued by God's pocket? I no longer cared, because I was now consumed with excitement, and the future couldn't look any better. Mummy told me I was going to join a new school up a mountain in Switzerland. A mountain in Switzerland – where Mary Plain and Heidi came from! This felt like familiar territory. What's more, I was assured there would be real children of my own age to play with there, and they were all part of our world family. I couldn't wait.

6

Post-War Europe 1946

Through peaceful alpine pastures a narrow-gauge train travels steadily up and down the Swiss mountainside between Montreux, on the shores of Lake Geneva, and the peak of the Rochers de Naye. At some stations along the way its single track doubles up, to allow a descending train to pass another train going up. And it was at Glion Station one day in the summer of 1946, as two trains stopped beside each other, that Chérie, in one of them, suddenly spotted Bill in the other. She dashed out of her carriage and ran round both trains to speak to him.

'Bill!' she called, knocking on his window. 'Welcome back!' He looked surprised, but he and his travelling companions waved back cheerfully. Nothing much could be said through the train window, but Chérie gestured that she'd been up at the village of Caux, obviously Bill's destination, and she was now heading back to London. 'Catch up soon!' she shouted, waving, before hurrying back to her own train.

Chérie's fellow travellers laughed at her impulsiveness, but one in the group, her mother Dulcie, was disapproving. 'Really, Chérie,' she said in a quiet aside as their train moved off. 'You *can't* go throwing yourself at a man so publicly! Anyway, our train might have left without you, and you'd have missed the connection at Montreux!'

Chérie patted her mother's knee affectionately. 'Always the worrier, Mama!' she said, feeling pleased with herself. 'Anyway,' she confided in a whisper, 'it's been four years since I last saw Bill. If he's forgotten all about me, then at least he remembers now.' 'But if you've truly given it all up to the Lord's will, there's no point forcing the pace,' Dulcie insisted. 'Yes, of course I've surrendered it,' Chérie said firmly. 'But I just have an inkling…' She silently committed her future to a higher authority once more as the train continued its steep descent to Montreux.

The women travelling together were some of a mass of volunteers who'd just spent six weeks halfway up that mountain, turning the run-down Caux Palace Hotel into a fully-functioning conference centre. They'd scrubbed walls, floors and bathrooms, polished wood, brass and chrome, hung curtains and made beds. Now this vast building, which had been bought by 60 Swiss families to be a centre of reconciliation after the war, had been cleaned and refurbished. It had been renamed Mountain House and was ready for hundreds to attend its first MRA conference in July 1946.

The speed with which this hotel complex in Caux was transformed reflected the urgency felt by Frank Buchman and his followers. The World War had ended, but they believed the battle of ideas was far from over. If suffering and bitterness were left to fester in war-torn countries, they feared further cycles of collapse and revenge, as witnessed in Germany after the First World War. Fascism had been defeated for now, but they considered that communism, the official doctrine of the USSR and China, posed a similar threat. Buchman believed MRA could help provide a moral dimension to democracy and peace, which could prevail if they moved quickly. Eighty years on, environmentalists use similarly pressing language when urging people to 'wake up and change', and seize this crucial moment before it's too late to save the planet. The MRA team were convinced that the future of the world depended on immediate action, although at that time nuclear catastrophe was seen as the imminent threat rather than climate change.

Frank Buchman had arrived back in Britain from America in April 1946, three months before the opening of Caux. Accompanied by more than a hundred MRA workers, he had crossed the Atlantic on the newly derequisitioned *Queen Mary*. Chérie and her co-workers, who'd returned to London from Cheshire at the end of the war, were out in the street to greet the party when they arrived in coachloads at Berkeley Square.

During the war Buchman had suffered a severe stroke, and it was a shock for many to see this formerly energetic man now walking slowly, hunched over a stick. As he entered the front door of 45 he was offered a seat in the hall under the large winding staircase, which was packed all the way up to the fourth floor with his London team, gathered to welcome him back. After years apart and the death of many colleagues in war, it was an emotional moment. Everyone was eager to start a new chapter of the work.

The theme of this post-war phase was to be reconciliation and renewal. They believed this would come about through inspired new leadership, especially in the fields of politics and the labour movement. 'Labour, led by God, must lead the world,' Buchman would say, 'otherwise the materialism of Marx or fascism will take over.' To this end there would be regular conferences at the new Caux centre, as there had been during the war at Caux's American counterpart on Mackinac Island (pronounced Mackin-awe) in Michigan. Ambitious missions were being planned that entailed MRA teams visiting strategic places and using books, songs and, increasingly, theatre to spread their ideas. During the war drama had been put to use in America, and was about to play a major part in the ongoing work of MRA worldwide. Among those arriving with Buchman on the *Queen Mary* were the entire cast and production team of a stage play called *The Forgotten Factor*. It addressed industrial and family relations in crisis, and was ready to be shown across Europe.

It was into this flurry of activity that Bill returned in the summer of 1946, after his final army posting in Blackburn, Lancashire. With his Cambridge degree and officer's training he could have pursued a solid conventional career path, but his decision to work full-time for MRA had been made. 'What was clear to me then', he wrote later, 'was the absolute priority need in the world for a group of completely available people, fully committed to being open to the will of God for this shattered world.'

Bill's first move as a civilian was to head for the new conference centre in Switzerland, where he was in time to greet Buchman and his colleagues from America. The reunion of friends that day at the entrance to Mountain House in Caux was euphoric. Then Buchman suddenly looked around and asked, 'Where are the Germans?' It was a question that dismayed many people present who'd suffered in the war, and who hadn't expected to be confronted with 'the enemy' quite so soon. However, Buchman insisted, 'You will never rebuild Europe without the Germans.' Hurried arrangements were made to raise a German delegation for the summer conference, despite tight restrictions on Germans leaving their country so soon after the war. The Allied Control Authority finally allowed 16 Germans to visit Caux that first year, including the widows of two men executed for plotting to kill Hitler.

A few months later, in November 1946, Bill stood on a crowded stage at the Westminster Theatre in London alongside more than 60 colleagues, all in uniform, who'd served in the forces during the war. It was Remembrance Sunday, and the theatre was being dedicated to the men and women of MRA who had died in the war. Hundreds of people had contributed to the purchase of the building, for the purpose of presenting drama productions of hope and inspiration to counter the cultures of despair and nihilism. It was seen as a practical way of honouring the sacrifice of fallen friends by building the peace.

A photo of the dedication ceremony shows Bill and one

of his teammates from Egypt, Matt Manson, standing in the front two rows. They are watching Bill's cousin Agnes as she reads out the last letter of her brother Sergeant Nigel Leakey, with whom Bill went to school. Nigel had died aged 28 fighting the Italians at Kolito, Ethiopia in 1941, and had been awarded the Victoria Cross for gallantry.

Bill's thoughts also went to Tom Shillington, buried in the desert, Geoffrey Currall, killed in Italy at the Anzio Beach landing, and Mike Sitwell, a third close friend who died during the D-Day invasion of Normandy. Bill's friends, lost and living, seemed to merge together that day. He firmly believed his colleagues had not died in vain. They'd given their lives to win the war. But now their battle for a free world continued.

Back at Hays Mews, Bill rejoined the book team while assessing the future. He noticed changes. The work was growing, and so too was MRA's structure and organisation. Even Frank Buchman was initially uncomfortable with some developments. In the 1920s and '30s, the American had enjoyed an informal fellowship, allowing for spontaneity and flexibility. The operation had felt close in spirit to that of the early Christians, before church buildings, hierarchies and prescribed laws sprang up. Oxford Groupers had often followed random individual directives in their quiet times. As a contemporary had put it, if you'd suddenly felt called to 'go to Basingstoke', then off you went to Basingstoke, with minimal – if any – consultation. Their life had been frugal and monastic, yet free from rules and structure.

By the late 1940s and '50s there were many more full-time workers, too many for each to liaise as closely with Frank Buchman as they had before. He remained the cherished leader, and his workers continued to write regular, detailed letters to Buchman, reporting on their lives and activity. But increasingly Buchman's immediate team helped manage his mail and pen his replies.

As a registered charity, Moral Re-Armament also owned substantial properties, including the two international conference centres at Mackinac and Caux, the Westminster Theatre, and headquarters in cities all over the world. In London, after the war, five more Mayfair houses were donated to MRA, to add to 45 Berkeley Square and Hays Mews. The houses 12A, 40, 41, 43 and 44 Charles Street, obtained at knock-down post-war prices, were rapidly put to use as communal homes and workspaces. This was exciting to Bill and his colleagues. The donation of all these properties appeared to indicate people's readiness for the new ideology, and the momentum of MRA's work seemed unstoppable.

As the operation grew, new routines and practices evolved. These had originally been considered unnecessary as long as people followed God's direction and absolute moral standards. In keeping with prevailing principles of the time, these 'standards' assumed no marital relations outside marriage and no same-sex partnerships. But almost inevitably, as the community developed so did unwritten behaviour and dress codes. The Mayfair homes were considered on a par with embassies, receiving visitors constantly, so the dress code was smart. Those wanting to relax in shirtsleeves, slippers or hair rollers did so in the privacy of their bedrooms.

There was no smoking or alcohol on MRA premises. The influence of Buchman's strict Lutheran and Pennsylvanian Dutch background was strong. He was a stickler for high-quality housekeeping and hospitality as a means to make people feel respected and welcome. Accordingly, good cooking was the order of the day, along with tidy bedmaking and table-laying, complete with perfectly arranged flowers and table napkins. Each December at least one giant Christmas tree, always a real one, dominated the hallways and sitting rooms of MRA buildings. The branches would be decorated with genuine candles, which would be lit, with all electric lights switched off, while the household sang carols around the tree.

A younger Bill might have balked at the mandatory nature of some of this, but after the army he embraced it with enthusiasm. Serving others selflessly was a way to reach people, and discipline was how battles were won. With no parents and his siblings scattered, MRA had become Bill's family and MRA centres his home. On his travels he carried photos of Frank and his wartime friends, not of his relatives.

One morning after returning to London from the first conference at Caux, Bill decided to consult Frank Buchman about his future. A posse of assistants including a doctor had accompanied Buchman since his stroke, so a private appointment was duly made, and Bill was summoned to an upstairs sitting room at 45 Berkeley Square.

'Well come on in, Bill.' Buchman's eyes lit up brightly as the younger man walked in. 'Captain Conner! It's good to have you back, soldier. And all signed up for the new battlefront, I hear!' Buchman had hauled himself to his feet, leaning heavily on his stick, and the men shook hands warmly. Bill plunged straight in. Yes, he was back. He was in it for the long haul. And he'd come to talk about Chérie.

Over the years Bill had generally adopted a dismissive attitude to Chérie's obvious interest in him, but his friends had challenged him to drop the façade. He'd faced the fact he was strongly drawn to her, and was now even considering proposing. During the war, thoughts of Chérie seemed an indulgent distraction. In any case, having chosen to live by 'absolute purity' and shun the attentions of women, he'd found it easier to go to monastic extremes and ignore his feelings altogether. Even now, with friends urging him to seek God's guidance on marriage, he half expected, half hoped even, that Buchman might raise some kind of objection.

But Buchman had moved on from an earlier stance that appeared to discourage his workers pairing up. His secretary Dr Morris Martin writes that Buchman's original reluctance arose from his belief that sex and money, as basic human desires, needed to be sublimated to truly serve God. He'd also regarded marriage and children as impeding the Oxford Group's progress by setting conflicting agenda and reducing his team's flexibility. But times had changed. The young men and women enlisted by Buchman at university age were now in, or approaching, their thirties. Many newcomers to the work, like the journalist Peter Howard, already had a wife and children. And if the new MRA centres and campaigns needed hosts and managers to nurture young recruits and create a sense of community, then married couples who prioritised 'the work' over all other concerns were ideal for the role.

So suddenly, as post-war life resumed, a wave of MRA marriages was taking place in Britain and elsewhere with Buchman's blessing, even though he himself remained determinedly single and celibate. Within weeks of his arrival from America in 1946 he'd attended seven of these weddings in England and Scotland, and others took place at Caux, including, the following year, the marriage of Bill's sister Erica to Edward Evans. The marriage surge reflected a universal trend as couples reunited after the war, but in MRA circles getting married went beyond personal fulfilment. It represented a stepping up of a spiritual commitment in partnership with the new spouse. It wasn't a chance to opt out, build a nest or make private plans, but a time to contribute more.

'Is God calling you to this marriage?' Frank asked Bill.

'Well… yes, I think perhaps He may be,' Bill admitted cautiously.

'Is Chérie feeling called?'

'I don't know for sure, Frank. I rather think she may… Our friends seem to think so.'

'So what are you waiting for, Bill?'

'Well, she's perfect, but I may not be ready… and being single has its advantages. After all, *you've* never…'

'This isn't about *me*!' Frank broke in firmly. 'It's about accepting a gift God's handing *you*, you lucky feller! Now get cracking, won't you? Or I might have to carry you up the aisle myself!' Frank waved his stick at Bill impatiently, but his eyes were twinkling. 'I'll need a date quickly, you know. My schedule's filling up fast!'

With this unexpected push from Buchman, Bill left the room with a spring in his step, yet strangely nervous too. The marriage idea may be rubber-stamped by Frank, but what of Chérie? Perhaps he'd been too cool with her and her attentions had moved elsewhere. He knew of others who seemed sweet on her. And was he ready for this? Becoming an 'MRA couple' would be a rapid promotion within the work, almost like becoming an officer. Was this really for him?

Bill prayed. He had a quiet time with close friends, and he sensed a forward momentum that felt right and which suddenly he had no desire at all to stop. He booked a restaurant table for two outside London where they wouldn't be disturbed. He borrowed a car. And he wrote a note on fine writing paper inviting Chérie for an evening out.

For Chérie, her engagement to Bill was a fulfilment of her own prayers, and an assurance that following the Almighty brought abundant rewards. Bill was always embarrassed at the thought of his gauche marriage proposal in a layby on the A40. He'd hoped to reinvent himself as the suave suitor, managing the occasion with aplomb, the candlelit dinner setting the mood before, and not after, he popped the question. But the traffic on the way out of London was slow, and the small talk in the car a little strained. Finally, Bill's nervous impatience to get to the point of the evening had him halting at the side of the road, to brusquely propose then and there. To Chérie, who accepted him immediately, it couldn't have been more romantic in a movie. The handsome hero of her dreams had finally broken his reserve and confessed his deepest feelings for her.

The wedding was arranged in London for 7th December 1946, a couple of months away. The date was partly to accommodate Frank Buchman's busy diary, and also to enable Chérie and Bill to later join an MRA team heading to still-occupied Germany. Their engagement was exhilarating for the pair, moving so quickly from restraint with the opposite sex to a degree of closeness. Now they had outings á deux to the theatre or park, and exchanged passionate letters and even hugs and kisses, strictly in private. Bill began to show a more relaxed, open side of himself, barely seen since his mother's death. He'd surprise Chérie with a spontaneous posy of flowers, or loving words scribbled in a secret note, while she, for whom even the old reserved Bill would have been sufficient, simply glowed with contentment.

Given the food rationing that continued well into the 1950s, and their lack of salary or savings, the couple expected a simple, austere wedding. But the generosity of friends astounded them. Gifts poured in to make the event splendid by any standards. Someone had already provided them with Chérie's gold, opal and diamond engagement ring. She was then loaned a bridal gown in antique silk that fitted her petite five-foot form exactly, and came with a Brussels lace veil. Meanwhile the singers at Hays Mews created a choir for the church service, and had a special arrangement of *St Patrick's Breastplate* sent from Ireland.

Even the honeymoon at Parknasilla, one of Ireland's finest hotels on the coast of Kerry, was a gift they hadn't expected.

A further bonus was that Chérie's father Roy had recently returned to Britain from Hamburg, where he'd been commanding a hospital set up in the former German Luftwaffe quarters. Now he was in charge of the Queen Alexandra Military Hospital at Millbank, and had moved with Dulcie into a large London mansion flat in Welbeck Street, Marylebone. The large apartment rooms were perfect for hosting the wedding reception, and a team of young women from Hays Mews organised the catering.

One wedding present was a short black and white film of the event, made by a friend called Jimmy. Home movies were an exciting novelty at the time, and the use of explanatory captions instead of a sound commentary gives this one the look of a Buster Keaton or Charlie Chaplin film. Like most luxury commodities, film stock was in short supply after the war, and Jimmy found he'd overshot before the service started. There are brief glimpses of Chérie and Bill and the bridal party, but the film mainly features the wedding presents, the beaming faces of helpers in aprons waving Chérie off from her parents' flat, and the guests arriving for the service at St Peter's Vere Street.

Both the film and the wedding photos have a military flavour. Bill wore a morning suit, but many guests wore uniform, including Bill's brother Arthur, his best man Reggie Hale, and his new father-in-law, who was then a colonel. The wedding cake, made by Dulcie, featured the insignia of the Royal Irish Hussars, for Bill, and the Royal

Army Medical Corps, for Chérie's father. On top of the cake sat the gold harp emblem of the Irish Hussars, and the first slice was cut by the newlyweds with a regimental sword.

The photos show Chérie looking radiant and Bill happy and relaxed. The one exception is a shot of the couple standing on either side of their guest of honour, Frank Buchman, dapper in his tails and white carnation buttonhole. Bill is firmly holding the right arm of Buchman, who has discarded his stick. The three stand, straight and formal, fixing the camera with an intense, solemn expression, indicating this was not simply a marriage but also a joint commitment to a life of service alongside their leader.

In this context, and given the pressing world needs felt by the MRA team, it was perhaps surprising that the wedding was followed immediately by a flight to Dublin and a blissful honeymoon at Parknasilla. This was probably not only the first but also the last time they ever had a vacation alone as a couple, as holidays didn't feature much in their life ahead. Yet they expressed no regrets, and Bill became a keen advocate of honeymoons to launch couples into married life. They would speak with pride of this romantic time in the land of their two respective Irish grandfathers. In a family photo album there's a faded sepia postcard of Parknasilla, a five-storey country house facing out to sea. Bill has scribbled on the back, 'We were the only guests here when we arrived from the Royal Hibernian Hotel Dublin for the greater part of our honeymoon', and after their years of communal living they must have revelled in the privacy.

The fortnight also introduced a note of reality into the relationship. They both admitted to highs and lows as they got to know each other for the first time. Chérie would say she'd been so 'swept off her feet' by Bill before the wedding that she'd believed it impossible to ever fall out with him. She was quickly proved wrong when Bill took her out to sea in a dinghy, claiming to be an experienced sailor. The weather turned stormy, the boat listed wildly out of control, and they were lucky to make it back alive. 'What were you thinking of?' she snapped furiously, as Bill struggled to prevent them capsizing. 'You said you knew what you were doing! Are you barking mad?!'

For Bill, that moment of truth had arrived in Dublin where they'd attended a service at St Patrick's Cathedral. Arriving late, Bill tried to steer Chérie into the vacant seats at the back. But Chérie advanced up the aisle, aiming determinedly for the crowded front pews. 'Stop here. This'll do fine,' Bill hissed at her, to no avail. He blanched as they forced people at prayer to slide along to make space for them, and felt a surge of fury with his new wife, which he admitted later was quite disproportionate. Their tempers recovered and the honeymoon resumed. But they would refer to these incidents as evidence that marriage has to be worked at, and that their practice of quiet times, with a readiness to apologise, was the key to a good partnership.

Back in London, they were now an 'MRA couple', and they threw themselves into the new role. Chérie took on household management in various MRA properties, and did less secretarial work. Bill kept some responsibilities on books and publications, and together they hosted receptions and welcomed visitors. They readily adapted back to being part of a fighting force, conscious that even though they were now together, they shouldn't flaunt their special relationship in a distracting or self-centred way. They were back on a mission, and their private life had to take a secondary place.

7

London, Germany, Bristol
1947–54

When the world had still been at war and Bill was an Army Education Officer in Cyprus, he'd written to Frank Buchman, 'You would be very thrilled by much that is going on in these countries in the way of unshakable bridge-building between races, factions and classes as a result of the leadership of MRA people… The Area Commander is going to send out *Battle Together For Britain* to every officer and O.R. – as the most effective statement of what we fight for'. Bill names the Cypriot team members he's working with, and tells Buchman that together they've sent him a gift of Cyprus embroidery 'for your home of the moment'. He ends, 'This brings love and gratitude and the thoughts of the MRA fighters of the Middle East – which are constantly with you and the team with you. Loyally, Bill Conner'.

The letter is part of a large collection of correspondence now in the Oxford Group Archives at the Bodleian

Library. It conveys Bill's strong personal devotion to Frank Buchman, and in this Bill was not alone. The same powerful allegiance to Buchman appears in all the letters sent from the MRA workers to their leader and friend. They wrote to him frequently about local goals and challenges, team achievements and also any significant personal news.

Another handwritten note from Bill to Buchman, two years later, signs off: 'Our thoughts and prayers are constantly with you Frank, Affectionately and loyally, Bill and Chérie Conner'.

This one, sent from a flat in central London, announced the arrival, three days before, of the couple's baby son Patrick on 18th September 1947. The birth was, Bill writes, 'a physical and spiritual battle that lasted 18 hours but the certainty of guidance was there all the time'. Bill's euphoria at this 'human miracle' is tempered by assurances that an expanding family in no way compromises his and Chérie's commitment to their calling. While describing his joy at seeing Chérie 'so thrilled and motherly', Bill quotes some of her thoughts about motherhood, written during a quiet time: 'Mary said, "I am here to serve the Lord". The birth of a child is meant to be in service to God. As such it is a great privilege, and nothing to be personally proud, afraid or ashamed about, but rather to glory and rejoice in as something apart from myself'.

Bill goes on to describe their flat, which is 'three minutes from the Westminster Theatre and six of us live there'. Chérie would be staying in her nursing home for a fortnight, and that night in the flat there was to be a meeting with local colleagues to see how to counter a Communist

Party plan to spread its influence on Westminster City Council.

For a while Bill and Chérie remained in London with their young son, while occasionally supporting campaigns further afield. Some of their co-workers were heading to Japan, America, South Africa and the Middle East in response to requests for an MRA presence. But for the moment their own sights remained within Europe.

Chérie's German language skills had proved useful in London and Caux, and in the autumn of 1948, she and Bill joined an international MRA group of 250 travelling through Germany for three weeks. Both Chérie, who'd lived in Berlin before the war, and Bill, who'd fought the Germans in North Africa, felt compelled to join the tour. There's no record of where they left one-year-old Patrick but it's likely he was cared for by Chérie's parents, who'd recently returned to London from a posting in Singapore.

Europe's reconstruction was a top post-war priority for MRA. Hitler's defeat had left Germany in ruins and its fascist ideology leaderless and discredited. The joint occupying forces – America, Britain, France and Russia – didn't want to repeat the mistakes of the Treaty of Versailles after World War One, which had imposed crushing penalties on Germany and enabled Hitler's rise. Instead the Allies were looking for ways of restoring democracy, economic growth and stability, while creating structures that could bond the new Germany with its neighbours in peace.

Stalin's Russia had its own view on filling the 'ideas vacuum' after the collapse of Hitler's National Socialism.

Russia was determinedly promoting communism in the East of Germany, which it controlled, and this strengthened the resolve of the Americans, British and French to rebuild the other German regions as a buttress to protect the 'free West'. The Second World War had finished, but the Cold War was only just beginning.

Aware of MRA's wartime campaigns and the Caux conferences, some leaders in the Allied zones endorsed MRA's attempts to offer an alternative ideology to communism, and urged Buchman to get to work in Germany. One supporter was Lord Pakenham, the minister in charge of the British zone, who told MRA workers that, apart from food, 'the kind of work you are doing is the only thing which will do any good in Germany now.'

Movement in and out of Germany was still highly restricted, but with this official backing the flow of Germans to Caux had increased. By 1951 around 4,000 German delegates had attended conferences there. They included statesmen like Konrad Adenauer, who visited Caux in 1948, a year before becoming the first Chancellor of the Federal German Republic. MRA groups were invited back into Germany, stage plays were written and translated into German, and special publications were produced, including the booklet *Es Muss Alles Anders Werden* (*Everything Must Be Different*).

Bill and Chérie kept photos of the German mission they joined, but left no written record. However, the letters home of a French fellow-traveller, 19-year-old Jacqueline Piguet, paint some vivid impressions of the journey. Jacqueline describes how their cavalcade of buses visited the cities of Ulm, Munich, Stuttgart, Frankfurt, Düsseldorf, Essen, Wuppertal, and towns in between. They brought with them the cast and stage equipment of a musical revue called *The Good Road*, which was performed at each stop. The show had been created at Caux, Jacqueline says, 'to bring to a post-war Europe the heritage and values of democracy', with songs that celebrated how, 'with new hearts and new people, everything can change'.

The scale of destruction in the bombed-out cities of Germany shocked the French teenager. As a schoolgirl she'd fled her home in Alsace and lived under German occupation, hoping Germany would one day suffer as badly as France had done. 'But I never imagined such suffering as I saw here', she says. Nonetheless, people meeting them after the shows were generous, offering gifts of flowers, cakes, even a slice of rye bread. One old woman 'dressed in tatters' brought an envelope containing 100 marks and a note saying this was 'to bring this hope to more people'. Jaqueline realised how desperate and cut off from the world the Germans felt.

Many of the MRA group wore national costumes, on and sometimes off the stage, to demonstrate the wide range of countries represented who wanted to reach out to Germany again. As guests of the regional governments, the troupe was billeted in barracks, hostels, homes and even a large boat on the Rhine. The accommodation was basic. One American barracks was considered comfortable as it had some heating and two hot taps between 100 people.

Leaving Frankfurt, the visitors were granted special permission to visit the air base from which flights were leaving every three minutes on a mercy mission to Berlin. Four months earlier the Russians had blocked all rail, road and canal access to Berlin in protest against the new Deutsche Mark and America's aid plans for Germany. The blockade had stopped food, clothing, fuel and medical supplies reaching people in West Berlin. Now the Allied planes thundering over the visitors' heads were bringing vital relief in the famous Berlin Airlift, which continued for almost a year. It was the first major international crisis of the Cold War.

Witnessing the huge aid operation was sobering. 'With some anguish we realised this extraordinary effort of the airlift is not, and cannot be, a solution', Jacqueline writes, 'because thousands of planes, thousands of litres of fuel and tons of food cannot stop the advance of ideas. It brought home to us why it was worthwhile giving up our normal and comfortable life for this adventure'. Everyone had sacrificed something to be there. Chérie and Bill had left their baby. Jacqueline Piguet had given up a year of college. Some participants stayed on in Germany after the tour, working there for several years.

Much of the ongoing MRA focus was on the Ruhr region. This was the heart of Germany's coal and steel industries, which were central to the country's regeneration plans. Over the next years, workers and management from the mines and factories spent time at Caux, including Communist Party members influential on the workers' committees. Many took up the MRA challenge to build productive working relationships instead of stoking confrontation. Meanwhile the trust built at Caux between senior French and German politicians, including Chancellor Adenauer and the French Foreign Minister Robert Schuman, helped facilitate the Schuman Plan. This scheme placed French and West German coal and steel production under a single authority as a means of ensuring future peace. It was a starting point in the supranational co-operation that evolved into the European Union.

Returning to London, Bill and Chérie stayed informed on events in Germany, while juggling work and family. Their baby was one of many who rapidly followed the post-war MRA marriages and further changed the culture of Buchman's work. For a community used to fast-changing plans, long working hours and global travel, babies and children added an extra challenge that had received little advance thought. Chérie and Bill didn't anticipate any difficulties. Both had grown up in a world of nannies, governesses, boarding schools, and absent parents. Moreover, their life of 'faith and prayer' meant trusting in a loving God to look after all areas of their lives. They believed the 'right plan' would always reveal itself.

Black-and-white family photos of the couple with their baby leave little doubt that Patrick was loved and enjoyed, and in his early years Chérie and Bill were mostly hands-on parents. Bill remained the more mobile of the pair, occasionally travelling, while Chérie stayed with her child, supported by other mothers and young women in the MRA community in London.

Bill even bought a house at this time, using his share of an inheritance from his father's Irish estate. But his purpose was to invest, not to create a home or put down roots. In the post-war years large Victorian villas in the London suburbs were, like the MRA houses in Mayfair, available at greatly reduced prices. For £2,000 at mid-century values, Bill was able to buy a large house in Croydon. It needed work, but was already divided into four self-contained flats. Bill realised it could provide a small income, which would be useful back-up when working without salary. What was more, Chérie's father Roy was retiring from the army around this time, and was looking for a home in England. He and Dulcie agreed to move into one of the flats in this house, do up the whole place, and manage the letting of the other apartments. This suited both parties, as Bill and Chérie were turning their attention to a new industrial campaign in Bristol. They could free themselves of responsibility for the property, while Roy and Dulcie were glad to have a home that brought with it refurbishment tasks they'd both enjoy.

Number 9 Chichester Road stood at the top of a hill not far from East Croydon Station. Nowadays the site is covered with 1970s' town houses. But after the war the road comprised imposing, detached houses with curved front driveways and three-quarter-acre gardens. Roy happily applied himself to painting walls, fixing sash windows and clearing cellars, while snapping up bargains at a local auction house to furnish the flats. Dulcie sewed curtains, covered chairs and, with Roy, rescued the neglected garden.

Meanwhile Bill and Chérie moved with three-year-old Patrick to the West Country. It was 1951. A retired businessman and his wife, Geoff and Freda Sanders, had offered them a share of their home in Bristol. This arrangement, whereby MRA supporters of means helped unsalaried full-timers, was typical of the way MRA operated, and the match was a good one. The Sanders had no children and warmly welcomed the young family into their house, which was close to the Clifton Downs and Torwood House School for Patrick, and provided easy access into the city.

Chérie counted her blessings. Some of their friends had barely stopped travelling, despite becoming parents, but here there was every possibility of even expanding the family. And late the following year, as Patrick turned five, Chérie gave birth to a daughter, Judith Maye, in a Clifton nursing home. Chérie later recalled pushing a pram on the Downs in the spring, a froth of white blossom on the hawthorn trees, and Patrick beside her chatting to his glove puppet animals. 'I was so happy I'd burst into song,' she'd say. 'A favourite was *Oh What a Beautiful Morning*! from the musical *Oklahoma*, only I'd sing "*Oh what a beautiful baby, oh what a beautiful boy*"… I didn't expect so many gifts to be showered on us.' There would be future sacrifices to make, she was sure, but for now she revelled in her good fortune.

Chérie and Bill joined a large and longstanding MRA team in Bristol, a city still recovering from the war. As a major port and aircraft manufacturer, Bristol had been heavily bombed in 1940 and 1941. Around 13,000 people had been killed, and more than 80,000 homes destroyed, along with schools, factories, shops and public buildings. The air raids were described by the city's Mayor at the time,

Alderman T. H. J. Underdown, as 'a veritable volcanic cataclysm' with fires raging from building to building 'like a huge fiery furnace'. The raids had continued for months, with some lasting for twelve hours on end.

Despite the onslaught, Bristol had remained one of Britain's principal food and oil ports through the war, and the port receiving most of America's war supplies. Prime Minister Churchill had written to Mayor Underdown that he had 'heard with pride of the courage, resolution and patience with which the people of Bristol have answered these detestable attacks', and the Bristolians' resilience was seen as a model worldwide. The Mayor attributes some of this fortitude to his predecessor Alderman Burgess. Two months before the air attacks began, Burgess had distributed around the city 50,000 copies of an MRA leaflet called *Morale – How To Play Your Part*. Signed by the Mayor, his Deputy and other senior civic leaders, it was republished in other places under attack, including the island of Malta during its two-year siege by Germany and Italy.

The leaflet suggested five steps everyone could take to keep up their spirits, under the following headings:

Forget yourself in helping your neighbours
Keep the moral standards of the nation high
Be a rumour-stopper
The secret of steadiness and inner strength is to listen to God
Forearm yourself by listening to God first thing every morning

Some people no doubt baulked at the religious tone of the manifesto, but according to Mayor Underdown, the message was widely welcomed, and locals clubbed together to publish it on full-page spreads in Bristol's three daily papers. The Council's Emergency Committee used it in setting up neighbourhood 'fellowships' that offered support after each air raid. The Mayor also commended the 'conspicuous service given by the Moral Re-Armament Players who visited the City at the time of Bristol's severe trial and gave performances of *Giant Otherfellow*, a striking play with music and song… heartening the troops, munition workers and the people in the most heavily blitzed areas of the City'.

At the end of the war Bristolians involved in these endeavours called for more full-time MRA workers to join them, hoping to advance MRA's industrial strategy in their city. When Frank Buchman had launched Moral Re-Armament in London in 1938, he'd said, 'Only a new spirit in men can bring a new spirit in industry. Industry can be the pioneer of a new order. When Labour, Management and Capital become partners under God's guidance, then industry takes its true place in national life. New men, new homes, new industry, new nations, a new world.' Buchman envisaged fairly treated labour and philanthropic management working together to revolutionise industry for the common good. In so doing he hoped to attract fascists and communists alike to a new ideology.

The Ruhr region of West Germany seemed to be developing some models of collaboration, while also demonstrating the tough ideological battle required to achieve it. It was common knowledge that the communist Soviet Union, already controlling East Germany, was taking any opportunity to extend its own influence and power westward. Strengthening communist influence among the workforce of the industrialised Ruhr was a key part of the Russian strategy.

After the *Good Road* campaign that Chérie and Bill had been a part of in Germany, the North Rhine-Westphalia government had invited MRA workers to continue working in the Ruhr. A young Norwegian called Jens Wilhelmsen was one of them. Their purpose, Jens said, was 'to foster democratic attitudes, a sense of responsibility for reconstruction and a better social climate in the industries of the Ruhr'. Sleeping on sofas in workers' three-room family apartments, Jens spent several years in what he calls this 'ideological wasps' nest'. One worker told him, 'If the western occupation forces were to withdraw now, there would be a capitalist dangling from every lamp-post. There is a lot of class hatred here.' In 1948, 70 per cent of those on the Ruhr mining industry's *Betriebsträte* (works councils) were KPD (German Communist Party) members.

Jens writes that MRA's aim in the Ruhr was not to oppose the communists but rather to permeate the party with a new approach, and win them over. Most KPD members who started to engage with MRA had, Jens says, no intention of leaving their Party or their committee, hoping to make changes from within. Some of them were voted out. However, before long a large number of Ruhr militants had replaced the language of class war with that of co-operation and trust. There was talk of an enlightened management approach emerging, and a new union culture. These were making possible power-sharing legislation, raised production and ultimately the regrowth in Germany that came to be termed an economic miracle. Jens and his colleagues in industry were convinced that without the spread of this collaborative spirit, the European Coal and Steel Community would never have been created in 1951 by the Treaty of Paris, a cornerstone for the European Union. German industrial workers started to be seen as a source of inspiration, and a group of Ruhr coal miners were invited all over the world to share their experiences.

Bristol was, of course, quite different from the Ruhr. It was known for its port and its aircraft and car production rather than coal and steel, and labour militancy was less obvious. However, when Chérie and Bill arrived, Bristol was still highly industrialised, with factories and a bustling port at the heart of the city, a far cry from the yachting marinas, apartments and restaurants that have replaced them now. Working conditions for the port's dockers were shockingly harsh and dangerous by today's standards. Not surprisingly, worker-management relations were strained.

As they made friends with dockworkers and their families, Chérie and Bill learnt that the dockers were employed casually, with no guaranteed income. They heard how degrading it was every morning to gather in a 'pen' on the docks in the hopes of being picked by a foreman for work that day. Missing out left the men unpaid and desperate, and a culture of threats and backhanders had developed, along with seething resentment between workers and against foremen, managers, or inactive union reps. In addition, frequent accidents were caused by outdated, unsafe loading machinery, or toxic cargo materials. Finding their employers unsympathetic, the workers resorted to strikes, but stoppages often led to dismissals and ship owners moving their business elsewhere. This cycle was starting to afflict all Britain's major ports.

In this troubled atmosphere the MRA team worked hard to bring labour and management together, just as their colleagues were doing in the Ruhr and in other British cities. Their purpose was to facilitate understanding and agreements for the benefit of both sides. They didn't propose specific solutions, but tried to help opposing factions explore 'what's right, not who's right'. It wasn't an easy task. Opponents often accused the MRA workers of having a hidden agenda, one side calling them 'communists', while others said they were 'management stooges'.

Opposition came not only from within the industrial world. MRA continued to be fiercely attacked in the press, with claims that Buchman was pro-Hitler or a pacifist circulating for decades. One of MRA's most outspoken critics was Tom Driberg, a well-known journalist, Member of Parliament, Anglican churchgoer and Labour Party Chair. Rumours that he was also a KGB agent were confirmed after his death by Soviet defectors and espionage experts. But whatever his motivation, his safe position at the heart of the British establishment enabled him to conduct a powerful campaign against Frank Buchman and his work, and for decades his fiercely hostile book *The Mystery of Moral Re-Armament* remained the standard 'authority' on MRA in British libraries.

Buchman urged his teams to accept opposition as a natural response to, and even proof of, their effectiveness. They were, after all, in a battle of ideas. He had no desire, nor money, for legal suits. Some historians have suggested that Buchman's reluctance to engage in public debate was a drawback for the movement, as the mud thrown often stuck in people's minds. But MRA workers became accustomed to it and carried on.

In Bristol, life was varied for Bill and Chérie. The Bristol team, some full-time, some with 'day jobs', met frequently. One day they might be knocking on the doors of dockers' homes inviting them to a public meeting. On another they could be taking international visitors to meet local MPs or union officials. Sometimes Bill drove to London or Tirley Garth to confer with other teams, or accompanied Bristol delegates to a Caux conference. There were no formal line managers. Decisions were made on the basis of 'guidance', agreed with colleagues at local and national level, while liaising with Buchman.

On quieter days Bill might drive the family to the beach at Weston-super-Mare, or to see his sister in the Midlands. Erica's husband Edward was taking over the supervision of the family estate from his elderly parents, and was exploring ways to apply MRA to land stewardship, farming, staff relationships and global food production. With Edward's three sisters and two brothers also working with MRA, and colleagues constantly visiting them, Whitbourne Hall had become something of an MRA centre in the Worcestershire countryside.

At his shared home in Bristol, Bill was an affectionate father who, like many men of his time, was happy to leave the practicalities of child-raising to the womenfolk. In the confines of the home he showed his softer, more mischievous side. He enjoyed using private jokes to give his children a light steer on good manners. One involved him tracing the letter 'M' with a finger on his lapel, where a badge might be worn. The ritual was used to discreetly discourage Patrick if he was licking his knife or blowing bubbles in his milk. The 'M' referred to Molesworth, a messy, rebellious prep-school boy from one of his son's favourite comic books, and it was a reminder not to follow his example.

Bill came up with another coded message when Judi became an assertive toddler. This involved the secret letters 'PHCHT', which Bill would whisper with mock menace when she became bossy. Even before she could read she knew this stood for *Patrick Hasn't Cleaned His Teeth*. Bill didn't want her being a 'tell-tale', let alone that most alarming of prospects, a 'controlling woman', something Buchman sometimes spoke of with distaste. Bill's playful side quickly disappeared when visitors arrived or a meeting approached, and the children knew there was another side to their father's life that called him away in the middle of games.

On her part, Chérie was an affectionate, attentive mother, who approved of Dr Benjamin Spock's bestseller *Baby and Child Care*. Spock urged parents to trust their own hunches and treat children as individuals. His relaxed approach to feeding schedules went against the old 'leave babies to cry' practice. But Chérie never followed Spock to the letter. For now she was the classic stay-at-home mother approved of by Spock. But her commitment came first, and like Bill she was prepared to serve anywhere they might be called, with or without the children.

Thanks to the supportive MRA community in Bristol, Chérie never felt housebound. Her hosts Freda and Geoff were willing babysitters, and the household included Judith, a Swedish girl whose *au pair* support was part of her MRA training. Chérie could attend meetings and make her own contacts. She and Bill made many good friends in Bristol, especially among their co-workers. Both locally and worldwide, MRA was a tightly bonded fellowship.

One friend in the Bristol team was Elisabeth, who'd been a land girl with Chérie in Cheshire. Elisabeth had also married an MRA full-timer, a handsome, multi-talented linguist called Frank Bygott, whom Bill had met at his first Oxford Group house party. The couple had a son and daughter the same ages as Patrick and Judi. The sudden discovery that Frank had advanced leukaemia came as a devastating shock to the whole MRA team. During his final days, Chérie sat with Elisabeth by Frank's hospital bed, singing the favourite hymns he requested. After his death Elisabeth took her children to live at her parents' country vicarage in Gloucestershire. When Chérie and Bill visited them, Frank's baby daughter Jane would reach up to Bill, longingly. It was heart-breaking for the grieving family and friends to see the toddler apparently mistaking Bill for her own father. They were all bereft.

Not long after their friend's untimely death, Bill and Chérie moved back to London. They had been invited to host one of the large MRA homes. Two years in Bristol left them with cherished memories, but now they welcomed a return to the capital and a more direct engagement with MRA's global work.

8

Mountain House

Caux, Switzerland 1959–61

Miraculously, in the nick of time, I was whisked away from the daunting challenges of school in Kensington, and was off to live somewhere else, far away. God's pocket had worked its magic. And the new home could hardly have been more different from central London. I was off to live in a fairytale place, halfway up a Swiss mountain.

According to family photos, and a much-repeated story about me falling from the top *couchette* of an overnight train without waking up, I'd been here before. But I didn't remember much about it, and this was a whole new adventure. I was taking a plane for the first time, and flying above the clouds with my mother, destination Geneva.

We travelled by British Overseas Airways Corporation, and I was chuffed to be invited to join the BOAC Junior

Jet Club. The stewardess gave me a shiny gold membership badge with a viciously sharp pin, and a logbook to record all the flights I was told I'd make. A big suitcase carried all my clothes, my teddy, my doll and some books, but no library books, so I knew I'd be staying at the new home for a while.

From Geneva Airport, someone Mummy knew drove us alongside a very long lake, and all around us were tall, snowy alpine peaks. Mummy pointed out towns along the way – Vevey, Lausanne, Montreux – and occasionally she showed me glimpses, high up ahead, of a white palace with towers and turrets, hanging to the side of a mountain.

'That's Mountain House, that's where we're going!' she said excitedly when she first spotted it, and I wondered how we'd ever get up that high. 'It was once a luxury hotel called the Caux Palace!' she told me. 'Film stars and royalty stayed there. Now people still come and stay, but it's for everybody. It's a meeting place where people find answers to problems and make the world a better place.' That sounded a bit like the Charles Street houses, but this building looked far bigger than all of them put together.

As we came closer, the car turned away from the lake onto a road which zig-zagged up the mountain. The Swiss chalets we passed had sloping wooden roofs like my cuckoo clock and Heidi's home. We twisted our way through a town called Glion, and on up towards Caux, Mummy grasping an armrest and steadying me at every bend. Now the ground and the buildings outside the car were covered in thick snow, and the lake was a long way below. My ears blocked up, like they had on the plane, and I felt a bit sick.

With a final lurching curve in the road, the car arrived in the dark shadows of a massive building, its rows of windows stretching high into the sky. Mountain House at last. But the car turned away from it, up a short driveway, and parked at the entrance of a smaller building. I counted four, maybe five, floors but it looked cosy compared with the palace towering above us across the road.

'This is the Hotel Maria!' Mummy exclaimed happily, her tone reassuring me that this was a good spot, and one she knew well. I soon learnt that if we'd continued a little further uphill in the car we'd have passed the village shop and reached a branch in the road. To the left a car could carry on snaking up the mountain. To the right, the tarmac flattened out beside a line of flagpoles and parked cars to one side, and the grand entrance doors of Mountain House to the other.

That was the usual drop-off point for visitors to Caux if they'd travelled up by road. And if they'd taken the blue mountain train up from Montreux, then Caux's tiny railway station, its bar smelling deliciously of French cigarettes, was right next to Mountain House. Adult visitors sometimes received an extravagant musical welcome on their arrival at those big front doors, and I would play a part in those welcomes. But all that lay ahead, and I was pleased with our quiet arrival at the more modest Hotel Maria.

Stepping from the car, the air was icy and sharp, not at all like the thick stuffiness of London. And I was walking on deep, firm snow, sprinkled with grit. The hall we entered had a few chairs and tables, and was otherwise empty and quiet. Its hard, polished floor made our footsteps loud, and smelt different from London floors. Years later I still come across that distinctive 'Swiss smell' in random places, and it takes me back to the corridors of the Maria and Mountain House.

It appeared that some of the children I'd be joining at Caux School lived here in the Hotel Maria too, and I made the best of starts when we took our bags upstairs, and discovered my new roommate, Marion. I took to her immediately, and knew that with a friend like this school could be fun.

Marion had a blond fringed bob, and was seven years old like me. I liked her cheeky smile and infectious laugh. We found the same things funny, and could set each other off into giggling fits, sometimes with just a word or a catch of the other's eye. What was more, Marion's Canadian mother Auntie Margie and Scottish father Uncle Matt were also warm, twinkly people, who clearly knew my parents well. To begin with they, like Mummy, had a bedroom close to ours in the Maria, although these rooms were soon taken over by other carers when our parents had to travel.

Marion had been at Caux School for two years. Before that she'd lived in Paris, in a large shared house like my London home. It was a relief, after my niggling worries at the last school, to have a friend who was not only part of the 'family' but also knew her way round here. There was so much to find out. Where do we have breakfast? Who takes us to school? Who are the other children? How do I wear '*strumpfies*'? (These were thick woollen *strumpfhosen* leggings worn by continental children long before tights replaced socks and stockings in England.) And what on earth was *bircher muesli*, *schnitzel*, *emmental*, *fondue*, *pasta* and that creamy stuff in glass jars called *yaourt*? I hadn't come across any of these tasty items in 1950s' England. 'We have black cherry jam on Sundays,' Marion told me. 'It's the best ever! And the yoghurt's lovely too. It's a bit sour on its own, but you stir in brown sugar, then it's very good.'

Along with these important insider tips I picked up some rules: No running in the Mountain House corridors, no using the lifts as they're for grown-ups, and always say 'Bonjour Monsieur' or 'Bonjour Madame' or 'Bonjour Monsieur, Dame' to strangers passing by who aren't part of our bit of Caux, and probably speak French.

Having a roommate was a delight after my lack of young company in Charles Street. In our twin room at the Maria, Marion and I would chat away, play with our dolls and share books. I particularly liked Marion's Canadian picture book of catchy verse. The poems used transatlantic words I'd never heard before, like 'sticky-icky molasses', which intrigued us. 'Molasses is what you'd call black treacle,' a grown-up explained, and we loved the idea of someone carrying yukky gooey treacle in their coat pocket. We'd *never* be allowed to do that ourselves, and we enjoyed chanting the repetitive and mildly subversive lines as we tramped around Caux:

What have you got in your pocket?
What have you got in your pocket,
Early Monday mor-ning?
Sticky-icky molasses!
Sticky-icky molasses!
Early Monday mor-ning!

Mummy bought me children's books in French, hoping I'd soon be bilingual, but I struggled with the words. One book featured a girl called Martine, another a cartoon dog, but I could only tell the story from the pictures. At school and around the conference centre everyone seemed to speak English, and by the time I left I'd only learned the most basic French.

One group we assumed to be French speakers around Caux were the blue-overalled workmen who were refurbishing the Mountain House dining room and repairing other buildings. We were told to treat these men with respect, and make sure we said our 'Bonjour Messieurs' when we passed them. Marion and I once decided it would be funny to say something different to them, something completely nonsensical. 'Bajee, Mossy' was one variation we tried on them when adults weren't listening, and we almost cried with hilarity at our joke and the builders' bafflement. We later learnt that most of them were Italian or North African, so French probably wasn't their first language either.

In spite of a few tame efforts like this to pretend to push the boundaries, we generally accepted that we were living in a very grown-up place where good manners were expected at all times. We also became used to big ideas being discussed around us to put society to rights. The conversations passed way above our heads and we didn't attempt to keep up. We were innocents in a world with no television, radio or neighbourhood friends outside Caux School to link us with popular culture. All our influences came from our carers and teachers, and the rest of the MRA team around us, and we had little idea of the rough and tumble of the world beyond.

One day Marion saw a friend of our mothers breastfeeding her new baby in private. Neither of us had had any contact with babies, nor any experience of adults baring their body parts, and the activity fascinated us. The young mother had told Marion that mummies often feed their babies milk like this, so we started cradling our dolls in our arms, pretending they were drinking. Getting dressed we'd look with scepticism at our own flat little chests. 'How is it possible to make milk?' we asked. Auntie Margie smiled at us. 'You're much too young for that,' she said cheerfully. 'You have to be real mummies first.' That was unimaginable. Adult lives were beyond comprehension, and our interest in babies quickly faded.

Despite a brief scrap after Marion scribbled the words of a song in heavy pencil over the pristine pages of my Junior Jet Club logbook, we were firm buddies. Disagreements among the children were in any case nipped in the bud by the grown-ups. An apology was always required if a culprit was easily identifiable, and if that wasn't forthcoming there would be a short quiet time for both parties to reflect on who had to say sorry. We soon learnt it was less hassle just to say sorry quickly, even if we didn't feel it, and even if it wasn't our fault.

Finding the way around the village of Caux proved rather easier than unearthing the unwritten rules. I soon discovered that the Hotel Maria was one of three former hotels dotted around the village, which provided additional accommodation to Mountain House. Although they were no longer public hotels they had kept their names: the Grand Hotel, the Hotel Maria, the Hotel Alpina. A few chalets also belonged to the Caux complex. Together the buildings could host hundreds in the MRA community along with the thousands of conference visitors who came here all year round.

These buildings became familiar to us children, but we were almost always in the company of an adult and knew we couldn't explore or play in them freely. I quickly became used to pushing through the heavy wood and glass front doors of Mountain House into its spacious entrance hall, always dark as it faced inwards towards the mountain. Crossing the hall you walked through to the sunny side of the building. To the left was the *promenoir*, a long wide gallery with big windows overlooking the gardens. To the right was the conference hall at the heart of the building. This huge space was carpeted, and had a low stage facing rows of chairs, ready for meetings. The room had pillars with sweeping arches and a lofty painted ceiling. A massive bay window gave panoramic views across the terrace and lawns to the lake below and mountains beyond. On the opposite side of the hall to these windows, a wide flight of stairs led up to the entrance doors into another auditorium: Caux Theatre.

When there were no meetings on you could pass straight through to the back of the great hall, where swing doors led to a staircase and lifts. From there you could go down to the dining, kitchen or office areas, or up to the bedroom floors. At every landing, if you turned a corner near the lifts you'd find yourself at the start of a long, long corridor with dozens of bedroom doors. Each corridor seemed to go on forever, as the far end was out of sight thanks to a slight curve in the middle of the building. We children knew that the best rooms faced the lake and had balconies, and these were where guests and VIPs, and sometimes our parents, stayed. We mainly went to Mountain House for meals, slipping in through a back door opposite the Hotel Maria. This was the quickest way to the kitchens, a cafeteria and, beyond that, the main dining room. The hotels and chalets had smaller kitchens and dining areas too, and sometimes we'd eat there.

Within this large complex of properties, the most homely building of all was one that none of us children slept in overnight at that time, yet it quickly became the most familiar. The Chalet de la Forêt, presumably once a private home, was tucked away at an upper edge of the village, and every morning we'd make the short walk up the looping mountain road we called 'Twigglytwog' to reach this modest but charming property that housed Caux School.

'The Chalet' was the perfect picture-book wooden Alpine lodge, complete with sloping roof, overhanging eaves and shutters on every window. It stood beside a dense pine forest, and in winter months skiers swished past on a narrow ski track between the chalet and the tall, dark trees. In spring we picked armfuls of wild narcissi that grew in abundance in pastures above the forest, and in summer we'd hear cowbells tinkle and chime from that same paradise of lush grass and wild flowers. All year round the air was crisp, and laden with powerful scents of nature: pine needles and sap, alpine herbs, grass, cow dung, sawdust. A short, steep walk uphill from the schoolhouse brought us to Haut de Caux, a hamlet with a seasonal ski lift. There the tarmac road gave way to smaller mountain tracks heading up to the peak of the Rochers de Naye or horizontally into sloping woodland. Walking downhill from the Chalet at the end of each day we'd glimpse Lake Geneva sparkling way below us through the trees.

In this busy conference village the Chalet de la Forêt was a refuge, offering some routine, and rooms of comfortably hobbit-like dimensions that were homelier than the cavernous hotel chambers. There were 13 of us at Caux School when I arrived, aged between six and nine years, and organised into three classes. We had certain things in common beyond being English speakers and following a broadly British syllabus. All our parents, like our teachers and carers, worked with MRA and knew each other, so there was no gap between school and home. No one would ask us why we lived here, or what our parents did, or that most impossible question: 'What is Moral Re-Armament?'

My new friends seemed to be as English as my

classmates in London. But I soon learnt that while most had British fathers, Anne and Elisabeth had Swiss mothers, Edward's mother was Dutch, Angela's was German and Delscey and Geoff's was South African. Sometimes we were also joined by two Romanian princesses who lived near Geneva, the ones I'd played dolls with in London. And not long after I started, an American girl called Jessie became the newest arrival.

Some older Caux children, including Jessie's siblings, attended a bigger English school in Glion, down the mountain. We knew the big kids by name but didn't see much of them. At one stage a group of German children came to stay in Caux at the Hotel Alpina, where they took lessons in their own language. Some of them were close to us in age, and we occasionally played with them or went on outings together.

'Isn't it marvellous to have so many playmates?' Mummy often commented. But my initial glee was somewhat reduced when I realised life here had a downside. We rarely saw our parents, even when they were at Caux, and it wasn't long before Mummy and Daddy set off on their travels. Any expectations of spending regular time with them were dashed. Those storybook images of children living with their parents remained an ideal far-removed from our life in this enormous community.

Slowly it also dawned on me that I not only lived apart from my adored brother Patrick, but we were now in separate countries. 'Where do your brothers and sisters live?' I asked my new schoolfriends, and discovered most of them had no siblings. Marion, Anne, Angela, Jean,

Elisabeth, David and Edward were all 'only children'. In the minority were Delscey and Geoff, Princesses Helen and Irina, and Jessie. I reckoned I was halfway between the two groups, having a brother I rarely saw. Even when he came to Caux once we spent little time together. With our five-year age gap it was hardly surprising he had companions his own age, and it never occurred to me to ask for more time with him – or, for that matter, with my parents. I knew I couldn't influence the grown-ups' agenda.

In London I'd already started to learn that the 'global family' always came first. But here in Caux, with my parents about to leave me, the priorities were even clearer. Married couples generally stayed together, but wider family relationships seemed to be played down. There were some exceptions. The princesses' father was a king, and it seemed their family time together was important. There was also a young man from India who was always introduced as 'the grandson of Mahatma Gandhi', so I thought his family must matter too.

But the idea of relatives seemed to be of little interest when it came to most of us children, and nobody talked about my grandad. In fact, it was only years later that I discovered that several people I'd seen around Caux were related to me. One was Agnes Leakey, Daddy's Kenyan first cousin who'd grown up with his family in England and was like a second sister to him. But at Caux I only knew her as someone who spoke in conferences about forgiving the Mau-Mau killers of her father, and who sang the *Nkosi Sikelele* anthem with other Africans. The audiences went very quiet when she talked about her father's terrible death. The fact he was my great-uncle passed me by, and Agnes was just another kind face we saw at Caux from time to time.

Confusingly, the grown-ups often spoke about the importance of family life, yet that didn't mean families should be together. We children were taught not to be clingy or demanding of our parents' time. That would be selfish when they had important things to do. When our parents left or returned we knew not to make a fuss. 'It's not fair on your parents, nor the children here without their parents who mustn't feel left out,' we were told. Caux was a place where everyone must feel included, so there couldn't be cliques or special relationships. 'There's no need for a best friend,' our headteacher said, 'because everyone must be treated as a best friend.'

The travels of our parents followed no particular pattern that we knew of. If they were around in the school holidays or at weekends we might see them. There could be meals and walks together, or even a ride with them on the little train up the mountain, or down to Montreux to drink hot chocolate in a café. But we couldn't assume anything, and we didn't know when these treats might arise. If they stayed long enough, in rooms close to ours, we might have some chats or stories at bedtimes or before breakfast. But even in adjacent rooms we still shared a corridor with other people. Communal living was our normal. As to where my parents went on their travels, I knew very little. I have few memories of Mummy at Caux, and barely any of Daddy.

Despite the constant separations, I can still recall

the names and faces of all my friends' parents, all warm-hearted, delightful people. Years on, I wonder how I could have known them this well, and Marion suggests that, 'Although we all longed to have our parents to ourselves, when they *did* visit we often had to share them.' Caux School offered no parents' events such as school plays. It would have been impossible to gather all the parents at once. Instead, they might be invited to join us for meals sometimes, and we'd all meet them together.

Marion recalls her parents joining us for a day when we were on a school holiday trip, staying in another part of Switzerland. 'We *all* wrote my mum and dad welcome cards, and the chocolates my mother brought with her had to be shared between *everyone*!' Again this would have been to avoid anyone feeling left out, or pining for their own family. But it was an inconsistent practice, and Marion was envious when she saw others enjoying the one-to-one time with parents that she'd been denied. We could never admit to our sadness. Negative talk would only result in a talking-to and a sense you'd let the side down, so we learnt not to question grown-up judgements.

In photos I've seen of the Caux children at this time, whether in term-time or holidays, the adults with them are almost always teachers or carers. And it was the carers above all who kept us going while our parents travelled. They were the 'people who look after us', like Mary PB had when I was younger, and were all MRA full-timers like our parents. These young women stayed in neighbouring rooms, or sometimes shared ours, and saw to our needs around the clock. They'd dress us, get us to school and back, and keep us fed, occupied, washed and in clean clothes. They were probably also very good at distracting us and keeping us busy, since tearful farewells were almost unknown as our parents left. The carers worked closely with our teachers, joining in with walks or picnics. Each managed one child, or occasionally two, and we knew we could rely on them as our personal designated adult while our parents were away.

During my year and a half at Caux I had four successive carers, and liked them all in their different ways. First there was Phyll, a jovial and energetic Geordie, with striking dark eyebrows and wavy hair. When Mummy left the Maria for the first time to join Daddy somewhere, Phyll and I moved into a room together. Marion, whose parents left about the same time as mine, had a Swiss girl called Iris looking after her. With her red-blond curls, pale delicate skin and blue eyes, I thought Iris looked like an angel, but a warm and happy angel. All the carers were kind and upbeat. There were no hugs and kisses, but in those less demonstrative times we didn't notice. Even our parents treated us with some formality unless we were alone.

After Phyll I had the twinkly-eyed Betty Forsyth from Ireland – or Eire, as she encouraged me to call it. She taught me other Gaelic words like *coleen* and *caed mille failte*, and told me I was very Irish myself. Apparently my father came from a long line of Irish Conners and O'Connors and he'd started life in County Cork. This was exciting news for me, as I'd never thought of my parents coming from anywhere in particular. I also loved the idea of being Irish. It made me feel special.

I had a brief spell in the care of Molly, a quieter, rosy-cheeked Englishwoman, and then in my final months at Caux I was reunited with Mary PB. It felt good to be back in her familiar company. On our first meeting I solemnly presented her with a bundle of *J. M. Conner* fabric nametapes, the ones sewn onto my clothes labels. I'd seen them in Mummy's sewing bag in her room, and decided there wasn't much point in her keeping them. The gesture felt important to me, and while Mary seemed a little surprised, she appeared to take me seriously and appreciate the symbolism.

The date of this handover to Mary was Monday 13th February 1961. I know that precisely because every Christmas my godparents with whom we'd lived in Bristol sent Patrick and me each a pocket diary. My brother had been to Caux that last Christmas of 1960, and having seen him write entries in his diary I'd decided to do the same. My records are minimal and matter-of-fact. The only mention of Patrick comes on Thursday 12th January 1961: *In the morning I ate in the cafétéria and then wrote thank you letters and then I went skating and then at 9.30 Patrick went to England.* A month later comes Mary's arrival: *In the morning Mary Pelam* [Pelham] *Burn started looking after me. And in the afternoon we went for a L-O-N-G walk. And we found the first primrose. P.S. Mummy left for Luzerne.*

From January to February my diary registers three bedroom moves, from the Grand Hotel to the Hotel Maria, then to Mountain House, then back to the Maria. I would have been used to these shifts by then. Caux's Allocations Team was always juggling room plans to make space for visitors. My initial switch from the happy room-share with Marion was supposedly made so that I could move in with my new carer Phyll. But when I later asked Mummy if I could room with Marion again, I was told, 'I'm afraid not, I gather you girls giggle too much!' This directive no doubt came from the school, ever anxious to discourage private jokes and cliquiness. Nonetheless the bond between us two survived, and our companionship was a precious escape, easing the bleakness when Mummy left.

It helped to be with friends, and thankfully the adults around us were kind and protective. And yet... it was hard to feel settled here. I was a small person in a big place and whatever it was, this wasn't a home. I hadn't expected to see so little of my parents, and was beginning to realise that I'd joined an all-year-round boarding school.

9

London & the World Mission
1953–55

'Will we *ever* get used to all these *stairs?*' Chérie gasped, arriving at the fourth-floor landing and dropping her bags. 'Of course you will,' said Bill, following behind with a baby and a suitcase. 'People have been running up and down these stairs for 150 years. Keeps ya fit!' Patrick joined them last, carefully carrying a box of Matchbox cars.

The family was moving into 28 Wilton Crescent, in an elegant sweep of Georgian terraced houses in Knightsbridge, close to Hyde Park and Harrods. It was the home of Roland and Mary Wilson and their daughter Margaret, and they'd bought it seven years earlier both for the family and the work of MRA. '28' was yet another building bought for an extraordinarily low price. Few post-war families wanted its nine bedrooms, with a further three in its mews cottage at the back, but the house was perfect for accommodating MRA workers and their guests passing through London. At mealtimes there could be 14 or more seated around the long table in the ground-floor dining room, while the drawing rooms on the first floor provided space for receptions or meetings.

Bill and Chérie had been invited to host the home while Roland and Mary spent a year in Africa. MRA's work was expanding worldwide, and Frank Buchman would gather large teams of old hands and new recruits to travel with him. The Wilsons were in the former category, having known Buchman for 20 years, and Roland had been the Secretary of the Oxford Group in Britain since its incorporation before the war.

It was typical of Buchman that his suggestion the Wilsons join him for a year came at short notice. He expected his team to be flexible and to involve themselves in the world's crisis areas. The Wilsons were ready to go. Across Africa, countries were seeking independence, and tensions between nationalists and their colonial rulers, and between rival nationalist groups, were causing turmoil. The Mau-Mau uprising was raging against the British in Kenya, the 1952 Revolution had undermined British rule in Egypt, and a bitter war against France seemed likely in Algeria. The fierce suppression of nationalism in Morocco and Tunisia, and new apartheid laws in South Africa, indicated how far the colonial powers would go to entrench themselves in power. The Soviet leader Nikita Krushchev saw these upheavals as an opportunity to gain lasting influence in Africa, so Russia was backing freedom fighters where it appeared strategic, and training key nationalists in Moscow.

The MRA team for their part were determined to fight for peaceful transitions to democracy in Africa. Frank Buchman had links with nationalist leaders across the continent, and MRA teams were already at work in Ghana, Nigeria, Kenya, Northern Rhodesia (now Zambia) and South Africa. An MRA Assembly held in Lusaka in 1953 had been one of the first multiracial gatherings ever held in Southern Africa.

It was against this background that Roland and Mary accepted the invitation to Africa and Bill and Chérie moved into their home. As 'hosts' at 28 on behalf of the Wilsons, they saw to the welfare of a busy, disparate household, while Bill again pursued his interest in the Middle East and the friendships he'd made there during the war.

Frank Buchman had been urged by both Arab and French politicians in the region to address the conflicts in Morocco and Tunisia. He also had senior connections in Cyprus, Turkey, Egypt, Saudi Arabia, Iraq and Iran. In 1954, unable to visit them all himself, Buchman dispatched two Arabic-speaking colleagues to tour these countries instead. One was British – Francis Goulding; the other, American – Harry Almond. For some of the time they were accompanied by two former generals, one Egyptian, one British, and two former naval officers, one German, one French, all supportive of MRA. This motley crew was characteristic of the teams Buchman would send out, representing diverse national outlooks. He also knew the military element would carry weight with government officials in these countries.

Back in London, Bill kept tabs on the tour's progress and followed up as new contacts from these places travelled through London. Sometimes they stayed or came for meals in the MRA homes or accepted invitations to assemblies in Caux and Mackinac Island. One guest that year was the Greek Cypriot leader Archbishop Makarios, who attended a dinner at 45 Berkeley Square just before he was exiled to the Seychelles by the British for being, as the government viewed him, a troublesome nationalist figurehead in Cyprus.

Dr Abdu Sallam in Egypt remained a good friend of Bill's and they kept in close contact. Abdu, having given up a promising surgeon's career to work as a doctor in a poor farming area, was soon to join a group of professionals implementing President Nasser's new land reforms. Later Abdu told Bill how, in 1956, shortly before the Suez Crisis, the Russian Foreign Minister Dmitri Shepilov visited Egypt and went to see the villages where Abdu worked. The Russian was incredulous at the way land ownership had been transferred peacefully and effectively to the *fellahin* peasants. According to Abdu, the minister claimed such changes were 'impossible without the Marxist incentive' and presumed the first village he'd seen was a set-up, until he visited several others like it. Egyptians like Abdu could see the challenges to their new country as they threw off colonial rule, only to be wooed by Russia.

Engaging with players in this turbulent global landscape, it was only a matter of time before Bill and Chérie would travel themselves. But for the year while the Wilsons journeyed through Africa and on to the Caux Assembly the following summer, living at Wilton Crescent worked well for the whole family. The Wilsons' daughter

Margaret, who'd stayed behind, was the same age as Patrick and the two got on well. A cheerful girl with long fair plaits and an English-rose complexion, Margaret seemed to accept her parents' travels and share her home willingly. Her bedroom on the third floor of the house was also the nursery, serving as a playroom by day for Patrick and Judi too. A sliding cupboard door in the room concealed a gas ring and a sink, and the children's meals were often taken upstairs.

Looking after Margaret in her parents' absence was a young Englishwoman called Stephanie, and she was soon joined by Mary Pelham Burn, who moved in to help care for Patrick and Judi. The two women, both aged around 20, were extremely competent in their childcare skills, but they were primarily volunteers for MRA. Young recruits often undertook such roles at an MRA centre as an alternative to joining a campaign 'on the road'. Women volunteers would typically be secretaries, carers or cooks, while the young men tended to join press, transport or publications teams. As theatre and film increasingly became a way of spreading MRA ideas, newcomers with singing or acting talent might find themselves performing in new productions alongside sympathetic professionals from the theatre world or Hollywood.

Young MRA workers like Stephanie and Mary were expected to feel as responsible for the global work as Buchman, while pitching in with the practical needs of their community. Household decisions at Wilton Crescent were made together after quiet times and sharing their thoughts. Sometimes this happened round the big dining table at breakfast, before everyone dispersed to their various occupations.

At times the three children of the house joined the meals in the dining room. Otherwise they lived in their own upstairs space, among the books, toys and games they shared. There were also outings to the park, or occasionally to the Harrods pet department, reputed to sell anything from lion cubs to a baby elephant. On hot summer days the children could splash outside in a paddling pool on 28's roof garden.

'We always believe "where God guides, He provides",' Chérie told her mother, 'so I shouldn't be surprised. But just as Bristol was perfect for us, so is Wilton Crescent! The children are very happy, and you won't believe this: we even have a school for Patrick in the basement.' It was true. Rooms at the bottom of the house had been turned into a small infant school for the children of full-time MRA workers. Known simply as 'Dot John's School', it was run by two volunteer teachers dedicated to MRA, Dot and Kay. Margaret had been going to the school since it began a year before, and initially Patrick joined her. Every day they were both taken round the block to enter school via the back door, from the mews behind. Dot insisted on this, so that there would be no distinction between the two children living upstairs and all the rest.

Somewhere high above the school, Judi would be with Chérie or Mary, oblivious of the children below and happy to see Patrick and Margaret return in the afternoon. During that year she grew from being a baby pushed to the park in a pram to an accomplished tricycle rider. One advantage of communal life was the sharing of equipment, so prams, bikes and clothing were easily acquired from older children.

Margaret's parents wrote to her frequently from Africa. In one letter her mother Mary said she'd delighted some African children by showing them photos of Margaret and Patrick playing in the snow. Another was written after Mary's birthday in June 1954 and addressed to 'Darling Margaret, and Patrick too', thanking them for their birthday mail. She described 'the card from Patrick with all the patterns, and a picture of the Queen's ship going under Tower Bridge, with lots of writing on it saying *happy day*. I was very pleased with it'. In another letter Mary reminded Margaret that God wanted her and Roland to be there in Africa and not at home.

Shortly after the Wilsons' return to London, Bill and Chérie turned their minds to travelling too. Campaign plans were becoming increasingly ambitious and required more people. Initially Bill travelled alone, leaving Chérie and Mary with the children, and in December 1954 he flew from London to help with an MRA World Assembly held the following month in Washington. Senior figures from Asia and Africa attended, and a photo Bill kept from that time shows the Egyptian Government representative, Brigadier Abdel Fettah Hassan, presenting Frank Buchman with a Damascus silk scarf on behalf of his people.

Participants at that Washington conference had a direct influence on a new phase of MRA's global work, in which Bill and Chérie played a part. It was a phase geared to supporting the newly independent African and Asian states, now free from colonial rule. In April 1955, the Bandung Conference took place in Indonesia, bringing together leaders of these 'new', non-aligned countries to discuss their own economic and cultural co-operation, and resistance to colonial influences, whether from the capitalist West or the communist East.

Buchman kept in close touch with some of the Bandung delegates. He was determined to promote MRA as an alternative philosophy to both the Western and Eastern models of society. While he and his team were considering ways of achieving this, a former Foreign Minister of Denmark called Ole Bjørn Kraft had an idea. He rallied a group of European government ministers, past and present, who wanted to help Buchman, and suggested they could travel in a private capacity to talk with non-aligned government leaders about MRA's ideas.

Buchman was with colleagues in California when they received Kraft's proposal, and within days the idea of a small private tour had suddenly mushroomed into the 'World Statesmen's Mission'. 'We have got to reach a billion people in Asia!' Buchman exclaimed with passion, as the team pooled their ideas. 'Let these men go there and let them take the play with them. Make it a "world mission".'

The play of which he spoke was *The Vanishing Island*, a satirical stage musical about the war of ideas, being written by Peter Howard. It portrays two countries: one totalitarian, thriving on hatred and intent on world domination, the other a self-absorbed capitalist democracy, pursuing the freedom to do as it pleases. They clash but find a way to work together to everyone's advantage by seeking 'what's right, not who's right'.

And so it was that, within the next couple of months, the modest group of European ministers and ex-ministers found themselves part of a sweeping global tour of 250 people from 28 countries, travelling across four continents. The plan was that while the senior figures on tour engaged with their local counterparts at each stop, *The Vanishing Island* would also reach the country's leaders and as wide a public audience as possible.

It was a huge undertaking to arrange at short notice, especially in the days before broadband or even good phone lines. Urgent exchanges generally had to be cabled. MRA workers worldwide, including Bill in London, sought out participants for the Mission, and helped create and support welcome committees in the Asian, Middle Eastern and African nations to be visited. There also had to be funding, transport and accommodation for the travellers. Not least, a full-scale musical had to be produced, with programmes and literature printed in many languages.

Within weeks, the script and music of *The Vanishing Island* were finalised and rehearsals underway at Mackinac Island. Professional leads included Ivan Menzies from the British D'Oyly Carte company, and the producer, choreographer and musicians dropped other projects and gave their services with some excitement. Thomas Peluso, a music director for NBC radio, worked through three days and nights to arrange the scores in time, and told the cast, 'This is the greatest thing I've ever done... the most unique thing in my 42 years as a conductor.' The show previewed in Washington and Los Angeles before the tour officially began in Tokyo.

As the troupe flew off to Japan, controversy was already raging. Some officials in Washington had been stung by the play's caricatures of corrupt Western businessmen, journalists and politicians. Word went out to all US Embassies on the tour route that the play 'ridiculed Western democracy, emphasised neutralism and represented an overall gain for the Soviet concept'. But the tour went on. The target audience was in any case the non-aligned countries rather than America or Russia, although the message of working together across divides was intended to be universal.

While Buchman and his colleagues in Los Angeles and Mackinac co-ordinated with teams worldwide, Peter Howard and Buchman's secretary, Morris Martin, managed the travelling company, and full-timers were mobilised in every country of the tour to handle the logistics. Bill, in London, writes how he 'was suddenly asked, "Can you go to Cairo? You know Cairo well. There's an urgent need there"'. He immediately agreed, although the show by then 'was already in Karachi, heading rapidly for the Middle East, so two or three of us went out somewhat apprehensively'. Each set-up team had to find accommodation for 250 people, plus a venue and audiences for the show. In some cases they also had to put together a welcome committee if one wasn't already in place.

There are no records of Bill's day-to-day experiences, but some of his colleagues wrote vivid accounts of the challenges. One was a young Frenchman, Michel Sentis, dispatched from Paris to the Philippines, and later to Vietnam, to prepare for the group's arrival from Tokyo. He had never been to Asia before, and knew little about these countries. Arriving in Manila, the absence of a certain government senator, supposedly his principal contact for the tour arrangements, left him perplexed. Moreover, he'd been told there'd only be a few dozen on tour. Suddenly there was talk of 200 or more – plus a stage show. The arrival of two energetic Australian full-timers raised his spirits, as did the appearance of the missing senator, who rapidly set up a local welcome committee.

But to Michel, the obstacles still seemed overwhelming. He quickly learnt that anti-Japanese feelings ran high here. The Philippines had not yet resumed diplomatic relations with Japan following its wartime occupation of their country, which had ended only ten years earlier. In Manila Michel saw signs of war devastation everywhere, and he wondered how on earth people here would receive the three senior Japanese parliamentarians about to arrive from Tokyo with the World Mission.

Meanwhile, the Roman Catholic Archbishop of Manila, Monsignor Rufino Santos, had been warned from Rome not to get involved with the Mission. In this predominantly Catholic country, Michel wondered if the tour's initiation by a Danish Lutheran politican and an American Lutheran pastor (Buchman), and its inclusion of Muslim and Buddhist participants, had caused this caution from the Vatican. But in the nick of time, Buchman sent over an American Catholic lawyer friend, Joe Scott, who knew the Philippines well. Together Joe and Michel called on the President of the new republic, Ramon Magsaysay, a forward-looking leader.

'The idea of welcoming the Japanese at the heart of an international mission won over the President immediately', Michel recalls with relief. Magsaysay instructed Michel to cable a presidential invitation to the Japanese, welcoming them at his palace, and assuring them that visas would await them on arrival. Joe Scott went on to smooth the way with Archbishop Santos, persuading him of the healing value of the Mission at this time. The objections seemed to evaporate, and *The Vanishing Island* was permitted to play at the 1,500-seat auditorium of the Jesuit University in Manila.

A month after Michel arrived in Manila, three chartered planes landed there, offloading their 250 mission participants. The next day President Magsaysay received the party in the Malacañan Palace, seat of Spanish and American colonial rulers until the Philippines gained its independence nine years before. In a huge reception room dominated by Venetian glass chandeliers, the visiting Japanese politicians, on behalf of their Prime Minister Ichiro Hatoyama, offered their heartfelt apologies for the behaviour of the Japanese in the Philippines during the war.

Michel writes, 'Joe Scott and I were there alongside the international delegation when these apologies were solemnly presented, with a series of humble bows, by these eminent politicians. Magsaysay responded, visibly moved. We had just witnessed a historic moment of the post-war reconstruction'. The Japanese envoys had also been authorised by their Prime Minister to propose opening negotiations to settle the Philippines' war damages claims, and within a year a Reparations Agreement was signed between the two countries.

The following evening Michel saw the Japanese speak again, after a performance of *The Vanishing Island*. 'When one of the Japanese, Niro Hoshijima, came to the front of the stage with his interpreter, his first words, spoken in a language still carrying hated memories, triggered a roar of protest from the audience. The interpreter quickly translated the words "we come here to present our apologies", and in the complete silence that followed the audience listened. When the Japanese finished nobody dared move. Then someone in the audience clapped, and the whole crowd followed suit. One person stood up, and then more than a thousand Philippinos rose to their feet applauding'. News of the apology and its acceptance quickly spread around the city.

Far away in Iraq, American full-timer Harry Almond was also preparing for the Mission's arrival, and his account has the same 'seat of the pants' feel as Michel's. Harry and his wife Beverley had started off in Tehran, after the Shah had invited the Mission to visit Iran once they'd left Pakistan. But the American couple had rushed on to Baghdad after hearing that a key government host there had been called away on official business and preparations had fallen through.

With only a day to go before the 250 travellers arrived in Baghdad, Harry and Beverley hurried up and down Al

Rashid Street reserving hotel rooms. There was no time to organise airport buses for the following morning, so multiple taxis were ordered to collect the party, but when the planes landed these cars were nowhere to be seen. It was only as the visitors started emerging from the arrivals hall that Harry and Beverley saw, to their relief, 'a plume of dust on the horizon' and a line of cabs start to appear. Assigning people to taxis, giving out hotel names and paying drivers felt utterly chaotic to Harry, who still hadn't even secured a theatre for the show to perform in. He was astounded when Peter Howard, leading the Mission, announced that this had been the smoothest arrival of the tour so far.

Harry's challenges continued. The Royal Theatre, the best venue for *The Vanishing Island*, was locked up, and keys couldn't be found. Nonetheless Harry had seat tickets printed, and brazenly went to see the Mayor of Baghdad to present him with a bunch of them, thanking him warmly for the use of the theatre. 'These he accepted with appreciation', says Harry, 'although he had no idea what was going on. *De facto* occupancy of the theatre had been obtained using a gardener's key, and we trusted that the tickets given to the mayor assured official recognition'.

When Bill joined Harry and others in Cairo they had an easier time. For one thing, Colonel Gamal Abdel Nasser, the effective head of state and soon to be Egypt's President, had been one of the first national leaders to invite the Mission to his country. As a result they were to be government guests for two weeks, with *The Vanishing Island* playing at the famous Cairo Opera House. The

Ministry of Information was arranging hotels and local transport, and Bill found himself working on the visitors' schedule and delivering invitations to the show.

There was a reason Egypt was well-prepared. Back in May, when *The Vanishing Island* was in rehearsal and tour plans barely underway, Abdul Hamid, an Egyptian diplomat at the United Nations in New York, had visited Mackinac Island. Hearing about the proposed Mission to non-aligned nations he'd cabled Cairo directly, suggesting Egypt invite the international group. An invitation from Nasser had been wired back almost immediately, referring to MRA's important work in 'restoring the lost dignity of absolute moral standards and creating a world that works'.

Bill was thrilled to be back in Cairo. Egypt was now a proudly independent republic following the army coup three years before, and Bill found the country much changed. This was a year before the Suez Crisis, but a phased withdrawal of British troops was already taking place. Nasser was delighted to show the international visitors a country standing up for itself. Bill found Egyptians optimistic, seizing on the Mission to build new links with the wider world.

Shortly after the Mission arrived in Cairo on 12th August 1955, Colonel Nasser received the visitors at his palatial offices. A photo shows the group packed together, some on the ground level of the grand hallway, some on the broad, curved staircase and the landing above. Downstairs at the front stands Nasser, standing between a Ghanaian leader and a German miner from the Ruhr. Nasser told the group, 'Your principles and objectives are highly appreciated in Egypt, where all efforts are being mobilised to restore moral values, social justice, human dignity and freedom.' Over the next fortnight the visitors met with government ministers, trade unionists, teachers and Cairo's diplomatic corps.

Having travelled on with the Mission from Asia, the young Frenchman Michel Sentis worked with Bill and the others to ensure that every foreign ambassador in Cairo received an invitation to *The Vanishing Island*. At the Hungarian Embassy the chargé d'affaires accepted Michel's invitation immediately, and suggested Michel join him in the box he'd been offered at the Opera House. Michel enjoyed the irony of sitting beside the representative of a Soviet-controlled republic in the ornate 19th-century theatre built for royalty and colonial rulers. The Hungarian approved of the message of the play, interpreting it as supporting Kruschev's policy of 'peaceful co-existence' between the Soviet bloc and the west.

Follow-up visits were made, and Michel again called on the Hungarian official. He put the case that co-existence only really works when people on both sides of the East-West divide change their outlook and tackle the world's needs together. The MRA men gave examples of personal change in their own lives, and the diplomat apparently determined to improve relations with his wife, who'd refused to join him in Cairo. Michel wrote that 'this visit was important to me, because I discovered that, behind even the most determined of ideologically-committed people, there is a human being who can be moved by feelings deeper than his intellect.'

The Mission went down so well in Cairo that it was invited to make an extra stop in Alexandria. However, plans were well advanced for the next dates in Nairobi, so it was decided to insert a visit to Alex between Nairobi and Istanbul. Bill went on ahead to help set up first in Alexandria, then Istanbul.

In retrospect it seems strange that Bill didn't accompany the group to Kenya, because his first cousin Agnes Leakey Hofmeyr was one of three Kenyans on the Mission who were pivotal to the East African leg of the journey. From the age of eight, when her mother died in Kenya, Agnes had lived with Bill's family in England, and his mother Maye was both Agnes's aunt and her godmother. Bill and Agnes had grown up together and met the Oxford Group at the same time.

In addition to losing her mother so young, Agnes had faced further family tragedies. Maye had died when Agnes was 19. Five years later her oldest brother Nigel was killed in Abyssinia in the war. Agnes had married a South African MRA colleague, Bremer Hofmeyr, soon after the war. But her world had again been shattered when, only months before this global tour, Agnes's father Gray Leakey and her stepmother had been killed by the Mau-Mau on their Kenyan farm.

Along with Agnes and Bremer on the Mission were a Kenyan brother and sister, David and Mary Waruhiu, with whom they had a particular bond. The father of these two Kikuyu Africans had also been murdered by the Mau-Mau. The wounds of these devastating events in the two families were raw, but all three shared a strong spiritual faith and had determined to surrender their bitterness and desire for revenge. They believed passionately in the power of love and forgiveness to break the cycle of hatred.

The three of them had already spoken publicly on the world tour about finding an understanding of the Mau-Mau fighters, and the strength to forgive them. Now they were bracing themselves to speak about this again in the hardest place of all: their own Kenyan home territory, possibly in front of their families' killers.

The Mau-Mau uprising was continuing in Kenya, as it would for a further four years. In Nairobi, where *The Vanishing Island* was performed, people could move freely, but in many other parts of the country public events were banned. Nonetheless, David Waruhiu's request for a gathering on his home Kikuyu territory was granted. He invited some of the travelling group to join an outdoor sheep roast there, after which a few of them would speak to his people.

Agnes recalls in her memoir the hundreds of Kikuyu people who gathered around them on a hillside, and the gasp when David introduced her as the daughter of Morungaru, her father's Kikuyu nickname, meaning tall and straight. 'I spoke from my heart', she said, 'and apologised for the arrogance and selfishness of so many of us whites that had helped to create the bitterness and hatred in their hearts... A murmur of understanding rippled through the vast crowd. Afterwards many of them came up to me and said how sorry they were for what had happened to my family... I was touched by what they said, and all traces of bitterness that lingered in my heart were washed away. I felt that they were my friends. For us the day was a healing of the heart'.

The following day Agnes and Bremer travelled with a South African nationalist friend to Agnes's derelict family farm in Nyeri. This was where her stepmother and their cook had been killed by 60 Mau-Mau attackers, who had then carried off her father and buried him alive. The house had been looted and abandoned, and they sat on the veranda taking it all in. Afterwards they visited the cemetery in Nyeri where Agnes's father and stepmother had been buried together.

The small party rejoined their fellow travellers for a showing of *The Vanishing Island* to Mau-Mau detainees in the Athi River prison camp. After the performance, Agnes noted how some of the Mau-Mau covered their ears when white people spoke from the stage. But 'gradually the hostility melted', Agnes wrote, as the white people spoke of their mistakes and their decisions to change their ways. As they were leaving one prisoner gave them money, pooled together from the inmates' meagre camp earnings. He told them, 'We want to help you. If we had known there were people like you there would never have been Mau-Mau.'

There were many possible reasons Bill didn't accompany Agnes to Kenya. There could have been logistical issues, such as limited travel places. It may have been Bill's own choice, to avoid reminders of his own past trauma. Bill had an ingrained horror of appearing 'soft' or emotional. In his view a person should surrender their grief, fear or pain and press on. But it's most likely that it never even crossed anyone's mind. The army-like discipline of MRA drove Bill and his colleagues to put the World Mission before anything else. And to Agnes, the support of the global family, which included her husband, no doubt felt sufficient. While family life was promoted by MRA in principle, creating a society in which such values would flourish long-term was considered the highest priority. For Bill, Agnes and their colleagues this wasn't a hard option. Their certainty that their work was making a difference to the world gave them the same joy and satisfaction that Bill had experienced as a soldier.

This high level of commitment to an idea beyond self-interest was not, of course, exclusive to MRA. It applied to many others caught up in the war of ideas, whatever 'side' they were on. Ruth First and Joe Slovo, who were contemporaries of Bill and Chérie, devoted their lives to communism in Southern Africa. Passages in their daughter Gillian Slovo's family memoir resonate strongly with those who grew up with MRA parents. 'We were brought up in a political culture which used self-sacrifice as its fuel', Slovo writes. 'It never went away, this conflict between the demands of "one" and the needs of the "whole". Our parents were rebels, they saw a wrong and they fought to make it right. To do that they had to turn away from the subjective. Their eyes were on a greater prize than self – they were fighting for humanity'.

Bill's focus, too, was on a battle for humanity and, most immediately, on his next tasks in Egypt and Turkey, before spending the summer at Caux, where the World Mission would end. Plans were being made for *The Vanishing Island* to tour Europe over the coming year, and both Bill and Chérie had decided to join that next campaign together.

Arrangements for their children fell easily into place. Patrick was eight, and had started boarding at a prep school in Worcestershire, a few miles from his aunt and uncle's home. Judi, meanwhile, had been invited to live at Mary Pelham Burn's family home in Sussex. Mary's parents, Ian and Pamela, were MRA supporters, eager to support Chérie and Bill. They suggested Judi might stay long-term, with Mary still taking primary responsibility for her. 'Once she's almost four Judi could go to school with Amelia,' Pamela pointed out, referring to the youngest of her seven children.

It was another perfect solution, even though Chérie had to fight back twinges of regret at not seeing her daughter start school. When she'd dropped off Judi and Mary in Sussex, Chérie admitted to feeling quite lost without the children. 'Now let's not be weaklings,' Bill coaxed her from the driver's seat as they headed back to London. 'Patrick's in an excellent school. And Judi's in a wonderful home. They won't give us a second thought!' 'I suppose we'll need a prep school for Judi before long,' Chérie sighed deeply. 'One step at a time, eh?' said Bill. 'She won't need to board for a while. And anyway, girls' education isn't as crucial as it is for boys!'

Chérie watched the country fields and hedgerows flashing by the car window and wondered about this. She thought of her own piecemeal schooling, and every spare penny of her father's salary going toward her brothers' education. She regretted her lack of formal learning.

But settling back in her seat, she quietly committed her misgivings to the Almighty, and resolved to focus on the pleasure of once more working alongside Bill.

10

Europe, USA 1956–58

In the 1950s the MRA team tended to assume critics and doubters were suffering from some kind of moral compromise in their lives if they didn't accept their ideas. Some commentators have suggested this supposition, and the lack of interest in public debate with dissidents, might stem from an anti-intellectual streak in Frank Buchman. MRA came to be considered intense, aloof and cult-like, and it perhaps wasn't easy for its converts to appreciate how daunting the movement might seem to outsiders.

Bill and Chérie were not alone among their colleagues in having relatives who were mystified and alienated by their work. A cousin of Chérie's puts a fairly positive spin on it in a family history, 'As a child I understood that Chérie and Bill had a very busy and important life. They belonged to the Oxford Group, or Moral Re-Armament (MRA). I remember visiting their large home in upscale London where they often hosted important guests. They also took frequent trips to the Middle East on diplomatic missions'. But misunderstandings were rife, including one false rumour that Bill had appropriated his house in Croydon from his parents-in-law.

The varied ways full-timers handled the question 'And what do you do?' didn't always help. There was no standard answer. The response, 'I'm a full-time worker with Moral Re-Armament' could induce blank stares of indifference, hostility, or fear of a lengthy explanation. 'Charity work' was too bland, 'full-time Christian work' too churchy, 'life-changing' too sinister, and, 'I'm a revolutionary, remaking the world' only made sense to people with radical ideological interests themselves.

Nor was it easy for them to describe how they spent their time. There was no formal routine, beyond a daily quiet time for private prayer and reflection, and their roles frequently changed. On Bill's marriage certificate in London he's registered as a 'book publisher'. On Judi's birth certificate in Bristol he's described as an 'industrial consultant'. Later in his life he was labelled a 'Middle East specialist'.

In the latter half of the 1950s, with both children at school, Bill and Chérie moved between London and the MRA centres in Europe and North America, supporting various campaigns and taking part in conferences. They were often involved in what is now known as track two diplomacy: behind-the-scenes conflict resolution carried out by non-governmental players. Bill was in his element in this field, well before this term was coined in the 1980s.

Their first project was the European tour of *The Vanishing Island*, which started in the main cities of

Switzerland, and went on to the four Scandinavian capitals, then Italy, France and Germany. As with the World Mission, the logistics of moving 200 people around the continent took energy and manpower. Beyond the practical needs of a theatre production were those of publicity, transport and accommodation. Another key activity was meeting the audiences after each show, and keeping in contact with those wanting to become involved.

One follow-up took Bill to Algeria in January 1956, during the brutal War of Independence there. The Mayor of Algiers, Jacques Chevalier, had seen *The Vanishing Island* in Paris and invited an MRA group to visit his city, hoping the spirit of MRA could encourage a peaceful settlement. Bill travelled out with Matt Manson, Harry Almond and two French colleagues. They talked with the Mayor's contacts about the MRA approach, sharing stories of change and hope, and they invited people on all sides to attend the next Caux conferences. But positions were already bitterly entrenched and the country was in turmoil.

By contrast, its neighbours Morocco and Tunisia were both on course to achieve their independence from French rule only a few weeks later, in March. On their way to Algiers, the MRA group stopped off in Morocco, where friends of Frank Buchman had been building bridges across the nationalist-colonial divide for some years. Harry writes in his memoir, 'We continued to the capital, Rabat, to see Prime Minister Si Bekkai and other friends regarding their nomination of Frank Buchman for the Nobel Peace Prize'. According to Buchman's biographer, he was frequently put forward as a Nobel candidate by politicians in many countries, but he never made it beyond the shortlist. This didn't bother Buchman, and he'd once responded to a nomination, 'But I haven't made peace between nations. Let's get on with the work!'

Bill and his companions found turbulent Algiers very different from Rabat. Here they witnessed mass street demonstrations against the visiting French Prime Minister Guy Mollet, who was resented by both Algerian nationalists and the French *colons* settlers in Algeria, who dreaded independence from France. Harry writes, 'We watched as the mob of protesting *colons* surged forwards. They picked the Premier's car up off the pavement and gave it a good shaking before setting it down none too gently. Mollet's face blanched, and the car sped off to the Palais de Gouvernement', where the French leader remained indoors for the rest of the week.

'Conner, Manson and I stayed on', Harry continues, 'visiting various people at the mayor's suggestion. One evening we were driven into the countryside to show an MRA film in a local cinema. It was well attended, in spite of armed guards at the entrance and the orange glare on the horizon of burning barns and haystacks'. Sadly the cycle of violence was already underway, and it was six years before Algeria was independent.

When Bill returned to Chérie and *The Vanishing Island* tour in Europe, he found that his sister Erica and her husband Edward, having left their country estate and children in good hands, had joined the mission for a couple of months as it moved through France and

Germany. Edward's memoir describes life on the road. 'After five years of intensive rooting into the feudal system at home', he wrote, 'the quality of teamwork and initiative required to be of some use in that international group was quite a challenge'.

Their tasks were varied. In Dortmund Edward was even recruited into the show itself, joining a chorus of 'businessmen' satirising grasping Western capitalists. 'One of my chief memories in the Ruhr', he writes, 'is of acting as a steward with the job of marshalling the huge crowds that tried to get into the hall. There were no tickets, and as far as I remember no charge for admission. Once or twice we stewards had to hold hands and form a human barrier to stop a dangerous number of people getting in'.

After the performances they'd talk to audience members in the foyer. 'A man came up to me one evening in Dortmund and we got into conversation. He pressed me and Erica to come and stay with him and his wife and tell him more'. The show was moving on the following day, but Edward reported the man's interest, and it was decided he and others should stay behind to spend more time with people like this. But as they stayed on, Edward and Erica became wary of their hosts. Their questions focused on MRA's strategy around the world, while they seemed exceptionally well informed on MRA's work in the Ruhr steelworks. Then they mentioned that West Germany was awash with East German spies. Edward checked back with their German colleagues who agreed their hosts were very likely to be agents themselves. 'So we disengaged politely and moved on', says Edward. 'The next stop was Berlin'.

This was five years before the building of the Berlin Wall, and trains still ran between the east and west of the city. Edward recalls people from both sides flocking to the show. 'At the climax of the play, when someone declares, "Together we from East and West can dare to build a world for all men everywhere", a great roar (or was it a sigh?) came up from the audience.'

Shortly after this, Edward attended a weekend retreat for some of the travelling group where 'we sought to renew our commitment to Jesus Christ and the Holy Spirit, the true source of the ideology for democracy that we were promoting'. It's not clear if Bill and Chérie went too, but such times were set aside to refresh the teams' faith and dedication at the heart of this work. Frank Buchman encouraged his followers to be true to their own cultures and faiths. He was outspoken about his own Christian faith, but had no desire to convert others to his religion. Essentially he wanted people to drop their self-will and follow their inner calling, whatever their background.

Sometimes Buchman worried that teams were going off-message. When *The Vanishing Island* tour reached Britain in the late spring of 1956, Buchman flew to London where the musical was on at the Prince's Theatre. He took the team to task for judging success in terms of full houses and large-scale results, insisting that the quality of changed lives should be their key concern, not the quantity of box-office sales.

By July the focus was again on the summer assemblies. Bill loved being in Caux. 'It's the perfect place for a holiday!' he'd say, knowing the comment would annoy Chérie and their friends, since the Swiss operation involved a great deal of hard work. Bill put in long hours too, but to him this wasn't arduous and the idea of a vacation seemed a waste of time for anyone in good health. 'You couldn't ask for more than this!' he'd say, indicating the exquisite mountain views and clear air. His work at Caux centred on hosting guests, particularly those attending by his own invitation, among them Egyptians, Iraqis, Cypriots and North Africans. He also helped plan and run the conference programmes, and sometimes manned the Mountain House reception desk.

That summer of 1956, during Patrick's holidays and before Judi began school in Sussex, Chérie and Mary PB brought the children to Caux. They were given rooms in a chalet in the village. Photos taken with Patrick's Brownie box camera show Judi splashing in a wooden horse trough outside the chalet, and a family outing to the top of the Rochers de Naye mountain. Bill looks relaxed in shirt sleeves and sunglasses, but his mind was probably on the conference. Chérie spent more time with the children, and thanks to Mary's help she also worked on room allocations and serving afternoon teas.

One of Bill's more unexpected roles that summer was playing an extra in an MRA feature film called *Freedom*. A year earlier, Frank Buchman had challenged a group of Africans at Caux to write a play about their independence struggles. 'Africa is not meant to be torn apart between East and West, but to speak to both East and West with an answer,' he'd told them. 'Could you write a play that would do that?' Within 24 hours a Nigerian, a South African and a Ghanaian had drafted the outline of a play about freedom fighters in a West African country and their journey to a peaceful solution. Days later the play, called *Freedom*, was performed at Caux, and it went on to be shown at a number of European and African venues.

The following year *Freedom* was made into a film in Nigeria. More than 7,000 Africans took part, and it was billed as the first colour feature to be written and acted by Africans. One of Walt Disney's favourite cameramen, Rickard Tegstrom, and British film director Vernon Messenger, gave their services to shoot and direct it. A few crucial scenes were set in and around the United Nations buildings in Geneva, and Bill, Matt Manson and many other colleagues were summoned down from Caux to play UN delegates. For Matt this was one of many MRA productions in which he and his wife Margie used their acting and singing skills, usually in more prominent roles. For Bill it was a one-off chance to support the Africans.

Premiered in Los Angeles in February 1957, the film of *Freedom* became the next vehicle for spreading MRA's ideas, and within a short time it had been seen in 70 countries. Buchman and his teams quickly recognised that the film medium could reach wider audiences, and with greater ease, than a stage show like *The Vanishing Island*.

One place in which the film was put to use was the American city of Little Rock, Arkansas, where a crisis erupted in the autumn of 1957. The state governor and his supporters had called on the Arkansas National Guard to illegally prevent nine black children, the 'Little Rock Nine', from entering a previously all-white school.

Frank Buchman had long wanted to tackle racism and promote integration and equal rights in America, and black community leaders had attended MRA conferences throughout the 1950s. The crisis in Arkansas led to MRA's direct engagement.

At the time the trouble started, a group of black and white Africans was travelling with Buchman, and he urged them to leave for Little Rock immediately. They took with them copies of *Freedom*, and showed the film to prominent members of both white and black communities, the school authorities and the federal troops sent by President Eisenhower to protect the black schoolchildren.

One of those who saw the film was Daisy Bates, President of the Arkansas National Association for the Advancement of Coloured People (NAACP). Mrs Bates had famously recruited the 'Little Rock Nine' to defy the opponents of school integration, and had risked her life walking them to school each day amid jostling and threats from the white supremacist mob. After seeing *Freedom* she joined a delegation from Little Rock that went to Mackinac Island to seek solutions. The visit led to her approaching the Governor of Arkansas and working with him to bring about multi-racial schooling throughout the state. Their achievement became a celebrated model for other civil rights groups.

The Arkansas events also led to a renewed focus on the United States in MRA's work. Buchman told friends that he'd previously refused invitations to the southern states because he'd lacked the people and means to make an impact there. But new opportunities were arising, and

Chérie and Bill were among the many MRA workers invited from other countries to support the work in America.

In particular, Buchman wanted to make the most of a new musical play called *The Crowning Experience*, which directly related to racial division in the United States. Not long before the Little Rock Nine incident, two Broadway actor/singers had, independently, turned up at Mackinac and become captivated by what they saw. They'd been particularly impressed by the delegates from Japan and Germany who were working for lasting peace in their countries. They were also interested in the way the creative arts were being used to spread MRA's ideas.

Buchman immediately spotted the timely potential of the pair. One of them was Muriel Smith, a black Harlem-born mezzo-soprano who had created the role of *Carmen Jones* on Broadway, sung *Carmen* at Covent Garden, and performed in *South Pacific* and *The King and I* in London's West End. The other was Ann Buckles, a white actor from Tennessee, who had recently appeared in *The Pyjama Game* in New York. The actors' friendship was difficult at first, but Buchman saw their attempts to work together as a microcosm of a divided America. He urged two playwrights to write a musical for the women that could bring a message of healing and hope to the country.

The result was *The Crowning Experience*, based on the true story of educationalist Dr Mary Macleod Bethune. The seventeenth child of former slaves in South Carolina, Bethune had trained as a teacher and became one of the most important black educators and civil rights leaders in

America. She founded the first black college in the United States and became special adviser to President Franklin D. Roosevelt.

At the age of 79, Bethune had been at the 1955 MRA Assembly in Washington that Bill had attended. He'd watched as she'd spoken from the stage about the ongoing battle against slavery across the world. Of America she'd said, 'Only a basic change of heart in men and women of all races can handle the present integration programme. Law and law enforcement alone can never do it. The task of morally rearming the nation is the greatest job to which any of us can apply our energies and talents. To be part of this great uniting force of our age is the crowning experience of my life.'

A white woman from Richmond, listening to this in the front row, was shaken. At the end of the speech she rose to her feet spontaneously and responded. Her parents, she said, had been slave owners, and now she realised that she herself had felt superior and entitled to white privilege, despite calling herself a Christian. She apologised to Dr Bethune for her prejudice against black people. 'I'm glad to take this opportunity to shake hands publicly with someone of your race,' she said, 'because I helped to build racial bitterness. But I've decided to commit the rest of my life to building bridges between the races.' It was an electrifying moment, moving some in the hall to tears.

This dramatic exchange featured in the musical play about Mary Macleod Bethune, starring Muriel Smith as Bethune and Anne Buckles as a young white journalist who befriends her. *The Crowning Experience* opened in

Atlanta, Georgia in January 1958 and ran for five months to the first de-segregated audiences in Atlanta's history. Smith's voice soared through the final song *The World Walked Into My Heart Today,* reaching out to audiences in the southern states with its inclusive message:

> *Black and white and brown and yellow*
> *The bitter man, and the man who's mellow*
> *The statesmen, yes, and the ordinary fellow*
> *They all walked into my heart...*

'It was the talk of the town,' the African-American civil rights lawyer A. T. Walden told the press about the show. 'The atmosphere changed... Atlanta will never be the same again.' It was noted that integration policies proceeded calmly in Atlanta at that time, without the bitter confrontations seen elsewhere. Walden was later summoned by President Kennedy to report on what was widely seen as an important advance.

While *The Crowning Experience* was performing in the South, Chérie and Bill moved between Mackinac Island and the MRA centres in Washington and New York. Frantic diplomatic activity was taking place as colonies and protectorates around the world negotiated independence from their colonising powers. The talks often took place at the United Nations in New York, where assemblies allowed nationalist liberation parties to attend as well as official government delegates. Bill, with Harry Almond, Matt Manson and other colleagues, met with a wide range of diplomats and politicians gathering there, including many from the Eastern Mediterranean and North Africa.

One colony in crisis was the island of Cyprus. In his *Cyprus – An Unfinished Story*, French diplomat Daniel Dommel describes MRA's 'twin track' role in the run-up to Cyprus achieving independence in 1960. He traces the story back to the 1940s, when Bill, posted with the army in Cyprus, had met Archbishop Makarios through a Cypriot friend of Frank Buchman. In 1950 the Archbishop became the leader of both the church in Cyprus and the Greek Cypriots. He would eventually become the country's first independent president, although through most of the 1950s Makarios was mistrusted by British governments, and was portrayed as a shifty, violent nationalist in the British press. It had been during a breakdown in negotiations with the British government that Makarios and his advisers had first spent an evening at 45 Berkeley Square among the MRA friends Makarios liked and trusted.

While Bill and Chérie were in America, the situation in Cyprus was deteriorating. Britain wanted to hand over the country to a power-sharing Greek-Turkish government, but neither the Greeks nor the Turks in Cyprus wanted to share sovereignty. The large Greek majority led by Makarios wanted Cyprus assimilated within Greece, while the Turkish minority wanted partition, to avoid Greek domination. Each community looked to its respective mainland ally, Greece or Turkey, for support. Meanwhile Greek EOKA guerilla fighters had launched a violent campaign against the British, drawing fierce reprisals. The four-year War of Independence, or 'Cyprus Emergency', was underway, and a diplomatic solution seemed a remote prospect.

Makarios's representative at the United Nations was Zenon Rossides, whom Bill had met in London. Rossides liked the MRA approach of solutions based on 'what's right, not who's right', and he attended conferences at Mackinac Island and Los Angeles to find out more. Dommel writes that 'in November 1957, Bill Conner, Matt Manson and his wife Margie were in New York and invited Mr Rossides and his wife for dinner. As they prepared for the evening they had the clear thought not to talk about Cypriot independence but rather to concentrate on questions of personal character. The Mansons had just been through a difficult period. Matt had realised he had been overbearing with his wife, causing several crises in their marriage. He had recognised his full responsibility for this and had asked his wife for forgiveness. This became a subject of conversation with the Rossides'. Evidently Rossides, a distinguished lawyer and nationalist who'd spent two years under house arrest by the British in the 1930s, was impressed by Brits showing such humility and candour.

Archbishop Makarios had also just arrived in New York, and the next day Rossides told him about the dinner. Makarios asked to meet Matt and Bill, and he received them in his hotel rooms. The British men spoke about their time as army officers, expressing deep regret for the arrogance and ignorance often exhibited in countries like Cyprus by the British. 'The Archbishop was visibly moved', Dommel writes. 'Then Rossides asked them to repeat for

Makarios what they'd said the night before about reflective listening and the possibility of being guided by God by this means'.

Bill and Matt said they believed that Cyprus could become a 'beacon of hope', and the Archbishop 'an architect of peace and unity in the Eastern Mediterranean'. Rossides confided later that 'he had never seen Makarios so moved in the presence of strangers, and he was sure this meeting would be fruitful'. The friendships continued and Bill and Matt were later to meet up with Rossides and Makarios in Europe at crucial points in the independence negotiations.

Another person Bill and his team spent time with was the Iraqi Foreign Minister Dr Fadhel Jamali, who had hosted *The Vanishing Island* in Iraq. In July 1958, after meetings with Jamali in New York, his friends were horrified to hear reports that he'd been killed in Baghdad during the Iraqi coup that month. In fact he'd survived, but was imprisoned and sentenced to death. After three years Jamali was eventually pardoned and released into exile, resuming his ties with MRA.

Harry Almond describes in his memoir how the coup in Iraq removed a western ally and increased the Cold War tensions in the Middle East. Lebanon and Jordan were allied to the USA and Britain, while Syria, Egypt and now Iraq were close to Russia. That summer, as religious and political tensions grew in the Lebanon, the possibility of a war in that region involving the super-powers was very strong. An emergency session of the UN General Assembly was called, addressed both by President Eisenhower and the Soviet Foreign Minister Andre Gromyko. A draft

Middle East resolution was proposed by Gromyko, but the Arab states roundly rejected it, and they were called on by the Assembly to produce an alternative proposal.

The Secretary-General of the Arab League at this time, Dr Abdul Khalek Hassouna, was another longstanding friend, who had opened many doors for MRA in the Middle East. Hassouna was frequently in New York, since all the ten Arab countries represented at the UN were Arab League members. Hearing about the emergency UN session while in Japan, he flew to New York. Harry describes how, over six days, Dr Hassouna brought together all the Arab representatives in his rooms at the Hotel Pierre until they could finally agree to a joint proposal to break the impasse. Hassouna confided to MRA friends that he'd worked hard for a united settlement, even using music and poetry to build solidarity through their essential shared values. Their eventual proposal was presented to the General Assembly on 20th August 1958, and passed unanimously the next day.

The UN agreement attracted excited press coverage, and Hassouna's role in helping avert war in the Middle East was widely recognised. The London *Times* reported that 'overnight an almost magical transformation had come over the scene' (22nd August 1958). The *Washington Post* three days later called the unexpected Arab unanimity 'a triumph' for Hassouna. And the *State Times* of Jackson, Mississippi even ran the headline 'Survival clue? Arab nations display spirit of Moral Re-Armament at UN'.

But in the midst of the Middle East crisis, a different kind of emergency had arisen for Chérie and Bill. They had suddenly faced the worst nightmare of parents separated from their children, and it brought their family sharply back into focus. Out of the blue a telegram had arrived from Chérie's parents in Croydon, where Patrick had been spending part of his school holidays. The brief message read: 'PATRICK IN GOOD HANDS IN HOSPITAL STOP POLIO CONFIRMED STOP ROYDULCIE'.

11

London 1958–59

Chérie was shaken to see ten-year-old Patrick lying flat on his back in a polio ward. On the 14-hour Pan Am flight to London, with no chance of an update on his condition, she had faced her worst fears and put her trust in God's mercy and the doctors' expertise. However, by the time she'd reached the hospital the prognosis was encouraging, and she was hugely relieved to see her son smiling back at her.

Polio outbreaks were common in Britain through most of the 1950s, peaking each summer before the new vaccines became readily available. Chérie knew that children were the most susceptible to catching it, and those that survived were usually left partially paralysed. She'd seen pictures of patients strapped into metal cylinders and breathing equipment, and children with crutches and callipers, but with all the recent medical advances she'd never imagined her own family at risk.

Hearing the shocking news from England, Chérie and Bill's friends in America had rallied to help. They urged

Chérie, at least, to fly to London immediately, and pooled together their dollars for her plane ticket. Chérie was even given money to buy Patrick a present and managed to dash into a toy shop on her way to New York's Idlewild airport. An assistant suggested she buy the latest Model E Viewmaster, a binocular-like gadget for looking at lifelike pictures of dinosaurs and other wonders of the world. 'Perfect!' she said, 'I'll take it!' although doubts niggled in the back of her mind. What if his eyesight was affected? Or his arms? Or worse? But she willed herself to think positively.

Bill stayed on in the United States. The Lebanese crisis was escalating, and meetings were arranged in New York. 'My guidance is to stay,' Bill told his colleagues. 'This is very much Chérie's and her parents' department.' But that didn't stop him waiting anxiously for news, and when the first messages from Chérie in London were cautiously positive Bill felt immensely relieved and vindicated. Patrick's case had been diagnosed unusually early by his doctor grandfather, who'd had him admitted to a specialist ward without delay. Bill thanked God that his son was responding well and on track for a full recovery.

This was the kind of miracle they'd come to expect, and Bill and Chérie felt supremely looked after by a caring God. Chérie felt blessed yet again when Bill soon joined her and suggested they might stay on for a while in London, where one of the Charles Street houses needed hosting. Once Patrick had recuperated and was back at school, Chérie collected Judi from the Pelham Burns in Sussex, and she moved with Bill and her daughter into their new London home.

Wilton Crescent held fond memories for Chérie, and she hoped 43 Charles Street would be a similar set-up. But 43, she soon realised, wasn't quite the same. Wilton Crescent had essentially been a family home, and had kept its historic nursery floor. 43 was a more exclusively adult environment. It had a similar layout to the other London house, but it accommodated more people, and being at the heart of the MRA centre in Mayfair, the flow of visitors seemed even greater. Opportunities for private family times were limited, and there were no other youngsters in the household.

A friend advised Chérie to 'always create what you feel the need for' rather than complain, and she determined to make the best of it. In her second-floor bedroom Chérie tried to create some family space, with a supply of books, games, pencils and crayons, and a radio for listening to children's programmes. It was a comfortable room with a sofa and chairs, and like the Wilton Crescent nursery it felt removed from life on the floors below.

At heart Chérie knew the house still wasn't ideal for the children, but she put on a brave front when her mother noticed it too. When Patrick spent school holidays there, his visiting grandmother observed to Chérie that he 'looked rather lost in that large household'. Chérie dismissed the concern on principle, pointing out how neighbouring MRA families had made it work for them. 'Look at Ken and Stella,' she said. 'They've lived at Number 40 for years and made it theirs. They have some of their own furniture, and their two children go to local day schools.' Privately Chérie hoped they wouldn't stay in

Charles Street that long, but for now she was happy to be with her children. 'It will be fine,' she assured her mother. 'The children will be mainly at school, and in the holidays we'll find other distractions.'

One 'distraction' Chérie organised was a memorable few days later referred to as 'the Dormobile holiday'. It was in fact the only family holiday Judi could recall with her parents before her teenage years, and, apart from a brief camping expedition to Devon after that, the only one ever spent together as a foursome. The Dormobile in question was an MRA minibus normally used for group travel. Bill decided the long bench seats and floor behind the driver could sleep three, and Judi could lie across the front seats. Taking food, bedding and a camping stove, they drove off to the south coast, elated by the sense of adventure. To the dutiful Bill and Chérie, their wilful truancy felt slightly decadent, but they had no regrets.

School was the main distraction, of course, and Judi was quickly signed up for Glendower, a girl's day school in Kensington, where she'd have companions her own age and continuity after her year at school in Sussex. Glendower was recommended by parents based in the neighbouring MRA houses, and Judi was able to join their five older girls travelling to and from school. Chérie realised nothing could quite replace the fun of a school run with Amelia, yet Judi seemed happy setting off on her first day with her purple blazer and beret, Start-Rite sandals and stiff leather satchel.

With both children occupied in term-time, Chérie helped manage the household and entertain guests. Sometimes Bill was there, sometimes not. The Cyprus conflict was still headline news, but at last there had been some movement in negotiations, and Bill was making himself particularly available for his Cypriot friends. The latest reports were that the Greek Cypriots had largely accepted the idea of an independence without union with Greece. However, the crucial issue of sharing power with the Turkish minority was still a sticking point.

Bill and his colleagues again met Archbishop Makarios and Zenon Rossides in New York in January 1959. This time they arranged for John McGovern, a British MP, to meet them too. The exiled Greek Cypriot leader was feeling thoroughly shunned and victimised by the British, and McGovern offered to arrange a meeting for Rossides with Prime Minister Harold Macmillan. McGovern, as a Labour Party MP, was not the best man to set this up, but he contacted a Tory MP friend in the MRA network to arrange it.

As for Macmillan, he was concerned to break the deadlock, and keen to have urgent private talks to hear the Greek Cypriot position first-hand. However, the official letter he sent inviting Rossides to London immediately contained an unintended slight, suggesting Macmillan may not be present in person. The Cypriots felt this was an old game with the British: they showed willingness to talk, but avoided meetings in practice. So Rossides shrugged off the Prime Minister's invitation, assuming he didn't mean business. The diplomat left America saying he was off to Athens instead.

A strange series of events followed, during which this key Cypriot player appeared to vanish into thin air.

Rossides was urgently sought in vain by British embassies and MRA workers around Europe, and was finally found in time for what became a crucial conversation with the British Prime Minister.

In years to come, the unlikely discovery of Zenon Rossides, which enabled a pivotal meeting to take place with Macmillan, was often spoken of in MRA circles as an illustration of the miraculous way solutions can unfold. It all hung on a small incident involving Margie Manson, who happened to bump into the missing man at Geneva Airport. Unaware of the manhunt going on, Margie had been peacefully travelling home to Paris from Caux. The train taking her to Geneva for her flight had stopped at Lausanne Station, where she suddenly had the compelling thought that she must change trains. The faster Bern-Geneva Express had just drawn in on an adjacent platform. Margie knew she was in plenty of time for her flight and could trust the punctuality of Swiss trains. There was no obvious reason to rush. But she followed her hunch, conscious it might be 'guidance', and transferred to the express train.

Arriving at Geneva Airport well ahead of time, Margie walked straight into Mr and Mrs Rossides, who'd just flown in from the United States. The three friends enjoyed a leisurely coffee together, recalling their times together in New York. The Cypriot couple told Margie that the British government was still playing its games, so they'd come to Geneva to catch up on doctors' appointments, staying at the Hôtel des Familles.

'Well, guess who I met at Geneva Airport?' Margie said casually during supper that night, having arrived back at

MRA's Paris centre in the Bois-de-Boulogne, her current base with Matt. She was surprised at the excitement and disbelief that her story provoked. Supplied with Rossides' exact location, a British diplomat at the table sprang to the phone, knowing that his colleagues in London were trying to find the man for Downing Street. He was able to confirm that the Prime Minister's original invitation had been fully genuine, and the tentative tone entirely unintended.

The following day Bill flew to Geneva to persuade Rossides that Macmillan sincerely wanted to speak to him personally, and that the timing was crucial. After two or three days of hesitation, Rossides finally agreed to the meeting. A conversation in London was arranged in great secrecy to prevent false rumours spreading at this delicate stage of negotiations.

On the morning of 2nd February 1959, Bill drove Rossides to the garden entrance of 10 Downing Street, and collected him again after the meeting. Years later Bill checked the public records in Kew and found the official report of the encounter matched Rossides' own feedback. Historian Daniel Dommel, drawing on both accounts, writes, 'The atmosphere was rather cool at first… but it was not long before it warmed up. Rossides expressed deep regret for the violent excesses committed by his Greek compatriots in Cyprus, and particularly for the British victims of assassination'. This drew a number of questions from Macmillan about the MRA conferences Rossides had attended, causing the PM's Foreign Office adviser to record his impatience that they weren't addressing the central issue of Cyprus.

Rossides went on to stress the importance of a fair solution to unite all the islanders, a goal he claimed Macmillan's own seven-year proposal would not achieve. Greeks and Turks should work together in political allegiance, he urged, not as national rivals but with a single legislative system for all. Rossides also proposed an end to British military operations, and an amnesty extended so that Archbishop Makarios could return from exile. The Cypriot told Bill afterwards that when he'd asked the Prime Minister what message he should take back with him, Macmillan had replied, 'A message of hope and faith based on the spirit you brought with you this morning.'

That evening Rossides flew on to Athens, where he briefed the Greek Prime Minister Karamanlis, catching him just before he left for talks in Zurich with his Turkish counterpart. A couple of weeks later, a conference to reach a final agreement on Cyprus was arranged in London. It brought together all the parties involved: the Greek, Turkish and British governments, the Greek Cypriots represented by Archbishop Makarios, and the Turkish Cypriot leader Dr Fazil Kutchuk. There was now a strong chance that all parties would agree to a power-sharing independence.

But it was still not plain sailing. Makarios had moved a long way to accommodate the Turkish minority, and he knew that a failure to agree could be the worst outcome for Cyprus. But he also knew that many in his Greek community were uneasy with the agreement on the table, and he suggested modifications. His changes were roundly rejected by the other parties who were pushing hard for a deal. Makarios asked the conference for one week to consult his people and reflect. To his disappointment, he was only given one further day to decide.

The conference was always remembered for the Greek Cypriot leader's cliffhanging reluctance to sign, and Bill recalled the last hours vividly. At 5.45 on the morning of 19th February his bedroom phone had rung at 43 Charles Street. It was Rossides telling him that neither he nor Makarios had slept that night, and asking if he could join them at the Dorchester Hotel. Bill and a colleague went at once. Dommell records that 'they found Rossides in an agitated state, pacing and very disconcerted. There was a typewriter in the room and in it a sheet of paper with an unfinished rejection of the agreement. The phone was ringing off the hook with journalists impatient to know what decision the Archbishop had finally come to. Makarios was in a second room adjoining the first'.

Dommell continues, 'the MRA men didn't try to influence Rossides either way, only to support his conviction that a solution had to be just. They prayed with him that in the decision-making all fear would be banished, which in the climate of insecurity in Cyprus at that time was very concrete and tangible'. The two visitors then helped answer the phone and type statement drafts, allowing Rossides time to clarify his thoughts and consult Makarios next door. 'After a short while, he came back and announced that Makarios had decided to sign the agreement, that he was at peace with this course of action, and confident that the news would be well received.'

With the agreement in place, the Archbishop made a triumphant return to Cyprus after his three-year exile, and he called for the Greek community to work in unity with the Turkish Cypriots. The new harmony wasn't permanent, and tensions resurfaced before long, but the deal did result in Cyprus finally becoming an independent republic the following year. The new Greek President, Archbishop Makarios, and his Turkish Vice-President, Dr Kutchuk, both acknowledged the role played by MRA in helping break the standoff and bring about a settlement.

While MRA's influence was recognised in situations like this, behind the scenes the movement itself was going through a period of change in the late fifties. The work seemed ever-expanding, full-timers were growing in number, and MRA's outreach was more obvious through plays, films and public events. But away from the limelight Frank Buchman, who turned 80 in 1958, was struggling. He'd suffered heart problems, strokes and a bout of pneumonia, and was largely confined to bed or a wheelchair. Accustomed to directing the work worldwide, he was forced to delegate decisions and rely on second-hand reports. Full-timers like Bill and Chérie continued to write to him about their activities, but they knew he might not read their reports himself, and letters back were often written by his secretaries.

The 1959 summer conference at Mackinac Island was the last time Buchman had most of his full-time force with him in one place, and he delivered some tough training sessions. He expressed concern that his teams may be losing sight of their essential purpose: to change people and live selflessly 'at the cross', or its equivalent in non-Christian faiths. He challenged them vigorously to live their fullest spiritual commitment without 'bluffing' or being 'feathery'. And he urged them again not to strain for human measures of success, insisting that 'it is God who gives results'.

The team took Buchman's corrections to heart. Many wrote notes when he spoke, including Bill, who forty years later compiled a booklet from his jottings entitled *Builder of a Global Force* to inspire future generations. The booklet doesn't attempt any context, it simply lists direct quotes of Frank Buchman, such as:

'That is Moral Re-Armament – when a man can go in and want nothing for himself but to think only of the good of the nation.'

'That's what I want. To be in touch with the Holy Spirit – for a world in a very serious situation.'

'Your job is to do for your nation what the government ought to be doing.'

To a modern reader the words are astonishingly idealistic. But it was in tune with some of that post-war generation. The more Buchman challenged his team, the more determined they were to keep at it.

Buchman's stridency must partly have come from the fact his own time was running out. But he was also deeply concerned by Western complacency about the rise of communism. For years he'd said that democracy without a moral and spiritual ideology at its heart was no match for totalitarianism, whether of the far right or left. If the West had, for the moment, defeated fascism through traditional warfare, he wanted it to wake up now to the creeping advances of communism.

In Buchman's view the West had been too quick to accept Russia's offer of 'peaceful co-existence', while ignoring simultaneous statements by President Kruschev that 'communism will sooner or later rule the world' (1959). Buchman feared most westerners had adopted a live-and-let-live approach, assuming states still conducted global business formally, through treaties or war. They were out of touch, he believed, ignoring the subtler ways in which the Soviets were undermining the West by quietly infiltrating their media and unions and weaponising trade. He recalled Lenin saying of America, 'We will not have to attack. It will fall like an over-ripe fruit into our hands.'

At the 1959 summer conferences at Mackinac and Caux, public servants and journalists with access to intelligence sources reinforced this view of Soviet strategy. Russia's aim was reportedly to sow division between western countries, using trade agreements to build dependency on Russia and China, infiltrating Western labour movements and community groups, and undermining accepted standards of morality.

At the end of the Mackinac conference Bill carried back to London bundles of a new publication fresh from the printers and soon to be re-published in Britain, Germany, France and Italy. It was a slim grey booklet called *Ideology and Co-existence*, with 31 pages of dense text in small font. 'We are at war' ran the opening line. 'World War III has begun. Even while we were celebrating the end of the war of arms in 1918, the Soviet was planning to defeat and enslave the free world through the war of ideas.'

Over the following months millions of copies of this pamphlet were produced and posted out to homes across America and Europe. At 43 Charles Street, copies lay on a table near the front door in case of interest to visitors. Beside it were copies of another booklet, published earlier, entitled *Where Do We Go From Here?* This one presented a lighter, more accessible outline of what MRA was doing, using colourful cartoons, humour and sparse, snappy text. The graphics followed an 'average' man and woman investigating what this new 'ideology' was all about. It explained complex concepts in brush strokes: *The Nazi idea was: a new order through the rule of one race. The communist idea is: a new society through the rule of one class. The superior idea is: a new world through the rule of one idea: It's not **who's** right, it's **what's** right.*

The booklet coaxes and even jests rather than insists:

> *You don't think it's necessary to change?*
> *You think you can take all that's coming?*
> *SO DID THE DINOSAUR!*
> *This tough guy ruled in ancient days,*
> *But one thing he forgot:*
> *He failed to alter with the times –*
> *Today he just is not.*

In the hall of 43, Chérie flicked through the pages of one booklet, then the other. The pictorial, funny version was more engaging. But when Judi came home from school one day saying she'd been asked in class what her father did, the family at 43 generally thought that the newer booklet would best answer the teacher's question. It had more gravitas, someone suggested. So it was *Ideology and Co-Existence* that was tucked into Judi's satchel the following morning.

The incident made Chérie realise how little contact she had with her children's school life. But both children appeared to be happy, and that's what mattered. Chérie was grateful that her children were adaptable, and contributed in small ways to the Mayfair home. They certainly helped put visitors at ease in this imposing house. The American singer Muriel Smith always remembered having the front door of 43 opened by six-year-old Judi on her first visit. The Cypriot diplomat Zenon Rossides enjoyed some rare respite playing chess with Patrick at the height of the Cyprus crisis. And when Judi joined the crowds welcoming Chancellor Adenauer to London, Chérie felt sure her daughter would recall that moment of history as an adult, even if she had no understanding then of the man's significance and the reasons some people booed him.

Late in 1959, Bill heard that 40 Greek and Turkish Cypriots were being sent by their new leaders to the Christmas conference at Caux. He and Chérie decided to join them there. For a while now they had been considering moving Judi to a small English language school at Caux that had been set up for the children of MRA full-timers. The run-up to this Christmas conference seemed the perfect time to move their daughter, who had just turned seven. She'd be among friends of a similar age, most of whom stayed through the holidays, their parents joining them when they could.

'What clothing would you recommend?' Chérie wrote to her friend Margie Manson, whose daughter Marion had already spent two years at Caux School. 'There's no formal uniform,' Margie wrote back. 'Skirts and woollen leggings for winter are the order of the day, and strong lace-up shoes. She'll want a good wind-cheater and warm trousers for the snow. The school provides skis, ice skates etc – from which you can tell they just have SO much fun here!'

The prospect of a Swiss mountain school for her daughter, surrounded by people they knew well, delighted Chérie. What could be better? The only difficulty might be prising her daughter away from her settled routine at Glendower. Chérie prepared herself for a hard sell. But when the moment came she was surprised to find her daughter appeared to be only too ready to move on.

12

A Chalet School

Caux, Switzerland 1959–61

On an icy January day I walked up a snowy track with three other girls and a carer to the Chalet de la Forêt. It was the first day of a new school term. The chill made our cheeks smart, our eyes water and our breath puff out in clouds. But under our woollen layers and thick *strumpfies* we were toasty warm.

The village houses we passed looked deserted under their dense covering of snow, fringed with icicles. Occasional snow clumps dropped on us from branches high above our heads. I'd seen flakes of snow falling in London, but only in picture books had I seen a full winter landscape like this. I could imagine Mary Plain or Heidi enjoying themselves here. At the Chalet we stamped the snow from our shoes and shed our outdoor wear as we went in. It was how I imagined the interior of a gingerbread house: warm and homely, with small rooms, and wooden floors, walls and shutters.

The staff were more daunting, especially Dot John, the slim, wiry headteacher. She had a brisk, businesslike manner, and calling her 'Dot' didn't mean we could be chummy. She could wag a good index finger and cast sharp glances, and there was no question who was in charge. However, she gave us plenty of time for winter sports or summer picnics, birthdays were celebrated imaginatively, and we didn't work very hard, so she was probably kinder and more easygoing than I realised at the time.

We called all the teachers by their first names: Dot, Kay, Meili, Kathleen. At Glendower School this would have been unheard of. But here the staff were not only teachers but friends and colleagues of our parents too. So while the formalities of a 1950s' classroom were observed in most respects, our relationship with the teachers sometimes extended beyond the school day. We'd see them around Mountain House during holiday times, and Meili and Kathleen, both talented pianists, accompanied the Caux Chorus or soloists when they performed and sometimes sang themselves.

Much of the school routine felt familiar to me. We had three terms a year and classes on weekdays only. Lessons were taught in English and centred on English Language, Literature and Arithmetic. I don't recall any History, Geography, Science or even French, but my diary refers to Sewing and Music, and I started piano lessons with Meili, Kathleen and sometimes an American called Janey. Most afternoons were spent skiing, sledging or skating in winter, or walking and playing games in the summer. Two favourite outdoor games were dodgeball and tracking, a kind of orienteering in which one group pursues another through the forests, following a trail of clues.

In English lessons we were frequently given dictation to check our spelling and punctuation and practise handwriting. At Glendower I'd learnt a fancy cursive style of writing. Here a plainer print script was favoured, although my diary shows I still looped y, f and g. When I eventually returned to school in England, Mummy spoke to the new headmistress when she noticed I was being switched back to twirly writing. I ended up with a hybrid scrawl, mixing the two styles.

My favourite subject by far was '*lovely English littriture*', as my diary puts it. With Dot and Kay we worked our way through a number of classics, including Kipling's *Puck of Pook's Hill*, *Black Beauty* by Anna Sewell, and tales of Ancient Greece. Best of all was *The Little Grey Men* by the mysteriously-named 'BB'. Set in the English countryside, it described the epic travels of three gnomes who set off downriver to find a missing friend. Their encounters with wild creatures, friendly and villainous, and the suspense of the search had me longing for the next lesson to find out more.

At the start of each school day we gathered in a solemn circle in the largest room of the Chalet. Glendower's morning assembly had been attended by several year groups. But with only 13 of us in the whole school, Caux School assemblies were more intimate. First we sang a hymn, then Dot said a prayer, and then she'd call for a 'quiet time'. After a minute or two of silence, while we tried not to fidget or catch each other's eye, Dot would look round and ask, 'Does anyone have anything they'd like to share?' These were words I came to dread when I discovered that always remaining silent wasn't an option. We were expected to speak up and 'share' on a regular basis.

In London I'd learnt that quiet times were about listening to God and trying to find guidance. I'd seen my parents have quiet times in the mornings, and adults had them at meetings. If there was a problem, or a decision to make, people would say, 'Let's have guidance about that' and things were usually sorted out. When the grown-ups shared a thought it might be quite ordinary, like 'Talk to Mabel about her travel plans' or 'Write to Tim'. Or it might be a grand thought, like, 'God has blessed us greatly' or 'Africa needs Ajani'. It might be more of a hunch: 'The timing of that conference doesn't feel quite right to me.' And often it involved putting something right: 'I was insensitive to Charles. I need to apologise and share my own fears with him.' It seemed to be mostly about planning or behaving better.

Before coming to Caux I hadn't been expected to take much part in quiet times, so it was a step up to have them every school day. We were told that thoughts just arise naturally, and good ones would fit with the 'four moral standards' of absolute honesty, purity, love and unselfishness. If our hearts were in a good place we'd find out what God wanted us to do. But my thoughts used to wander, or disappear altogether, and few ideas of a godly nature seemed to crop up. Quiet times felt difficult, and the loving God, whose 'pocket' was supposed to be safe, started to feel like a hard taskmaster.

Worried that my thoughts wouldn't meet with Dot's approval, I started looking for shortcuts to produce something she liked. Some approaches worked quite well. Others I learnt not to repeat. Sharing something we'd done wrong and saying sorry went down well. This could be something like being late or being cheeky to someone. But you couldn't share any old naughtiness. For instance, it wasn't on to say, 'I'm sorry because I don't like X', especially not in front of X. That might tick the 'honesty' standard, but not the 'love' one. We'd be gently corrected or offered different words to use. Once I said I was sorry because I thought a schoolmate 'looked a bit like a beaver'. This was a genuine observation but sharing it didn't go down well. However other expressions of remorse, such as 'I'm sorry for talking behind X's back' somehow seemed to be fine.

It was a minefield, and I started refining my shared thoughts according to the feedback. I suspect we all became a little creative about it. After all, it made life easier, pleased the teachers and made us feel better about ourselves if we got it right. We even became a little competitive in our sharing. An original thought, as in, 'I'm sorry I played with Y's doll without asking her' or 'I thought we could invite that little Indian girl to play with us after school' would raise not only a positive frisson among the staff, but glances of envy from those of us who hadn't come up with it first.

Sometimes we were told to write down our thoughts, which could be even harder. I took to copying adult words or phrases I'd heard. On the 'Notes' page in my 1961 pocket diary is written: *I want to think for other people and to share and fight for others and they must fight for me. I want to fight Uncle Frank's fight and be a sevant* (servant) *of God.* One day, facing extreme writer's block, I realised quoting from a hymn might sound impressive. So I wrote down *Fight the good fight with all thy might*, a line we often sang in assembly. I noticed I wasn't alone in adopting this tactic.

Having quiet times was one of many ways our life entwined with the wider Caux community. School was not just about lessons, and my diary entries indicate how much we were an integral part of the conference centre.

Sunday 12 February
In the morning I went to the meeting to speak and give money to Caux. (Presumably this followed a modest fundraising effort in school, as we had no money.) *And in the afternoon I played dolls and wrote letters.*

Thursday 2 March
In the morning I went to school and then I came down to Mountain House for lunch and then we went on with school. PS We ate lunch at MH because all the workers were invited to eat their lunch there. (This would have been a special meal to thank the builders working at the Caux centre, possibly after the opening of the new dining room.)

Too young to fully understand what was happening here, or to make our own choices, we didn't question anything. We were often told the work was important and urgent, and that old or young, rich or poor, everyone had a part in remaking the world. So we accepted we were part of our parents' mission. I don't think any of us could have explained what this was, but we knew it involved people changing, enemies turning into friends, and problems like war being solved. We also knew it was God's work, and we were following God's plan.

Although this was serious stuff, some parts of our life were fun. The scale of Caux and its constant activity was exciting once you became used to it, and, moving constantly between the Chalet de la Forêt and the conference centre, we were rarely bored. In some ways Caux was like a massive theatre. Mountain House, with its great halls and spacious terraces, was the enormous stage, where the public 'front of house' events took place. Meanwhile 'behind the scenes', in scores of back rooms and buildings around the village, the enabling work happened: the planning, admin, printing, cooking, cleaning, laundry, rehearsing, writing, liaising, and childcare. Wherever you went people were busy, and the place buzzed with energy.

Even the offices with their clacking typewriters and telex machines were interesting, while the kitchens, a vast windowless world of meal preparation on the bottom floor of Mountain House, were awe-inspiring. Here the cooks, in crisp white overalls and headscarves, managed industrial-sized soup pots so big that two of us children could have sat inside them with the lids on. The fridges were ice-cold rooms large enough to walk into with enormous trollies. Near the kitchens was a tunnel-shaped machine into which, after meals, a team of men loaded hundreds of dirty dishes. The plates travelled on a moving belt, emerging clean at the other end. Sometimes we'd see one of our parents or carers stacking plates or manning a soup pot, as the workshifts were made up of full-timers and volunteers among the conference delegates.

The variety of people around us was also interesting, and among the dull tailored European suits and dresses we'd also see people in bright saris, kaftans, kimonos or sarongs. I particularly liked the flamboyant cloth headdresses of the Nigerian women, which mysteriously stayed in place. The voices around us spoke in many languages, although meetings in the main hall were usually in English. I became fascinated by the skills of the interpreters. Sometimes they stood beside a speaker on the conference stage, translating after each sentence, but often you'd see them sitting high above the hall in a row of soundproof cubicles, talking into microphones. I enjoyed putting on one of the headsets that hung on a rail at the back of the conference hall for anyone needing to follow meetings in their own language. It seemed extraordinary that I could select an option on a dial – possibly French, German, Japanese, Portuguese or Italian – and hear those wizard linguists upstairs interpret a speech from the stage almost in real time.

In the holidays we'd sometimes be given simple jobs to do in Mountain House. Over the brief three-month period that I kept a diary at Caux, I record that I *cooked supper, served at tables, scrubbed plates* and *picked flowers,* some of these on multiple occasions. There are also five mentions of *I played with* or *I looked after a baby,* variously named Francli, Heidi and Anew. This last 'job' actually meant that the baby's carer was looking after me for a while, or else that my carer was briefly looking after the baby as well as me. Either way, we were encouraged to feel useful and responsible. 'Helping' in the kitchen at Mountain House would have involved a similarly scaled-down role, and didn't happen often. Typically we'd be wrapped in a huge apron and assist with tasks like washing fruit, or stirring a cake mixture. We must have been more hindrance than help, but it kept us occupied.

Our most frequent task was laying tables in the dining room. This included folding paper serviettes, and in time we learnt all manner of decorative folds, from the simple triangle to the water lily. One style would be chosen for each meal, because it was important that the whole dining room, seating hundreds, should look elegantly uniform. 'Do everything beautifully,' the Swiss ladies in charge would say, 'because doing things properly is a way of caring for people and making everyone welcome.' So everything had to be right. Knives, forks and spoons dead straight. Glasses spotless. Napkins folded perfectly and placed in exactly the same spot at each setting.

Wherever you went in this huge building, it wasn't long before you heard singing. It might be the distant strains of a stage rehearsal, or a soloist warming up. Perhaps it would be the cheerful sing-song of a team working that dishwashing machine. Out on the terrace in the summer, or at the end of the *promenoir*, you could come across someone strumming a guitar, or a couple of people working on a new song.

Mountain House had its own theatre where talented actors and musicians performed. There was also an international chorus, drawn from members of the MRA full-time team, who sang in diverse languages, many dressed in national costumes. And often visitors to Caux would perform in their own languages. Songs were sung to celebrate new arrivals, to mark special birthdays or national days, or simply to liven up a solemn conference session.

We children were frequently invited to help welcome, or wave off, VIPs and special delegations to Caux. A documentary film made in 1960 fleetingly shows us on the front steps of Mountain House waving farewell to Chief Walking Buffalo of the Nakoda Stoney Nation, the same chief I'd seen in London. In cold weather we'd gather in the front hall, but for arrivals I preferred being outdoors on the tarmac, standing beside the flagpoles that flew the national colours of Caux's visitors. Then we could watch in suspense for that moment when the guests' vehicle would suddenly emerge from around the corner of Mountain House, and the chorus would stand by to burst into song.

My diary mentions seven such arrivals over February and March 1961. The guests are listed as *Mrs Falc an Italian lady*, *Uncle Frank* (on two occasions), *the Queen and princesses*, *an important man Mr Chiba had sent*, *the Howards* and *Sir Hamilton Kerr*. If it was a school day, Dot would have briefed us on who they were. Of the names listed here the most familiar was Uncle Frank. We knew he had a particularly significant place in our global family as he'd started the whole thing. The Queen and her daughters were Romanian royalty. Mr Chiba was a senior Japanese politician. Peter Howard was a writer, married to Doë, and he was almost as important in MRA as Uncle Frank. And Sir Hamilton Kerr was a British Member of Parliament.

The chorus was always good, but I enjoyed it most when an accordionist struck up a few chords and Swiss singers in national dress performed their joyful yodelling songs. We children loved hearing a good yodel, and would later try to imitate them with high-pitched *yodle-odle-deeees*. One of us, half-Swiss Elisabeth I think, wrote her own yodelling song – *Holl-yodel-dee, Holl-yolly-yolly-dee* – and we'd sing it exuberantly among ourselves.

We realised that the singing at Caux wasn't simply because people were happy or loved music. It was one of the things, like meetings and talks over meals, that everyone did here because it helped people do things differently. A visiting musician might well perform a concert of their own work. But on the whole the music was Caux music: written to demonstrate how the world could be changed. It was nothing like the songs on Daddy's radio in London, about love or sadness or kissing. I still remembered the words to *Sing Little Birdie* and *Huggin' and a'kissin' with Fred*, but I knew they had no place here. Apart from national songs like yodels or *Nkosi Sikelel' iAfrika*, and an occasional virtuoso performance, every song was on a Caux topic.

Of the regular performers at Mountain House, our favourites were the Colwell Brothers, a talented trio of

American siblings. The Colwells wore cowboy shirts, hats and boots, and they travelled the world singing country-style numbers accompanied by their own guitars, double bass and banjo. The songs were rhythmic and catchy, and we knew many by heart. Another American musician, Herbie Allen, sometimes played with the Colwells and he was a brilliant soloist in his own right. Herbie played an enormous xylophone at spectacular speed. We would stare, transfixed, while he fluttered and whirled his hammers up and down the keyboards as if he were in a fast motion movie.

We had plenty of chances to hear these musical heroes. In conference sessions they'd be called onto the stage for a song, and sometimes they'd perform to welcome guests or celebrate a birthday. It was the lively, memorable tunes that caught our interest, but we couldn't miss the moral messages in the lyrics.

One Colwell song went, *Oh when I point ma finger at ma neighbour, there are three more pointin' back at me!* The lead singer demonstrated by pointing his index finger at one of his brothers, showing his other three fingers bending back towards himself. He concluded:

Oh when I point ma finger at ma neighbour it just ain't honest-eeee,
'Cos in my heart I feel that I first must deal with the three that are pointin' at me!

We got the point. Don't judge others before you've sorted yourself out.

Another song was about quiet times: *Write the thought down, brother, write the thought down.* Others commented on adult practices that we hadn't fully grasped, but we got the general idea, including one that went:

The diplomats were meeting at a table round
Most of them spent every evening out on the town
So they were outmanoeuvred, to their great surprise,
'Cos they couldn't see things clearly through their bleary eyes.
CHORUS: Oh you can't live crooked and (beat) *think straight*
Whether you're a chauffeur or a (beat) *head of state*
Clean up the nation, before it's too late,
'Cos you can't live crooked and (beat) *think straight.*

Some pieces were more of a general rallying cry than a commentary on human behaviour. For instance, *This is it!*, while avoiding any specifics, made it clear that Caux had the ultimate answer to the world's problems:

This is it! No sense in looking any more.
This is it! It's what everyone is looking for.
This is it! Right here and not around the bend,
You've come to your journey's end!

On their tours the Colwells wrote special songs in honour of particular cities, nations or continents visited. One of these, *Africa's Got the Answer* had a strong bongo drum rhythm. The chorus went: *Though Africa's shaped like a question mark, Africa's got the* (beat) *answer* and one verse went:

> *Now somebody made a false remark*
> *When he called the African continent 'dark'.*
> *'Cos Africa's given the world a spark,*
> *With a uniting* (beat) *answer.*

Another was written for a British audience:

> *Listen to the lion roar! He is going to roar once more.*
> *It will ring to the furthest shore, 'til everyone can hear it!*
> *Let us rally once again. We will build a new world then:*
> *A commonwealth of selfless men, an empire of the spirit!*

These lyrics addressing Britain's new post-colonial status meant little to a seven-year-old, but it was another song we could parrot and clap along to happily. And somehow, despite the relentless proselytising, the Colwell Brothers delivered their songs with such good humour, self-deprecation and musical talent, they never came over as insufferable prigs. Listening to them perform was a pleasure that brightened our days.

Occasionally we children also performed at Caux. Dot did her best to prevent us becoming a showpiece in conference sessions. But we often sang for guests, or for special occasions. I enjoyed it when it was our turn to sing, dressed in our best clothes, with our hair tidily brushed and shoes shining. We had two particular party pieces, both from American MRA musicals we hadn't seen, but we learnt the words and actions, and the way to stand tall and sing out to the back of the hall.

The first number was *The Polar Bear Song*, from a children's show called *The Bungle in the Jungle*, set in a troubled forest of warring wild animals. Their problems are solved by a visiting bear from the Arctic Circle.

*The polar bear breezed in from the North, from the
land of the frozen sea
With his eyes so bright, and his fur so white! So
what can his secret be?!
(Shout) TELL US, POLAR OLD BOY!
(Looking curious) What can your secret be?!
(All singing the bear's response) It's a very simple
secret! It's the secret of M – R – A,
Taking honesty, purity, love and unselfishness
(absolute) every day.
(Shout) SO…
Rising in the morning early, taking time to be
guided and gay,
Then your eyes will brighten and your fur will
whiten,
And the bungle in the jungle will vanish away!*

The other song was from *The Crowning Experience*, a stage show soon to become a technicolour movie. Some months after learning *Sweet Potato Pie* we finally watched and heard it sung on a big screen when the film was released. An early scene features a makeshift school for African-American children, set up in a rural barn in Florida. 'The

William (Bill) Conner

Chérisy (Chérie) Conner

Six thousand people attend an Oxford Group house party at Lady Margaret Hall, Oxford, 1935

*Bill (4th from left) at an Oxford Group house party in Malvern, 1937.
Bill's Bristol colleague Frank Bygott (far right)*

*Chérie (3rd from right) with other wartime land girls in Cheshire, including
Elisabeth Burgess (2nd from left), and Margot Appleyard (2nd from right)*

*Troopers (left
to right) Tom
Shillington, 28, Derek
Skey and Bill, 27,
Oxford Groupers in
the Royal Armoured
Corps, Cairo 1942.
Tom was killed in the
Battle of El Alamein*

Dedication of the Westminster Theatre to fallen MRA war comrades, Remembrance Day 1946. Bill's cousin Agnes reads a letter from her late brother Nigel Leakey VC. Behind her to the left: Matt Manson (front) and Bill (second row) [Photo:Arthur Strong]

Bill and Chérie's wedding in London, December 1946, with Frank Buchman as guest of honour, Chérie's parents Roy and Dulcie Oram, and Bill's sister Erica and brother Arthur

Mountain House, Caux, Switzerland [Photo: Jean-Rémy Berthoud]

Konrad Adenauer (centre) soon to be the Federal Republic of Germany's first Chancellor, with Swiss Chancellor Oskar Leimgruber (right) at Caux in 1948

Robert Schuman, French Foreign Minister and a founder of the European Communities, Council of Europe and NATO, welcomed to Mountain House by Frank Buchman and by the Colwell Brothers trio in 1953

Bill, Chérie, Patrick and Judi in Bristol, 1952

A Pelham Burn picnic (Mary left, Patrick and Judi far right) Sussex, 1956

Chérie, Mary Pelham Burn, Patrick and Judi at Wilton Crescent, London, 1955

Amelia Pelham Burn (left) and Judi, Sussex, 1957

The MRA World Statesmen's Mission welcomed to Cairo by Egyptian leader Gamal Abdel Nasser, 1955

Archbishop Makarios (left), first President of Cyprus, with Cypriot diplomat Zenon Rossides (right) visiting 45 Berkeley Square London.

Frank Buchman with Chief Walking Buffalo of the Nakoda Nation and a First Nations delegation from Canada, at Caux, 1960

Marion and Judi (centre back) with Caux School friends at the Chalet de la Forêt, 1960

Judi, Anne and Angela with a birthday cake for Frank Buchman, Caux, June 1960

Angela, Marion and Judi at Mountain House, Caux

First term at Pippins School, Devon, summer 1961 (third row: Judi 2nd from left, Jane 4th from left)

Liz and Judi with their family of rabbits at Pippins School, 1962

Judi leaving for her first term at Winceby House, Bexhill, September 1963

Chérie and Bill in Brazil, 1962

Bill with American singer Muriel Smith on her Brazilian tour, 1962

9 Chichester Road, Croydon

film tells a true story,' Dot told us, 'which started 50 years ago when these children couldn't afford an education. So their teacher baked and sold sweet potato pies to raise the money to keep her school going.' We had no idea what a sweet potato was, but it sounded delicious, and the children's song was jaunty and fun. It always made our audiences smile too.

Make a dollar, maybe two, sweet potato pie,
For we all depend on you, sweet, sweet potato pie.
One for the doctor, two for the may-or, another for
the girl with the ba-by.
Supposin' **you** *should want one too? I hope it's 'yes',*
not 'maybe'!
Thanks for turnin' nice and brown, sweet potato
pie,
They will smell you round the town, sweet, sweet
potato pie.
Round and round and round the town…
SNIFF, SNIFF [blissful inhaling]… *potato pie!*

Even better than singing our songs was the chance we had to perform in a live stage musical called *Pickle Hill* at the Caux Theatre. The theatre was equipped not just with full lighting and sound systems but dressing rooms, a greenroom and wardrobe department. Backstage we were given our costumes, and mine was a plaid smock dress, with a big collar and floppy bow. 'That was worn by Joanna,' I was told as I tried it on. 'She's gone to boarding school in England now, so it's all yours. She's a little taller than you, but that's OK, the Pickle Kids would've all worn hand-me-downs!'

Pickle Hill was based on the real story of Bill Pickle, a bootlegger whose life turned around when he met Uncle Frank. Pickle was a colourful character with a white walrus moustache who sold illegal liquor to students at State College Pennsylvania. The students were known for being rowdy and violent, and during rehearsals we loved the scene when the drunken students sang raucously:

If you wanna be good, goo-ood, as they say you should, shou-ould,
Then keep outta my way, keep outta my way, keep outta my way at State College!

Before the show we gathered with the adult actors for a cast meeting in the greenroom. 'There'll be some key people in the audience tonight, and this play could make quite an impact,' someone might say, before a quick pre-show quiet time. Then the first actors were summoned, and we sat listening to the stage sound through speakers, waiting for our call. We only featured in one scene, so we didn't stay to the end, but our one song was generally a showstopper.

In our scene Frank Buchman makes his first visit to Bill Pickle's run-down home, known as Pickle Hill, where he lives with his wife and twelve 'Pickle Kids'. The children are curious to see this rare visitor, especially when they hear he wants to 'change' their father, but Bill tells them to keep out of the way. As soon as the guest has left, the kids rush back in, clamouring to know if their dad has 'changed'.

One of us had the cherished solo line, 'I've never seen anyone change before! What does it *mean*, Daddy?' Bill kicks the children out impatiently, assuring them nothing at all happened. The children groan in disappointment, and slouch off to the front of the stage to sing their song. They stand in size order, each delivering their own number in the line-up with a bob or bow when their moment came in the song.

> *Like the hours of a clock, we are all day long*
> *Si-ing-ing an endless song:*
> *ONE – TWO – THREE – FOUR – FIVE – SIX – SE-VEN*
> *EIGHT – NINE – TEN and then EEE-LEVEN*
> *We're… TWELVE Pickle kids who want to know*
> *The right way, not the wrong, to go,*
> *But whatever we do our dad says 'NO!'*
> *So we don't know right from wrong.*
> *Today some people came to call – we think it kinda strange!*
> *We'd like to know the answer now: IS DADDY – GONNA – CHANGE?*

I loved being part of this big pretend family on the stage. Against the glare of the lights we could only make out the front rows of the audience, but we'd see people there shaking with laughter and we lapped up the applause. We knew we provided light relief in the play, and the extreme cuteness of the smallest Number 12 Kid added extra charm. During my time in the play, that part was played by a tiny, delightful Moroccan girl called Jijah, the daughter of a Caux maintenance worker. Jijah was much younger than us and we didn't see much of her away from the theatre. But we were on nodding terms with the family, who lived in a chalet in the village.

I don't remember if my parents ever saw me in the show. However, Marion's parents were very much involved. Marion hadn't told me – she probably assumed I knew – that her parents played the star roles of Bill Pickle and his wife. Uncle Matt and Auntie Margie were both talented actors and appeared in many MRA productions. I must surely have recognised Auntie Margie straight away. But it took a performance or two before I realised that our stage father, the white-haired, moustachioed Bill Pickle, was actually dark-haired, clean-shaven Uncle Matt.

I envied Marion her glamorous parents. But however proud she was, Marion now says she'd have readily given up the excitement of their shows to spend more time with them. For the duration of that play it was the Pickle family that took her parents' attention, not their own one. We all craved time with our real family, yet we knew we couldn't ask for it. It would be selfish, and we had neither the awareness nor the words to discuss it. As for our parents, when they saw us singing our hearts out on stage or playing in the snow, they clearly thought we were having the time of our lives.

13

Normal Living

Caux, Switzerland 1959–61

It's not surprising that our chalet school was thought by our parents to be a child's paradise, and sometimes in winter, when we could ski, sledge and skate almost from our doorstep, it felt that way to us.

My diary indicates we had a short school day with no homework or exams, and winter afternoons were spent out in the snow. Every year the green lawn behind the Chalet Patinoire was watered and frozen over to create an ice rink. Some children had their own skates while others used the well-worn ones from the hut beside the rink. During my second winter I noted *I went to Montreux, and bought skates, a doll's bottle and doll's strumpfie*. It was early in January, so it's likely that Christmas cash gifts from family or friends had made this unusual shopping spree possible. The following day *I went skating with my new skates. I stayed all morning, then Mummy fetched me to eat in the cafétéria.*

When the school term began, winter sports – and mealtimes – remained my major focus.

19 January: *In the morning I ate with Jessie and Helen and then went back to school. In the afternoon I went sledging.*

20 January: *I went to school and I sledged for playtime. In the afternoon I skated and then tried on my skis and then had tea with Mummy in the Maria and washed my hair.*

23 January: *In the morning it snowed and it snowed all day and in the afternoon we sledged because the skating rink was not open.*

24 January: *In the morning I went to school and in the afternoon I skied and for supper I ate with Helen in Mountain House.*

While skating techniques were never formally taught, skiing was led by a much-loved Swiss instructor called Jaqui, known for his cries of 'Bend your knees!' In a basement store at the Grand Hotel he showed us how to measure up for wooden skis, and how to wax them to keep them slippery. Our nursery slope was a basin of land between the wide bends of Twigglytwog, but we quickly graduated to the steeper slopes of Haut de Caux, above the Chalet de la Forêt. I could soon descend with confidence, but took time to master the drag lift. The diary notes with triumph a day when *after lunch I skied and went up the ski lift and I did not fall off!*

When we weren't skiing or skating we'd be tobogganing at speed down Twigglytwog, and pulling our sturdy wooden sledges up the more direct 'Steep Path' for more. I don't remember many cars using that stretch of road in winter, nor any accidents. Often we'd drag the sledges up with us to the Chalet de la Forêt in the morning for use in break time, and then we'd slide back downhill after school. We relished the freedom, speed and fun of it all, and the rare chance to frolic. Out in the snow it didn't seem to matter if we sometimes shrieked with laughter or excitement.

Once there was a snowball fight in a car park near the Chalet Patinoire. It was organised by some older children, who'd built defensive walls of packed snow for each side. I don't recall our parents ever playing in the snow with us, apart from one day when Mummy unexpectedly had a go on skis. We'd visited an English family, not Caux people, who were staying in a chalet above the village. My diary entry reads: *I skied with Nigel Bowy. Mummy skied for the first time. Then we had a big tea and played and then went home.* Mummy was wearing an unsuitable straight skirt with thin nylon stockings, and had to pad out her borrowed ski boots with layers of extra socks. Her brief glide across a gentle slope near the chalet was all a bit of a joke, which she seemed to enjoy too. I noticed that our hosts, both adults and children, skied together and saw it as a family activity.

When the thaw came our afternoon activities changed, and from spring to autumn we'd be walked up mountain tracks into pine forests or through meadows flecked with wild flowers. Cowbells jingled in nearby fields and I'd imagine Heidi living nearby. Above the forest line we sometimes spotted alpine crocuses, orchids and blue gentians. Our destination was usually a viewpoint or stream where our carers would hand round Emmental and jam sandwiches before we played hiding games. Summer picnics were almost as good an escape from school and conference life as winter sports. But nothing quite matched the joy of sliding down the mountainside, shouting with fear and elation, without being watched every second.

Books were another distraction that carried me off to other places, and I never tired of reading, or being read to, in the privacy of my room. Violet Needham's adventure books, passed on by Patrick, were great favourites, most of them about a boy known as the Stormy Petrel who joins a rebel group in Eastern Europe. The best of the series, I thought, was *The House of the Paladin*, which Mary PB would read out dramatically. The story centres on attempts to rescue a young duchess held captive in a remote palace, and a colour illustration at the front of the book shows a man pointing a gun. The caption reads *'Hands up or I shoot!' cried Mr Hildebrand*. I could hardly wait, through all the plot twists involving poisoned chocolates, a villainous uncle and a deceitful governess, for this thrilling climax to arrive. Mary seemed as fired up as I was, and when we finally reached the crucial challenge we found ourselves screeching at the tops of our voices, 'Hands up or I shoot!' Our loud cry might have surprised passers-by in the corridor outside, but we were far too absorbed in the story to think of that.

My happiest and most settled time at Caux was a period during 1960 when I lived at the Mon Repos chalet. The 'Rippo', as we pronounced it in our English accents, was a short walk downhill from Mountain House, and although outside it wasn't as cutely picturesque as the Chalet de la Forêt, the wooden interior and small rooms gave it the same homely feel.

Staying in one building for a while was welcome respite from the constant room changes. But above all, it was fun to be here with Marion, Angela, Anne, Jean and Elisabeth, along with our carers and occasionally some of our parents. It was a children's zone set apart from the adult world of the conference centre. Here we could play together in the open-plan living and dining area, take some of our meals, and move freely upstairs to our bedrooms without a trek between buildings.

Mummy, and perhaps Daddy, stayed here at one point. I can picture Mummy in her bedroom with its windows looking out across the lake. Once, in that room, I put my bare foot into a slipper and yelled with shock and pain when a sleepy wasp inside it stung my toes. Another memory is of looking up from a book to see my mother, who was getting ready for bed, completely naked. 'Mummy!' I gasped in horror, quite unused to adult nudity. 'I'm *terribly* sorry, darling,' Mummy responded, looking aghast, and rapidly seizing her dressing gown for cover. 'I really wasn't thinking!' We children didn't know much about naked bodies, but we did know they should be covered in front of others. *And what if Daddy had been in the room?* I wondered with alarm. He might have seen her too, and how embarrassing THAT would be!

Most of our time in the Repos was spent with our carers, and mine was now Irish Betty. A Dutch girl called Maria joined the household in the autumn. We children were used to these ever-shifting arrangements, and it wouldn't have occurred to us that the young women in charge might have found the situation daunting. A hint of this appears in a letter written by Maria to her own family following her arrival. 'There are six girls of six to eight years old', she wrote, 'three girls like me who look after the house and three couples, but they are away a lot. It is a very funny family if you think about it: three fathers and three mothers. At the moment there are two mothers and one father'.

From our perspective, our carers threw themselves into their roles wholeheartedly, showing kindness and creativity and a lighter touch than our teachers. That Christmas Maria arranged a visit to the Repos from St. Nicholas and his companion Black Peter. Father Christmas didn't seem to come to Switzerland, so we enjoyed meeting Maria's Dutch version of Santa. And since he brought us small gifts and Black Peter scattered sweets and biscuits around the chalet, we didn't mind what he was called.

Christmas was an enchanting time at Caux. Carols were sung in the near-darkness around a huge indoor fir tree lit with flaming candles. Under the tree was a crib, and someone would tell the Nativity story. Some grown-ups went to church in the small Caux chapel or down in Glion. On Christmas Eve the Scandinavians made their traditional rice pudding, telling everyone to search for a lucky nut hidden inside, and we had to leave a little pudding outside 'for the elves'. There were iced biscuits, gingerbread houses and some discreet present-giving, and for a day or two Caux felt quite magical until, much too soon, the treats were gone and normal life resumed.

Birthdays were also celebrated enthusiastically at Caux. There was always cake, and our carers and teachers were good at thinking up surprises. My diary mentions *a treasure hunt and then birthday tea and films* for Geoff's birthday. A few days later it was Jean's birthday *and we tracked her and found her at school and then we had an indoor picnic on rugs and we played one game, then for tea we had records and an ice cream cake.* Another popular birthday activity was toasting dough 'dampers' on a bonfire. Celebrations were inclusive affairs. On one of my birthdays I was invited to the Mountain House cafeteria to have tea with an older woman I barely knew. 'It's her birthday too,' Betty explained, 'and it's always nice to celebrate these things together.'

For a week or two in the summer of 1960, a widowed friend of my mother came to Caux with her 12-year-old son David and daughter Jane, who was seven like me. They came from a different planet, it seemed to me, as they lived together in a cottage in Somerset, England with a granny and a great aunt. It sounded like the idyllic life of Milly Molly Mandy, my storybook friend who also shared a country home with her parents and relatives.

While I secretly envied their dream life, Jane was openly awestruck by Caux. Wherever she turned she couldn't believe the size of the mountains, the grandeur of Mountain House, the colours of the wildflowers or the freshness of the Alpine air. She would exclaim rapturously, 'How perfectly wonderful! How perfectly beautiful!' which I considered a very grown-up, and probably very English, way of speaking. Jane also displayed wild excitement when reunited with her mother after a few hours' apart. I watched in wonder as she raced towards her mum for a hug after a separation that we Caux children wouldn't even have noticed with our parents. I knew we wouldn't be allowed to be so demonstrative in public, however joyful we were. Unaware I was simply stifling my own longings, I assumed an attitude of disapproval. But deep down I yearned for Jane's spontaneity and the closeness she enjoyed with her mother.

Jane's brother David was a keen nature lover. We children watched spellbound as he caught and examined beetles and grasshoppers outside the Repos. One day we all set off on a day trip down the mountain and across the lake by boat to Évian in France. As the train descended from Caux and made its first stop at Glion Station, we were surprised to see David step out and run off along the platform. The adults worried a little, but knew he was a sensible boy, and on our eventual return to Caux he was found safe and satisfied after a day exploring the local flora and fauna. He hadn't wanted to waste a precious day of his holiday on a group outing with small girls, and who could blame him? For us it was an extraordinary and admirable episode, as none of us would have dared defy the grown-up agenda like that. We'd never even seen anyone try. When this family returned to Somerset they left their mark on us, having given us a glimpse of individuality that seemed rather attractive.

Within the Caux community and 'global family', one of the few ways we children could stand out as special was to wear a national costume indicating where we came from. These outfits were sometimes worn by adults to demonstrate and celebrate the wide range of countries represented at Caux, and the custom had been extended to the children. On special occasions my friends Marion, Jean, Geoffrey and David wore Scottish highland dress in their family tartans. Meanwhile Anne had a Swiss peasant *dirndl*, Angela wore a German one, Delscey wore a South African *voortrekker* dress and bonnet, and Elisabeth could choose between a Scottish or a Swiss costume, given her dual nationality. On my arrival in Caux I realised I'd miss out on this fun, as the English and Americans lacked these symbolic outfits and had to make do with ordinary clothes.

Then suddenly this situation changed. My Irish carer Betty arrived on the scene and not only persuaded me I was Irish, she presented me with my very own national costume. This was a high moment, if not THE high moment, of my time at Caux. Now I too had a special outfit to wear, and a credible identity. I was no longer a bland English person.

When Betty had first told me I was Irish I'd protested that I'd never even been to Ireland. Daddy had sometimes said he was Irish, but he didn't talk like Betty, so I doubted it was true. 'Oh, he's Irish all right,' she'd countered. 'He sounds as English as they come, but that's just English public schools for you. You're a real Irish Conner to be sure, a daughter of the High Kings, and you should be proud of it!' I loved her certainty, but still I pushed the idea aside, thinking my friends would say I was making it up.

Then one day, out of the blue, Betty gave me a perfectly fitting Irish national costume, a small replica of one she wore herself, and suddenly it had to be true. I was officially Irish, with a demonstrable place in the global family. This felt hugely significant. The treasured outfit had been specially made by someone Betty knew back in Ireland, and I can picture and feel each part of it. The coarse silk, emerald-green blouse. The black velvet cuffs and shoulder-pieces fastened with poppers – 'To spare them the wash,' Betty said. The white woollen shawl folded into a triangle, draped over my shoulders and fastened with a Celtic brooch. There was also a mobcap in the same green silk of the blouse, fringed with white lace, and a long red skirt of Irish tweed, encircled with a black velvet band above the hem. Nowadays the look might smack of 'Irish peasant who'd won the lottery', but it was perfect for 1960 Caux. 'It's just grand!' Betty kept repeating as she helped me dress. She seemed as pleased as I was.

My new national pride appears in my diary: *17 March 1961: St Patrick's Day Hooray. In the morning I went to school. After lunch we welcomed Uncle Frank. Then we selabrated [sic] St Patricks Day with the Irish blooded people and Simpsoms [sic]. We had shamrock.*

One day Betty told me to get quickly into my Irish outfit to greet a visitor. Shortly afterwards a friendly stranger turned up at the Repos. He had little hair, intense eyes and the strongest Irish accent I'd ever heard. 'He's an important Irish nationalist,' Betty had said. 'A passionate patriot. He's visiting Caux and asked to meet the little Irish girl.'

At seven I had little idea what this meant, and I still don't know who he was, but I was pleased to show off my Irishness. On arrival the man made a beeline for me when he saw me in my costume among my friends in their normal clothes. He whisked me up in his arms as if he'd known me a lifetime and set me on his knee. We weren't used to sitting on strangers' knees, but I was proud to be the centre of attention. While tea and cake were served the man told us stories about Ireland and sang us Gaelic songs. His charm and exuberance struck us children dumb, but Betty and the other carers kept the chat moving. It was as well I knew nothing of my Irish family history, as a mis-telling might have spoilt the mood. But the man didn't ask questions, and it's likely he'd been told Daddy was a reformed Protestant loyalist who supported the Republic. Whatever the brief, he seemed at ease, and I glowed with delight long after he'd left.

The peak conference seasons at Caux generally coincided with our school holidays, and our carers would take the children away to other parts of Switzerland. One Easter we were driven an hour and a half to stay in the countryside near Gstaad. My clearest memory of Gstaad is of a strange incident involving cows. We'd wandered into a small farmyard one day to look at these animals. As we peered over the split door of their shed, we noticed the tail of each cow was raised up high by string, which was tied to a wooden beam above them. We presumed this was to keep their tails clean. Then we noticed two of the strings were entangled, making the attached cows fidget and twitch. We wanted to free the strings, but didn't dare intrude. 'Let's throw water at it and the strings might separate,' I suggested.

The only containers we had were some giant snail shells we'd been collecting for no particular reason. So we filled them from a nearby trough and had a go at some coordinated water-flicking at the cows' tails. Of course it didn't work, and nor did it go down well with the farmer, who appeared on the scene shouting furiously as we ran off at high speed. Back at our chalet we explained ourselves to the carers, who were always quick to forgive our mild misdemeanours, but we were no doubt taken back to the farmer to apologise and explain ourselves before the event was forgotten.

In the summer holidays we had a longer break at Praz, a town by Lake Murtensee near Bern. At the top of the big old house we stayed in there was a lavatory unlike any I'd seen before. To use it you'd perch over a hole in a long wooden bench, with nothing between you and a black pit far below. Instead of flushing a handle, we poured water from a large jug down into the darkness. I used the toilet with trepidation, until it became routine.

The house was close to the lake, and we'd amble over to its shore with our towels and swimming costumes. In the shallow water I made my first attempts at breaststroke, reaching my arms down to the muddy lakebed when I wanted to stop. It took years to work out how to stop feet first.

One evening at Praz we stayed up late and visited a night bakery making traditional plaited bread. The walk along a moonlit road into the neighbouring town was an exciting treat. Another trip was to a women's prison in a bleak rural location. A prison now seems an unusual choice for a children's outing, but it probably arose from an officer or governor having contacts at Caux and offering a tour, and we seemed to take the experience in our stride.

Back at Caux, we knew people came there with all kinds of ideas and opinions, but the central message we learnt was that MRA was right, for everyone. It was 'the answer'. Whatever others thought of it, the MRA life was the norm. One of the Colwell Brothers' cheerful songs confirmed this, and its chorus would echo in our heads:

Normal living, normal living, normal living in the land!
If you think it's strange, then you'd better change
'Cos it's normal living in the land.

We got the message: if we didn't fit in we'd have to change our ways until we did. And it was easiest just to try to fit in in the first place.

Nobody had to tell us that some people had a different view of 'normal living'. I'd started to see this in London, and even around the village of Caux there were signs of 'us and them'. 'Us' was 'the team', who understood guidance and the four standards, and spoke about 'the work' and 'the battle'. 'Them' were the other people who either didn't get it yet or didn't want to get it, and weren't yet 'changed'. According to 'us', if more of 'them' didn't take up our normal living then the world would continue in a mess and there would be even more fighting and wars.

I could tell that the nice lady who ran the village shop, for instance, wasn't one of us. We knew her by sight, and we always said 'Bonjour, Madame,' and once we baked her a chocolate cake. But she wore lipstick and sold cigarettes. She also sold chocolate, postcards, cuckoo clocks and Swiss dolls, and we loved going to look at them. But she had no Caux books, magazines or Colwell Brother records. Adult chat in the shop concerned the weather or people's health, not Mountain House or 'the work' or Uncle Frank.

The café at Caux's railway station was also different. We never went inside, but we'd see its customers puffing on cigarettes and lingering over strong-smelling drinks. I liked the distinctive tang of French tobacco, but these were sights and smells we never came across inside Mountain House. Meanwhile, among the conference delegates we could spot the ladies with eye make-up, heavy perfume or trousers, and the men who slipped off outside for a smoke or a glass of wine.

These seemingly less desirable practices were not mentioned much. At school we were told, 'There are no rules. We're not an institution or an organisation or a point of view. We each have to find out what is right for us.' But there *were* rules, I could see that. Otherwise, why no cigarettes or lipstick or public hugs from our parents?

We also picked up on differences within the team at Caux. We were told that every person is equally important, and has an equally important part to play in changing the world. But some people were definitely more important than others. Uncle Frank for instance. He was always accompanied by some stern men pushing his wheelchair and carrying his papers. They stayed in the second-floor suites of Mountain House and conducted business there or in Uncle Frank's Dining Room, where he entertained special guests. This was much smaller than the main dining room, and it had upholstered chairs, crisp white table linen and heavy cutlery. Only adults waited on these tables as it was silver service. We knew Uncle Frank liked good, well-presented food, so meals in his dining room were extra special and often cooked in a separate kitchen. Once we were sent across the road from the Chalet Mon Repos to pick baby dandelion leaves for a special Pennsylvania Dutch salad, said to be his favourite.

Uncle Frank's special treatment wasn't surprising because we knew our parents held him in high esteem. They spoke of him both as their friend and their inspirational leader. But it wasn't easy for us children to love this ancient, mildly spooky person, and if I saw Uncle Frank and his retinue approaching along a corridor I'd disappear quickly to avoid an encounter. But in fairness, when we children did meet Uncle Frank on occasions, he had a kind sparkle in his eye that gave no hint of menace. He never said much, but would listen intently to what was said, or to a song or poem we delivered, and he'd almost always comment, 'Fine! Fine!' encouragingly in his American accent. A photo shows Anne, Angela and myself, in our best frocks and shoes, carrying a huge cake decorated like a snowy white mountain topped with pine trees and a chalet. Two adults hover over us, anxiously ensuring the candles stay alight, and we all look a little nervous. The cake was for Uncle Frank on his 82nd birthday.

For all the distractions Caux provided, I started, in time, to feel a return of the gnawing worries I'd experienced in London. The life of a grown-up seemed burdensome and the thought of becoming one filled me with dread. There seemed to be one right way to do everything, and all activity must have a purpose to it. But how were we to know what that was? If children arrived with parents new to Caux, we'd often be asked not just to play with them, but to 'think how you can help them'. How would we do that? I felt a heaviness growing inside. Life seemed difficult to figure out.

Even the Colwell Brother songs could be confusing. One of them went:

Be yourself, be yourself, how simple life can be.

If I was supposed to be somebody else, then why in the heck am I me?

Yet we children knew we couldn't just be ourselves, or say what we liked, because we mustn't be 'self-centred' and must always 'put other people first'. Teamwork was what mattered at Caux. And fitting in.

It didn't occur to me to talk to anyone about my disquiet. I couldn't put it into words anyway, and whatever 'it' turned out to be would almost certainly be my fault. Absolute Honesty, as we understood it from school, meant not stealing, cheating or telling lies. It didn't mean opening up about our thoughts and feelings. Sharing sadness or fears risked being labelled 'selfish' or 'unhelpful'. I'd heard grown-ups say sad people were often sinful, they weren't doing 'normal living'. It seemed easier to keep quiet if I was sad, and avoid scrutiny.

In the meantime I tried to avoid getting things wrong, especially after learning that the price of disobedience could be terrible. One day we'd heard some shocking news. A brother of little Jijah, the sweet Moroccan girl who played the smallest kid in *Pickle Hill*, had died in a boating accident on Lake Geneva. He was an older boy whom we'd all known by sight. His death was apparently a result of his own waywardness. He'd ignored his mother's instruction to stay safe indoors when a storm was due, and he'd gone out on the lake with his friends. Their small boat capsized and he'd drowned. It was very frightening. Wars and catastrophes had always happened far away. But now the dangers of the world were pressing in more closely.

Already harbouring these anxieties, I was dismayed to find that I too was apparently doing something wrong. Worse still, I never found out what it was. All I knew was that Dot took me aside one day in the spring term of 1961 and asked me if I had something I wanted to share with her. This generally meant she had something in mind but it needed to come from me. She sat me down a couple of times for quiet times, so I could seek God's direction about it. Reliving those conversations, I can recall my frustration.

Dot (*after class*): I wonder if we could have a little chat together.

Me (*heart sinking but attempting to look pleased*): Yes, of course.

Dot *(looking neutral):* Come over here and we can sit down together.

Me (*sitting obediently*): Yes.

Dot: Now, how are you, in yourself? Are you happy?

Me: Yes, I'm happy.

Dot: It's just… I have an idea there's something not quite right. Is everything OK?

Me: Yes, I'm fine I think. Thank you.

Dot: Are you sure there's not something you'd like to tell me?

Me: No (*thinking hard*) I don't think so. I'm fine. Really.

Dot: It can be helpful to get things off your chest.

Me (*trying to work out what she wanted*): Yes. But I am fine. Honestly.

Dot: Well, I think we'll just have a quiet time and see what we get. There might just be something you want to talk about.

Me (*realising there's no alternative*): OK. Yes.

Silence ensues for a few minutes. I stare through the window at the sky, wondering what I can possibly think of to satisfy her and get away. Then the worst bit, the sharing.

Dot (*breaking the silence, and smiling gently*): Well, what thoughts came to you?

Me: Erm, nothing really.

Dot: What, no thoughts at all?

Me: No, not really. Not that I can think of.

The grilling felt relentless, and it never occurred to me to ask Dot what she was getting at. It would have felt cheeky, like answering back, which was something we couldn't do. As always, I tried to conjure up something to say, and in one of Dot's chats I suddenly had an idea.

Dot: Have you anything to share?

Me: I thought I should be honest about laughing at a dirty joke with Catherine yesterday.

Dot: A dirty joke?

Me: Well, we were skating, and there was a brown mark on the ice. Catherine said, 'You know what that looks like?' and we were laughing because it looked like someone had 'done something'.

Dot (*not very interested*): OK. Any other thoughts?

Me: No, not really.

And so it went on. I really didn't know what she was after. I'd done something bad and was the only one unaware of what it was. It didn't occur to me to talk to my friends about it. We didn't discuss or query the teachers, as that would be talking behind their backs. I wouldn't talk to my carer Mary PB or write to my parents about it as I preferred them not to know. God's pocket wasn't much good, I thought, especially if I couldn't get good thoughts. In any case I reckoned God mainly spoke to grown-ups, as their thoughts seemed to override children's thoughts, just as it seemed Uncle Frank's usually trumped theirs. All in all I was disappointed because I'd thought I'd been meeting school expectations. But this felt like failure.

In my diary's brief entries there are no references to the chats with Dot, yet some interesting points emerge. I moved rooms much more frequently in the term when Dot was showing concern. On Sunday 1 January 1961, when the diary begins, I was living at the Grand Hotel. Over the next weeks I record the following:

Tuesday 17 January: In the morning I went skating then I moved to the Maria. Then I ate in Mountain House and then rested in the Maria and then invited Jean and Marion up to play with me. Daddy went to England.

Thursday 9 February: In the morning I went to school and… in the afternoon we did a bit of Scottish dancing. Then I moved to Mountain House.

Friday 10 February: In the morning I went to school and after lunch I did a bit of sledging and then Delscey came to room with me.

Thursday 23 March: Moved to the Maria.

Moving rooms is mentioned casually because it was routine. But having enjoyed the continuity of life in the homely chalet Mon Repos for a large part of the previous year, the frequent shifts between the larger hotels may have been difficult, even without the comings and goings of parents and carers.

Another feature of the diary is the frequent reference to health issues in my last three months at Caux School. These seem surprising as I was generally a healthy child.

Monday 2 January: I woke in the morning and I felt sick, so I stayed in bed all day.

Friday 13 January: In the morning I went to the infirmerie and then went skating…

Wednesday 25 January: In the morning I stayed in bed and in the afternoon I got up for tea and I played and then I went to bed again for supper.

Saturday 4 March: In the morning I served breakfast and then I went to the infirmerie and then lunch. After lunch I skied and then I cracked a bone so I had to have plaster of Paris and sling.

Monday 6 March: In the morning I went to school… and then I went to the Vevey Hospital to have an x-ray of arm.

Wednesday 8 March: In the morning I went to school and then I came back for half day and I went to the infirmerie and then I played with Anne.

Friday 24 March: In the morning I went to school and had lunch (which was only rusks and mint tea because I had a sore tummy).

None of this was dramatic, and the possible fracture turned out to be a sprain. I suspect I played up the trickle of minor complaints either to attract attention or miss school. After all, staying in my room with my books while dunking rusks in sugary mint tea was a blissful alternative to lessons. But some ailments may have been a product of anxiety, or simply normal childhood lurgies.

Any of these factors may have been clues to why Dot sensed I wasn't happy, but perhaps she also believed I was lying about my supposed ailments. My diary supports this view in an entry for Monday 20 February, when *I ate supper with Margret Burton (a doctor).* Dr Burton was a general practitioner, one of the doctors and nurses who worked voluntarily at the Mountain House *infirmerie*, and I remember that awkward meal in the cafeteria with this older woman I barely knew. The doctor told me a story about the boy who continually cried 'Wolf! Wolf!' when there was no such creature in sight, merely to attract attention. So when a wolf really did appear nobody believed the boy's cries. The moral was clear: false alarms can be dangerous. But I didn't think the tale related to me, and I told her I hadn't invented my aches or pains. The matter was dropped after that, or so it seemed to me. Neither Mary nor Mummy ever mentioned it to me. And Dot stopped questioning me, despite minor ailments continuing to appear in the diary.

Soon after this strange episode, the spring term came to a close, and I was told I'd be going to England for the holidays. I'd be seeing Mummy and Daddy and possibly Patrick again, and we'd be staying with my grandparents. The news came as a wonderful surprise, although as usual my diary just sticks to the bare facts, expressing no emotion.

Thursday 30 March 1961: In the morning I got up at qwater [sic] past 5 and then I went down to Geneva by car and got on an airoplane [sic] and flew to England.

I was accompanied on the journey by an MRA worker who also happened to be travelling to London. Mary PB had stayed on in Caux, and we probably all thought I'd return the next term, as my teddy bear, doll, books and toys also stayed behind. In fact, these belongings were to spend 12 years in Caux in a suitcase, which suddenly turned up one day in Britain when I was at university. Because I didn't return to Switzerland after that holiday. It turned out I'd now be going to an English boarding school.

14

Global Campaigns 1959–61

If 43 Charles Street had given Bill and Chérie a sense of living over the shop, the international conference centre at Caux was off the scale of unusual family homes. A few families staying long-term in this large, restless community had an apartment or suite of their own. But most Caux School parents were constantly on the move and had to stay in the accommodation that was available. Sometimes they had rooms adjoining those of their children, or at least in the same building. But not always.

The occasional inconvenience of this was far outweighed by the advantages of having Judi at Caux School. Back in England Patrick was boarding at his prep school, with relatives to go to in the holidays. Now Judi could have continuous care at Caux if needed. Chérie couldn't think of a school building more charming than the Chalet de la Forêt, or teachers more dedicated. What a matchless education the children would have there, and what adventures! On Judi's first day of term, Chérie watched from a window as the young girls set off to school from the Hotel Maria with one of their helpers. No more Number 14 bus to South Kensington, she thought with satisfaction. They'll have such fun, they'll hardly know we're not around.

The pool of young volunteers available to look after the children at Caux was impressive. A Swiss woman called Iris was resuming her care for Marion, while a Northumbrian called Phyll would soon take charge of Judi. Seeing them interact with the children, Chérie observed how competent the carers seemed for girls barely out of their teens themselves. A new thought arose in her mind. 'What if we parents start feeling replaced?' she asked Bill. 'I mean… might the children get TOO used to living without us?' But she'd known and accepted Bill's response even before he made it. 'This is living in faith,' he reminded her. 'If we're called to be on the road, we have to trust God will look after all parts of our lives – family too. In any case, there's nothing wrong with children learning to be independent.'

At daily team meetings in Mountain House Chérie noticed the many married couples and parents in the full-time MRA force now. It was quite a contrast to the pre-war years, when full-timers were mostly single. Many of the other parents here had travelled more than she and Bill had. Signe, a Norwegian friend who'd helped set up Caux School, had a daughter of Patrick's age. 'I've worked out that we'd lived in 82 different homes by the time Ingrid was two,' Signe once told Chérie.

'We were so lucky to have that time together in London and Bristol,' Chérie confided to Bill. She knew they were about to travel more and was determined to focus on the positives. In the context of the 'battle' and the dire state of the world, any daydreams about being a settled family again seemed to be self-seeking. Later in life she admitted to feeling some peer pressure on this. Putting work first was proof of one's commitment, whereas prioritising family was considered insensitive to other travelling parents and setting a bad example to new recruits. As much as Chérie longed to see more of her children, her sense of duty to carry out team directives and support Bill was stronger.

Buchman's high expectations of his colleagues can be seen in a letter to Bill dated 2nd May 1960. This was a year before Buchman's death, and shortly after he'd arrived back in Europe from America. The typed note would have been dictated to a secretary or possibly written on his behalf, and lacks the warmth of his previous letters to Bill:

> *My dear Bill*
>
> *Are you ill? I have not heard from nor seen you since we arrived.*
>
> *You learnt truth in America which is needed in the battle here. If you did not learn it, now is the time to do so. There is a desperate need and I do not hear of you meeting it.*
>
> *This is the place to fight.*
>
> *Sincerely*

The strangely critical and tetchy tone of this is mysterious, as there's no record of Bill or Chérie absenting themselves or losing interest. Indeed, with their children now taken care of in England and Switzerland, they'd freed themselves to be fully available for the work, and Bill never mentioned any dark-night-of-the-soul periods in his life with MRA.

Frank Buchman's biographer Garth Lean indicates that it was actually Buchman himself who was suffering an 'agony of spirit' at this time. In this final year of his life, the MRA leader was straining for new vision, new methods and a team that would keep rooted in an authentic, selfless faith experience. He sensed some of his people were too movement-minded, and too imitative of him to seek fresh inspiration for themselves. He feared for the future of the work, and blamed himself for not creating teams fit to impact the world more significantly. Yet Buchman was a sick man, lacking the strength to rally his colleagues personally, and forced to delegate almost everything. Lean describes a series of meetings he called for at Caux. 'Buchman was too weak to be there himself and had to relay his thinking and his criticisms at second hand. Some of these were inaccurate and others became distorted in transmission. Many of his old friends were left bewildered'.

The letter to Bill no doubt stemmed from the leader's anxieties. Yet Buchman had always insisted on plain speaking and on the MRA fellowship holding each other to their highest calling. He felt the more they could keep each other focused, the more the Holy Spirit – or its equivalent in other beliefs – would use them to change the world. 'Fighting for each other' to do their utmost was spoken of as a crucial part of teamwork.

Arguably the MRA workers' zeal and devotion to both the cause and its leader were at their most extreme in the

1950s and early '60s, giving the movement some cultish characteristics and whipping up the kind of pressure that most MRA parents felt to prioritise their work over family. However, Chérie and Bill would always deny that MRA was either sectarian or authoritarian. And Bill in particular would insist that following individual guidance or conscience was a safeguard against others imposing their will over them.

As to Buchman's abrasive letter to Bill, there is no record of Chérie and Bill's reaction, but it clearly didn't deter them. In the winter of 1959–60 Bill was involved in a conference attended by both Greek and Turkish Cypriots, and team meetings were abuzz with campaign plans for the year ahead. Over the following 16 months Chérie and Bill moved between London, Geneva, Paris, Nicosia, New York and Mackinac Island, returning for Caux conferences in between.

One MRA priority was to continue building human bridges between France and Germany, uniting Europe after the war years. Out of this work came a play called *Hoffnung* (*Hope* in English), which had been written and produced by 13 German miners. The play was based on their personal experiences of bringing hope to their divided country, and in 1959 they'd launched it in Germany before taking it to London and Britain's mining communities. Now it was moving on to Rome and Cyprus, India, Japan and the Congo. On formal occasions the miners wore their traditional uniform of dark suits with shiny buttons and plumed helmets, attracting newsreel coverage as they presented a new image of Germany. During the miners' tour some of their wives and children stayed in Caux, and Chérie was pleased Judi would meet the young Germans.

Bill and Chérie were part of a 60-strong taskforce supporting the *Hoffnung* tour when it went to London, Rome and Nicosia. It was February 1960 when the miners arrived in Cyprus, and the date of Britain's handover of power had just been pushed back for a second time. Tensions were running high and Archbishop Makarios was under attack both for signing the agreement in London and for his association with MRA. Nevertheless he'd joined the Turkish leader Dr Küçük in officially inviting the MRA group to Cyprus.

There was little time to prepare for the 36-hour visit, but the team managed to book a 1,000-seat theatre that was not only the largest venue in Nicosia but also one acceptable to both Greeks and Turkish audiences. They also arranged a translation system into 'neutral' English since the play *Hoffnung* was in German, a language that still rankled with some Greek Cypriots after the wartime occupation of Greece by Germany and Italy.

Chérie and Bill's Swiss friends Marcel and Théri Grandy, who hosted the MRA centre in Nicosia, reported back to Frank Buchman that 'the German miners took Cyprus by storm'. Marcel described how 'three hundred leading personalities of the island – Greek, Turkish and British – came to a reception at the Ledra Palace Hotel'. Despite a bomb exploding nearby the following night, the theatre was also full. 'It was probably the first time since the end of the emergency', Marcel wrote, 'that Greeks, Turks and British were to assemble together in such numbers'. Five hundred then attended a further reception at the Ledra Palace, where 'the manager, who had suffered under the German occupation in Greece, and to whom the Germans had apologised for his treatment, had the room beautifully arranged with drinks and sandwiches'.

The miners were received by each of the island's three leaders: Makarios (soon to be President), Küçük (soon to be Vice-President) and the British Governor, Sir Hugh Foot (later Lord Caradon). The visit led to further groups of Cypriots attending Caux conferences that year.

At Caux that summer the assembly ran from June well into October, with a steady flow of delegations arriving from the world's trouble spots. Bill and Chérie did their usual hosting and planning roles, with shifts on the reception desk or room allocations, but almost anything could crop up. One moment Chérie might be swathed in aprons stirring a huge vat of soup, the next she could be back in a dress and pearls, pouring afternoon tea on the terrace. Conference delegates often took turns on the kitchen work shifts too, in a practical expression of international collaboration that helped keep the centre's running costs down.

For parts of that summer Chérie and Bill stayed at the Mon Repos, where Judi and some of her school friends had moved with their carers. The chalet was handy for the conference centre and they could share some household meals. Occasionally they made a furtive outing from Caux with their daughter, taking care that other children didn't feel excluded. It wasn't at all like being together in a real home, Chérie thought, but at least the children were nearby and felt part of the Caux operation.

She found it heartwarming to watch the schoolchildren singing to guests or welcoming visitors on the steps of Mountain House. Sometimes they were even presented to 'Uncle Frank', and Chérie wished they'd seen him in his prime, when he was well, knew everyone by name and had an inspirational word for any occasion. When the children wore their national costumes Chérie was delighted to see Judi given her chance to shine in her new Irish outfit, gifted by her new carer Betty.

When school first broke up for the summer the children left for the village of Praz on Lake Murtensee. Chérie and Bill saw this as another wonderful gift, this time bestowed by their friends Professor Burnier and his wife Paulette, who generously made their home available in this way every summer. Letters from the carers in Praz spoke of swims in the lake, country hikes, the neighbours' rabbits and village festivals. It sounded like an excellent place for the children when Caux was so busy, and it gave Chérie and Bill peace of mind as they threw themselves into conference events.

A high point of their own summer was the arrival at Caux of their friend Zenon Rossides, now Ambassador to Washington, who'd been sent by the new President Makarios of Cyprus. The new Vice-President Küçük sent a respected Turkish lawyer, Mr Malyali, to represent the Turkish Cypriots. The two official delegates brought with them the first flag of the Cyprus republic to be sent overseas, and this was duly raised by Rossides at Mountain

House in front of 700 international delegates when, on 16th August 1960, Cyprus was finally declared an independent republic. The Cypriot diplomat who'd worked so tirelessly for this day told the conference, 'If there is a case where the spirit of Moral Re-Armament has worked successfully, it is certainly the case of Cyprus. It was that spirit which brought a settlement when it seemed hopeless, even by force.'

Another delegation at Caux that summer represented the Hindu, Moslem and Christian communities of the Indian state of Kerala, and included some former communists. Three years before, Kerala had become the first major state in the world to vote into power a communist government, but there had been a violent backlash and the Indian president had expelled the new regime. The Indian delegates spoke of coming to Caux to work across faith and cultural divides to build an 'inspired democracy'.

From the newly independent Republic of Congo, more than 100 politicians and community leaders arrived at Caux to explore solutions to its bitter civil war, in which the Soviet Union and the United States supported opposing factions. Other groups came from Kenya, Ghana, Sudan and Ethiopia, some as a result of seeing the film *Freedom*.

Meanwhile the German miners were back at Caux following a world tour, which had ended in Japan and America. Their visit to Japan had coincided with intense political unrest caused by the government's renewal of the US-Japan Security Treaty. The Germans met some of the student activists whose anti-American street protests had prevented the US President Eisenhower from visiting Japan a year earlier. The young dissidents were among 60 Japanese who accompanied the miners to Caux that summer. During the conference the students concluded that working together, MRA-style, would be more productive than confrontation. They followed the Germans' example and wrote a play called *The Tiger* about their change of heart. Before the Caux conference had finished, the miners had invited the Japanese students to perform their play in Germany, and the students had already left for the Ruhr. It seemed at this point that each campaign tour naturally generated a new one.

Once again, a central theme of this 1960 summer assembly was the global threat of communism. The Soviet President Kruschev had apparently said that year that he expected to see 'the red flag flying over the whole planet' in his lifetime, and MRA literature and plays were full of references to Soviet ambitions and the need to outmatch them with a bigger idea.

The starkest call to action came in the *Ideology and Co-Existence* booklet, which Frank Buchman promoted strongly when he opened this Caux conference. It was fast becoming the most widely-distributed publication MRA had ever produced. Buchman's biographer Garth Lean describes the booklet as 'also the most controversial', with its uncompromising anti-communist stance. In the context of the 1950s and '60s Cold War, the warnings may not have been so startling, but its blunt message was certainly designed to attract attention. 'Communism has a plan to take over our country,' it said. 'The choice for America is moral re-armament or communism'.

In years to come, many within the movement, Bill

included, came to see the booklet as a mistake. They felt it distorted MRA's message which was intended for everyone, regardless of their politics. As a result, it polarised people and understandably labelled MRA as anti-communist, pro-establishment and reactionary. 'Characteristically', writes Lean of Buchman, 'he did what seemed to him to be right, sometimes with the minimum of consultation, and let the sparks fall where they would'. He wasn't interested in engaging with critics. He simply wanted to forge ahead with his own 'proven' model.

For Buchman, communism was not so much a political creed as a materialistic and totalitarian attitude that was inherently inhumane. He believed it undermined people's freedom and spiritual life, as did corrupt forms of capitalism. Buchman hoped *Ideology and Co-Existence* would be a wake-up call, opening people's eyes to Russia's ambitions in the world. But as Buchman's biographers have pointed out, in the process it attracted uncomfortable bedfellows on the anti-communist far-right, and repelled some left-leaning and centrist supporters who felt MRA's mission had become narrow and fanatical.

With the MRA team reluctant to question Buchman and eager to show solidarity, many didn't spot these pitfalls at the time. Crises needed addressing, and everyone who came to Caux was considered a potential nation-builder who could find their ultimate calling here. Debate of the new booklet would have been seen as unhelpful navel-gazing. So for now *Ideology and Co-Existence* was generally embraced by the MRA team, and it was tirelessly promoted.

This single-mindedness, and the drive to present MRA as the sole answer to the world's problems, inevitably put some people off. Some longstanding backers became less comfortable with the stridency of the message and stepped back. These included Chérie's parents. On visits to England she found them generally supportive of her own work with Bill, and always ready to take the children in the holidays. Yet many topics were left undiscussed and fewer questions asked.

As to her wider family, Chérie knew some relatives regarded her and Bill's activities as eccentric, if not embarrassing. Explaining their activities could take time, and didn't offer much common ground. She found it hard to join in domestic chats about children and schools, difficult bosses or new kitchens. And the reasons she gave for missing a family reunion or for travelling over Christmas didn't always go down well. 'Global assembly', 'touch-and-go negotiations' or 'a statesmen's mission' were meaningful priorities to her and Bill, but left some others cold. Chérie would, in principle, have liked to see more of her relatives, but there was never enough time.

Bill was less conflicted. He enjoyed occasional encounters with his brothers, aunts and cousins, but Chérie noticed he didn't seek them out. The lack of gravitational pull towards his natural family didn't indicate lack of interest, she felt sure. She sensed it had more to do with his total dedication to his cause, supported by his school and army training. Chérie was proud of Bill's determination, and forgave him for covering up his softer side.

One way of spanning the natural family/MRA family

divide was to spend time with relatives who understood what they were doing, and were in fact doing it too. Bill and Chérie were particularly close to Erica and Edward Evans, who were also committed to MRA and had given a home to Patrick in Worcestershire. Bill's natural ease with his sister and brother-in-law largely arose from speaking the same language, knowing the same people and sharing a common goal.

There was little doubt Bill and Chérie were at their most comfortable among their close-knit team of global co-workers: people who, despite their different backgrounds, races and faiths, were bonded by a shared purpose. Visitors to Caux often said they were witnessing the socialist ideal of the 'brotherhood of man' lived in practice, and the MRA team would wholeheartedly agree. Being a part of this fellowship was to them a precious gift that they longed to share with others.

That August at Caux, Chérie reconnected with her old friend Elisabeth. They'd been wartime land girls together, then young mothers in Bristol. Since her husband Frank's death, Elisabeth had withdrawn from full-time MRA work to look after her two children. Chérie and others wanted to ensure Elisabeth still felt a welcome part of the team, and they'd invited her to bring the children to Caux. While Elisabeth's daughter Jane played with the Caux schoolchildren, and her son studied Swiss wildlife, their mother caught up with her old friends. She made it clear there should be no expectation of her returning to full-time MRA work. 'My place is at home, caring for Mum, Auntie and the children,' she said firmly when Chérie asked about her plans. 'My heart's still with the work, but my children need a mother, and I'm not going to go on the road like you do!'

Chérie appreciated the differences in their situations. She knew she'd feel the same if she lost Bill. However, she and Bill were planning to travel even more in the coming years. World needs were pressing, she told her friend, and Buchman was concerned they weren't making sufficient impact. New campaigns needed support, although where they'd go next – the Middle East, USA, Africa, South America or India – was undecided.

'Patrick will start senior school next year, at Bromsgrove,' Chérie told Elisabeth. 'It's where Bill and his brothers and cousins went, and it's close to Whitbourne, so it's a natural move for him. We're less sure about Judi. Caux School's been marvellous, but Judi's amongst the oldest there. We'll have to find her a British prep school soon.'

'Maybe I could help,' Elisabeth suggested. 'I could investigate local boarding schools near us. Jane would enjoy the company if Judi came to us on weekends out.' Chérie thought about the year ahead. Judi would be eight this autumn. There was no question of her following Patrick to Worcestershire. He and his cousins there were older boys, at single-sex schools. A parallel plan was needed for his sister.

A few British parents at Caux had opted for a Methodist boarding school for girls on the North Wales coast. Apparently it had a 'good Christian ethos', a head who was part of the MRA team, and it wasn't far from MRA's Tirley Garth centre in Cheshire. But when Chérie visited Penrhos College for herself she didn't warm to it. 'It seemed rather cheerless and remote,' Chérie reported back to Bill, 'and a big leap in scale from Caux School.' She recalled her own homesickness as a child when she'd boarded, first in Missouri in India, and later in Haslemere, Surrey. It had been hard leaving her home and she'd taken some comfort from having family or relatives nearby. Chérie decided to take up Elisabeth's offer to explore schools in the West Country, suggesting to her friend, 'The closer to you, the better.'

Over Christmas 1960 the Caux conferences resumed, and during Judi's spring term Chérie became increasingly sure it was time to move her daughter to a school in England. The headteacher Dot had taken her aside one day and confided that something might be amiss with the young girl. 'Nothing too serious,' she assured her, 'but she can be a little withdrawn, and reluctant to engage in school with her whole heart. I've tried to have guidance with her, but she doesn't open up.'

Then there was the matter of the aches and pains. Dot thought it was almost as if she wanted to be ill. 'When Joanna had appendicitis at Christmas, Judi suddenly felt sick too! She's twice been to the *infirmerie* at Mountain House after falls but nothing was broken. And when you're away she sometimes reports tummy aches. I talked to Dr Burton, who told her the "Wolf! Wolf!" story. But she just listened politely, apparently!'

Chérie had thanked Dot for her care and concern, but she wasn't worried. She considered her daughter healthy and resilient, and Judi's response was emphatically positive when asked about school. 'Yes, everything's fine. Really!' She seemed perplexed by the adults' digging, and Chérie decided she'd simply outgrown the school.

'She needs more challenge and stimulation,' she told Bill. 'Well, she's hardly short of that in Caux!' he smiled. 'Yes, but maybe not in her classwork,' Chérie persisted. 'At her age Patrick was taking Latin, Algebra, History, Greek, even a bit of science… He was a Cub Scout, and played rugger and chess. Judi doesn't get any of that.' 'Well, of course not – she's a girl!' Bill retorted, and Chérie, with a sigh, let the topic drop. When she thought about it in her quiet times she realised that what her daughter needed most was to be happy and secure. That had to be more important than what she learnt.

A plan began to emerge. Elisabeth wrote to say she'd found a delightful prep school in Devon, not far from her cottage, with available places. Chérie and Bill were in London when they heard this, and, as a first step, they immediately arranged for Judi to join them in her next school holidays. Nothing was mentioned to Judi about switching schools in case the idea didn't materialise. They hadn't even seen the place yet. But this did appear to be a timely opportunity to provide their daughter with the fresh challenges she needed.

15

Scrambled, Boiled, Fried

London, West Country, April 1961

Waking up on my first morning back in England, the bedroom smelt fusty, and the blue nylon sheets were slippery and cold. I missed the crisp cotton bedlinen of Caux, and the aroma of polish. A sash window was slightly raised, yet I could hardly tell it was open. In Switzerland the fresh mountain air would have blown through that narrow opening.

In the next room, amid clattering, a man was speaking earnestly without stopping. Then Mummy came in the door carrying a mug of tea. 'Here you go,' she said, 'some nice sugary tea before we get breakfast sorted. And you can have eggs – scrambled, boiled or fried – a real English breakfast!'

'Is that Daddy out there?' I asked eagerly, sliding up to a sitting position. 'Daddy?! Oh, no!' Mummy laughed.

'That's the newsreader you can hear, on the Home Service radio.' 'All in English?' 'Oh yes, definitely in English. It's the BBC. British Broadcasting. Remember *Listen With Mother*? You loved those radio stories when you were in London before. There's children's television too. You can watch some later on Granny and Grandad's TV.' 'Will Daddy get here soon?' 'Yes, he'll be here tonight, and he should be around for Easter weekend.'

I warmed my hands on the unfamiliar mug of tea, considering all the good things happening at once. No school. No meetings. Television. Grandad had found me a small bike. Mummy and Patrick were here and Daddy was coming soon. Last night we'd played a game called Contraband, and I hoped we'd play it again. We had to smuggle in whiskey, jewels and nylon stocking cards, hidden among ordinary luggage cards, and you won by telling whopping lies. That didn't seem to matter here, the whiskey or the lies, but I was sure Dot wouldn't like that. I tried to imagine what it would be like with all four of us in this one place with Granny and Grandad. We could stay indoors playing games and watching TV, without visitors! But I knew that wouldn't happen.

My diary sketches out that holiday weekend.

Friday 31 March 1961: In the morning I had breakfast and unpacked my suitcase and rode on my bike. Then I had lunch and rested and went for a walk and tea in a café and then I came home and saw TV.

Saturday 1 April: In the morning we had a tricky breakfast

(April Fools' Day) and Dad and I went down town on a bike. After that we came home and had lunch.

Sunday 2 April (Easter Day): In the morning we had a good breakfast and then I played and after lunch did the washing up. Then we had an ambassador's family here.

My new activities seem mundane, but the novelty of bike-riding, going into town with Daddy, playing badminton with Patrick and choosing library books again was thrilling. Discovering TV programmes like *Blue Peter* and *Crackerjack*, and seeing *Swiss Family Robinson* in a real cinema, made these days even more dreamlike. To top it all, we – which for a short time meant Mummy, Daddy, Patrick and myself – were staying together in something akin to a family home, even though it was Granny and Grandad's place. It was an apartment in a four-storey, yellow-brick Victorian house, in the London suburb of Croydon.

My grandparents occupied the ground floor, behind the big front door, while the other three flats had their own door at the side. The windows at the back of the house looked out across a spacious lawn and trees, above which a thin tower was visible on a distant horizon. This, Grandad told me, was the new Crystal Palace transmission station, which sent out our radio and TV programmes.

I'd visited Granny and Grandad's home when I'd lived in central London. Eventually I learnt the house actually belonged to Daddy, but Granny and Grandad had settled here with their own things and it always felt like theirs. It was full of Indian carvings and Chinese silk prints from their army travels. A glass cabinet displayed medals, old weapons, faded monochrome photos and sports team caps, but Grandad seemed just as proud of the furniture he'd bought at auction, which suited the scale of these large rooms. One of his best purchases was a heavy oak dining table, which not only extended but turned into a baize-covered billiard table when its top panels were removed. During mealtimes I'd fiddle with the tasselled billiard nets brushing my knees. When I was older I realised these grand pieces were too bulky for minimalist and compact fifties' homes, and it was only when I visited children in more modern homes that I saw how dated the décor was.

Apart from enjoying family time, I took pleasure in the small-scale living. Instead of bed sheets going off to giant laundry rooms, there was a tiny room off the kitchen where Mummy or Granny put them into a top-loading washing machine. 'It's my new twin-tub!' Granny told me proudly. 'Who'd have thought a machine could do our washing for us? We simply fill it with water through these hoses on the taps – and press a button!'

I didn't tell her about the much bigger washing machines at Caux in case it hurt her feelings. Everything here was toy-sized. The cooker only had four gas burners. The fridge was tucked under a counter. At mealtimes only six places were laid, unless there were guests. We'd wheel the food on a small trolley along a corridor to the dining room. And best of all, if there were just a few of us, we'd eat high tea watching television.

It was becoming clear to me that I had family who weren't part of the 'global family'. Within two weeks of arriving in Croydon there are several mentions in my diary of visiting relatives. On Easter Monday *my great aunt came to lunch.* A few days later *my great aunt and uncle came to stay,* and three days on, *my cousins and my uncle and aunt came to stay.* None of them are named. They were all nice, friendly people, but they didn't talk about quiet times or Caux, and some of the adults smoked and wore lipstick! I wasn't sure how everything fitted together.

Any hopes of remaining within this family cocoon soon evaporated. My diary confirms plenty of coming and going during those first two weeks in England, for all of us. After the Easter weekend there were a few busy days with visitors. Then Daddy took off somewhere, Patrick left to visit his friend Tom in Wiltshire and suddenly Mummy and I were also heading off, to Somerset.

If the purpose of our West Country trip was to suss out a new school, I didn't yet know this. For now, I was happy to be travelling with Mummy by train from Waterloo with the new sandals and bathing costume she'd just bought me. It felt like a proper holiday.

We were met at Taunton Station by Jane, the girl I'd met in Caux the previous summer, and her mother Elisabeth, who drove us along pretty country lanes to their home in the village of Forton. Flint Cottage was, as I knew it would be, a real Milly Molly Mandy home, complete with Jane's granny, known as 'Gaga', great aunt 'Hayhee' and brother David. As the week went on it felt increasingly like stepping into a storybook in which children only had to step outside the door and adventures awaited.

Thursday 13 April: In the morning David caught me some newts and one suffered so it had to die. After lunch we went to the sea and paddled in bear [sic] feet.

Friday 14 April: In the morning I played on the pulley in the garden and in the afternoon we went to the seaside and swam.

Saturday 15 April: In the morning I played in the garden and after lunch we went to the sea and swam and paddled. Just before tea we found a cuttel fish [sic] with its bone still on its back, but he was dead. Then we had a picnic tea and played and went home.

Sunday 16 April: In the morning we played and went to church, then played more and after lunch we went lizard catching and we found 7 lizards, 1 slow worm and 6 adders.

Monday 17 April: After breaky I caught spiders for my lizards and then I played and after lunch I played and after supper I had a game of Flounders.

Tuesday 18 April: In the morning I played in the garden and after lunch we went to Charmouth (the sea) and swam and paddled and rock pooled and had tea there.

The new interest in wildlife was inspired by Jane and her brother David, whose knowledge of beetles, butterflies, snakes and any other creatures he came across was extraordinary. We girls were in awe of him and his collection of specimens that he studied and painted in his cabin at the bottom of the garden. Jane showed me Gerald Durrell's books describing his real-life zoological trips across Africa, and these temporarily distracted me from my growing Enid Blyton addiction.

But if lizards and snakes dominated my diary, the freedom of uninterrupted, unsupervised play was just as memorable. Here there were few adult distractions and no guests to get changed for. We ran around in shorts, climbed trees and made up games about imaginary visitors from space, or explorers. Jane had books galore, as well as games, a piano and what appeared to be free access to the biscuit tin.

The happy week ended when we caught the return train, carrying an extra box containing my first-ever pets: a collection of lizards. On the way back to London we stopped off for a night to pick up Patrick. His friend Tom's parents, whom Mummy obviously knew well, made us welcome in a cottage not unlike Jane's. Tom's father even made me a cage for the lizards with glass panels, although the clever creatures managed to escape into the garden before they'd even settled in. Their liberation may have been a deliberate ruse on the part of the grown-ups, but whatever happened, I knew at once it was for the best. They needed to be in the wild, and they made terrible pets.

Returning to Chichester Road, there was finally some talk of moving me to a school in England. I welcomed the idea of leaving Caux, without the slightest idea of what an alternative might be like. As if to mark a significant new step in my education, Mummy bought me my first fountain pen – *an actual pen* – and suddenly my diary entries switch from pencil to ink, with smudges and splotches across the pages.

Before I could find out much about the new plan, there was a distraction. We'd been back three days when I woke up feverish, with a blotchy rash, and a doctor visiting the house confirmed it was measles. It was annoying to be hot and headachy, prodded with a cold stethoscope, and forced to drink '*awful stuff (two bottles of it)*'. But it was also worth it to have a solid week lapping up the attention of my family. Even the usually humdrum diary notes can't hide my delight.

Monday 24 April: I stayed in bed because of measles but I had a nice time cause Mummy read to me and Patrick gave me a jigsaw puzzle.

Tuesday 25 April: I still had measles so I still had to stay in bed but I finished my jigsaw three times. Then the doctor came and said I could be carried in to watch TV in my dressing gown.

The following day, when I was starting to get up for longer, I wrote that *Mummy went to see Pippins School where I might go,* taking a train all the way back to the West Country and returning the following day. The new summer term was fast approaching, and she must have felt the need to settle the matter quickly.

During our stay with Jane's family there had been no mention of the school, and presumably it couldn't be visited in the holidays. But now it seemed I'd be going to Pippins School in the town of Axminster in Devon. It was a few miles across the county border from Flint Cottage in Somerset, and Jane would be a day girl there while I boarded. This meant I'd have a ready-made friend, and could sometimes stay with her at half-term. 'Pippins is just like its name sounds: quite charming!' Mummy assured me after her visit. 'It's a prep school, which means it's for children up to 12 years old. And being small, it has a family feel. There's a lovely garden with a donkey and a pets' corner. So we could get you a hamster!'

This all sounded very acceptable, especially as I knew Mummy and Daddy would be going away again soon, so this special time together was coming to an end anyway. It never occurred to me that staying with them might be an option. Life didn't work like that. My parents were always on the move. But there was still plenty to look forward to. I was staying in England, I'd go to school with my new friend Jane and I'd have a pet.

Preparations were soon underway.

Friday 28 April: The doctor came and said I can go outside now. Mummy went shopping and bought most of Pippins School uniform. But she's going to make the Sunday dress. Daddy came home for his birthday.

Saturday 29 April: Daddy's birthday is today and we had a lovely birthday breakfast. Daddy and Patrick went to the seven asides [rugby at Twickenham] and I stayed at home and iced his birthday cake and watched TV.

Much too soon, my trunk lay open on the bedroom floor, ready to be packed. I tried not to think too much about school yet, and focused on the hamster.

Sunday 30 April: In the morning P and D went to Witborn [Whitbourne Hall] to go back to school. Great-aunt Vi and Uncle Aubrey came for two nights.

Monday 1 May: In the morning we watched May Day in Russia on TV.

Tuesday 2 May: In the morning Mummy bought a hamster cage for my hamster.

Friday 5 May: In the morning my hamster came. With food and everything.

There, abruptly, my 1961 diary ends, my journaling efforts only resuming in January after a new 1962 diary arrived from my faithful godparents at Christmas. Maybe I forgot to pack this one. Or maybe I already had a hunch the new school would be very different from the last, and I was readying myself for a fresh start.

*

Three sounds transport me back to my Devon prep school, each conveying the desolation that occasionally swept through me there. One is the insistent cooing of wood pigeons. The daylight through the thin dormitory curtains woke me early and I'd lie in bed listening to the pleading of these birds. They seemed to understand my despair at being trapped in an endless school term, far from anyone I really belonged to.

The others are night-time sounds, which would drift up the back stairs from the matrons' sitting room during our reading hour before lights out. One of these is the forlorn strains of the *Coronation Street* theme tune. I'd never actually seen the programme as ITV, the alternative to BBC TV with adverts, was discouraged in many homes, including that of my grandparents. But its slow, bluesy trumpet melody, punctuating every Monday and Wednesday school night for two and a half years, was both reassuring for its dependability and empathetic in its mournfulness. Matron's approaching footsteps as she came to turn off our lights at 8 o'clock would accompany the last weary chords of the tune, and I almost expect her to appear when I hear that music now.

Even more haunting is *A Scottish Soldier*, a song that spent 36 weeks in the pop charts during my first year at Pippins. Matron and her assistant Barbara must have loved it, as we often heard it those evenings rising from the staffroom, and the song tugged at my heartstrings. Andy Stewart is singing about a soldier who *wandered far away*, with *his heart crying* for the *hills of home*, and even with no claims to being Scottish, nor any particular place to pine for, I felt his pain at being separated from places he yearned to be.

Because those green hills are not highland hills
Or the island hills, they're not my land's hills,
And, fair as these green foreign hills may be,
They are not the hills of home.

Stabs of homesickness had also struck me hard when Mummy dropped me off for the first of my three summer terms at Pippins. In future I'd travel there in the reserved carriage of the school train from Waterloo. But measles had given me a late start, and Mummy and I travelled down by normal train, with Aunt Elisabeth driving us to the school. I'd expected Mummy to settle me in in some way, perhaps helping me unpack. But she never got beyond the grey stone paving of the hallway, where we chatted briefly to Matron and Miss Roberts Jones ('Call me Mip'), the headmistress. Suddenly there was a hug from Mummy, and she was off. The front door closed behind her and outside a car door slammed before Aunt Elisabeth drove her away to Axminster Station.

It wasn't like being left at Caux among people we knew, with Phyll, Betty or Mary in charge. Here it was just me with girls and teachers I'd never met before. At Caux everyone was in the global family, but I could tell nobody here knew that world. Beside me, Mip, Matron and Barbara the under-matron wore lipstick and smelt of cigarettes. Through the windows I could see girls in the garden chasing each other, giggling and shrieking in ways we wouldn't have done at Caux. So they probably weren't in the global family either. Mummy hadn't mentioned this. At least Jane would be here in the morning when the day girls came, a link to Mummy and my old life that I suddenly longed for. But Jane wouldn't be staying after class. She'd come in daily but I couldn't go home with her. The reality dawned on me that Pippins was cut off from everywhere I knew.

I was distracted from my emotional free fall by two smiling, breathless girls rushing in from the garden as if they were late for something. They greeted me like an old friend and linked arms with me on either side. Had they got the wrong person? After the restrained behaviour of Caux the girls' proximity might have felt awkward, even threatening. But they were so genuinely friendly and spontaneous it was comforting.

'Susan's your school "godmother".' Mip nodded at the older girl, whom she'd obviously briefed to be my guide. 'She's an old hand, you can ask her anything! And Amanda's in your dormitory – so you'll both be Roses. Susan's a Thistle! They'll explain it all and give you a good tour before tea.'

Warming to the girls' chumminess, I put up no resistance when they steered me off into the Common Room. 'This is where we play when it's raining. See? Books. Games. Gramophone if we need a dance!' Then out we swept through the open French windows across the terrace and onto the lawn beyond. Mip, Matron and Barbara had disappeared behind us. The gardens, I discovered, were our own domain.

Other girls ran up to us, and Susan and Amanda told me everyone's names, and gave them mine. Daphne, Roma, Jane, another Susan and her sister Rosemary, Small

Barbara… 'She's not so small,' Susan explained, 'but it sets her apart from Big Barbara, the under-matron.' A voice somewhere muttered, 'Big Barbara Brute!' There were chuckles, and I was surprised at the girls' cheek towards a grown-up.

The girls continued to propel me on round the garden, the babble persisting as they pointed out landmarks. A cedar tree in the middle of the lawn had ropes hanging from its lower branches. 'See that? We climb up and slip down the rope!' 'I'll show you!' 'Or just swing high. See, you sit on the knot and push off.' 'We queue up here.' 'Since when did you queue?!' 'Sometimes I do, so there!'

On we went to an area fenced with wicker panels. 'Da-DAR!' exclaimed Amanda, like a circus ringmaster. 'This is the pets' corner!' 'Come and see my rabbits.' 'Have you got a pet?' 'Yes, a hamster,' I said, pleased to have come prepared. 'He's still in the hall, I think.' 'Oh, hamsters are kept indoors,' said Susan, 'or in the shed. Big Barbara's probably put yours with the others. Just look at those gorgeous guinea pigs!'

'And don't forget Neddy!' 'Oh yes. See the donkey by the tennis courts? We're getting another one soon.'

'What about the camps?' someone broke in. 'Ooh yes. See the bushes? Behind the pets? And over there. And down behind the courts. We can go anywhere in the bushes and make camps.' 'You could join my camp if you like,' someone offered. 'Tessa and I started it last term. Come and see.'

I was acutely aware of being a new girl, but the friendliness was disarming. I felt accepted and almost dared to imagine enjoying it here. Then I stepped back through the French windows into the house and wasn't so sure. I heard the front door slam shut again, and remembered with a jolt that Mummy had left. I tried hard to look cheerful, but inside I felt alone and wary in this big grey building.

Pippins would once have been an elegant, finely furnished Georgian country home. It had been built on the edge of Axminster before the town developed its carpet factories and railway station. Now the house was institutionalised, with a sparse interior and bare floors. On the ground floor near the common room were classrooms, a dining room and kitchen. The junior classrooms and gym were across the garden in The Hut, named for its wood cladding rather than its size.

Once indoors, my guides led me up a curving stone staircase and showed me the dormitories: Rose, Thistle, Daffodil and Shamrock. In Rose there were eight identical iron-framed beds, each with a bedside chair. I wondered what it would be like to be with seven girls all the time, when I'd only ever shared a room with one person. Would we talk all night? What if I needed the toilet, or couldn't sleep?

Matron was in Rose unpacking a few last things from my trunk, ticking off items on a list as she went. 'Well, that's you done then,' she said cheerfully. 'And you're fully equipped for the term, excellent!' I felt proud of Mummy for getting it right. Matron patted the bed beside her. 'This is where you'll sleep, all made up and ready.' She pointed out my sections of the wardrobe and drawers, and the basins with our towels and washbags hanging on hooks with our names on. I thought of Mummy hand-stitching nametapes on all my clothes and wished she was still here.

It was comforting to realise that a few other girls seemed as lost as I was. Upstairs a girl was sobbing on her bed in Shamrock, and Matron went to sit with her. Someone else became tearful at teatime and left the table. Later, after lights out, I heard sniffles and nose-blowing. Neither the staff nor girls made a big deal of it, and I came to realise it was normal in the first few days back. I didn't cry that first night, but it was good to know I wouldn't be judged or told off if I did.

The routine at Pippins was quickly familiar, and its regular flow, week in week out, came as a relief, as did our unsupervised play. The schedule at Caux had been subject to change, and term-times blended with holidays. Our carers had steered us through each day, and we were rarely left to our own devices. I enjoyed the predictable patterns of each day here, and the time allowed for 'running wild' in the gardens.

Pippins had about 60 pupils, with four form teachers during the school day, and Mip and the two matrons in charge of 24 boarders outside classroom hours. Mrs Young taught the youngest ones, and the older classes were taken by Miss Tonge with the severe black fringe, Miss Ray, known as 'Rocket' as she 'blew up' occasionally, and the gentle Mrs Swift. Sometimes Mip took classes, and teachers helped out at weekends. Not surprisingly, given her mysterious insistence on the name 'Mip', our Head had a relaxed approach to life which came as a shock after

Dot's intensity. Mip probably dressed up for parents, but we were most familiar with her flip-flopping around the school in fluffy bedroom mules, cigarette in hand, with her adoring terrier Gillie padding behind.

The informality extended to Mip's daily pre-breakfast ritual. In term-time Mip slept, not in her cottage in a neighbouring village, but in a small bedroom wedged between the Rose and Shamrock dormitories. Her room was one of three in the building furnished with carpets and curtains, the other two being Mip's drawing room/office, and the staff sitting room. Before breakfast each morning, apart from Sunday, Matron would open Mip's door, and once dressed we'd troop in to see the headmistress, a few at a time. She would be lying under her sheets and silky eiderdown, her head propped up on pillows, and she'd be sorting through the early morning post. Keeping her own mail to one side, Mip would spread our letters over her quilt so we could pick out any for us. We learnt to spot our own letters at speed, and for most of my time at Pippins my parents' distinctive yellow and green-edged *VIA AÉREA* envelopes stood out easily.

If we were lucky we'd coincide with the arrival of Mip's elegant breakfast tray, brought up to her room by Big Barbara or Mrs Long, the short cook. On the tray's lacy cloth sat a dainty teapot, cup and saucer, and a rack of crustless triangles of toast. We'd watch as Mip settled this feast on her knees, poured her first cup and spread her toast with real butter and a dab of marmalade. Without fail one of us, chosen at random, would then be handed a piece of that precious toast.

This seemingly modest offering was to us a marvellous delicacy because the pupils' food was stodgy and dull. After the high-quality meals at Caux it came as a surprise to me. In Switzerland I'd enjoyed food almost unheard of here: pasta, muesli, Gruyère, sourdough bread, and *always* real butter. By contrast, Pippins' meals relied on thick white sliced bread, often stale, spread with white oily 'marge' and flavourless jam identifiable only as red or orange. So Mip's crustless toast with butter and marmalade was worth loitering for, whether or not we had letters.

The regular sight of the head in her skimpy nightie exemplified the easygoing ethos of Pippins outside lesson time, and I soon stopped thinking how unimaginable the idea of invading Dot's bedroom at Caux would have been. However, in the classroom and dining room traditional ideas on child behaviour prevailed, and there the staff, including Mip, could be strict. At meals we had to finish everything on our plates. I could manage most food, even the standard lunch fare of liver and gravy, but the dreaded spotted dick pudding was my nemesis, and the one thing that kept me struggling at the table when most others had left to play outside. Under the cook's watchful eye I had to stay and swallow every last blob of the suety slime.

At four o'clock every afternoon we'd be called indoors for high tea, the last meal of the day. This was a simple hot course, often baked beans on toast, followed by the white bread and jam filler and taken with a mug of milk. In my first week I discovered that, as optional extras, fresh fruit and a pot of Marmite could be provided by parents to enhance the meal. I thought I'd missed out for the term, but thankfully Jane's mum, Aunt Elisabeth, concerned about our diet, kindly ordered fruit for me.

Perhaps it was also Aunt Elisabeth who kept me supplied with sweets, as we each had a hoard, locked in a cupboard until after Saturday and Sunday lunches. At that point we could choose four each. Fairness in counting out our sweet allowance was crucial to us, and convention had it that one Crunchie or Mars bar equalled four individual sweeties, a sherbert fountain was worth three, and a Swizzel double lolly was two. We trusted Matron or a teacher to be the arbiter and they would slice the chocolate bars under our close scrutiny.

On weekday mornings, Jane and the other day children arrived in their parents' cars and for the next seven hours boarders and non-boarders blended together in a mass of blue and white gingham. A handful of young pre-prep day boys stood out in their grey shorts and white shirts, spared more formal attire since they'd all be moving on to boys' prep schools soon. With pupil numbers doubled, and our weekend mufti replaced by uniform, the atmosphere on Monday mornings felt more businesslike as we filed into The Hut for morning assembly.

While the curriculum here was more varied than Caux's, it still wasn't stretching, and was probably old-fashioned even by 1960s' standards. The giant world map covering one classroom wall still had large swathes of red to signify 'British territory' despite many former colonies having become independent nations. History lessons covered 19th-century British explorers like Livingstone and Stanley 'discovering' Africa, and geography focused on the natural resources and culture of Commonwealth countries.

In the Easter holidays I'd looked through Patrick's comic books *How To Be Topp* and *Down With Skool,* about scruffy Nigel Molesworth trying to survive a prep school called St Custard's. But the books related little to life at Pippins. For a start, Molesworth lives exclusively among boys, and finds 'gurls uterly wet and weedstruck [sic]'. St Custard's is a world of tuck boxes, sport, caning and bullying prefects, none of which featured at Pippins. And Molesworth, like Patrick, learns different subjects from us. In fact none of Molesworth's most detested topics, namely Latin, maths, science and modern languages, were part of my new school curriculum.

Nonetheless, I enjoyed the subjects we did cover. In nature study we made books of pressed wild flowers, and in sewing we made functional items like embroidered aprons, padded jewellery boxes and woven baskets. For PE we did rounders in summer. In winter Rocket took us for military-style 'drill' on the tennis courts or 'country dancing' in The Hut, where we learnt Scottish and English reels, waltz and polka steps, and Strip the Willow. Jane and I both took the optional after-school dance classes of Miss de Vos, a statuesque former ballerina, and piano lessons with the kindly Mrs Wilson, my favourite teacher whom I fantasised might one day adopt me.

At 3.30pm each weekday the cars collecting the day children circled the drive and the school numbers shrank again. The boarders donned their outdoor overalls and spilled out into the garden to play – unless they had dance, piano or riding lessons before tea and homework. Our free time seemed to stretch expansively before us, yet nighttime came early at Pippins. From six o'clock Big Barbara started ringing the bell at 15-minute intervals, calling us in for bathtime in groups, starting with the youngest.

Baths were sociable events, with four girls washing at a time in the bathroom's two parallel tubs. Matron hovered between them, refreshing the water, scrubbing our backs, and directing us in and out of the water. Above the baths hung a Mabel Lucie Atwell picture of a chubby child in pyjamas and dressing gown with a verse we knew by heart:

> *Please remember – don't forget – never leave the*
> *bathroom wet –*
> *Nor leave the soap still in the water (that's a thing*
> *we never ought'er!)*
> *Nor leave the towels about the floor, nor leave the*
> *bath an hour or more*
> *When other folks are wanting one – please don't*
> *forget, it isn't done...*

It was effective advice, as the floor and mats stayed remarkably dry given that 24 girls had taken baths in under an hour. The method we learnt of drying each leg and foot before stepping out of the tub became, for some, a lifelong habit.

Amid the bedtime banter and prattle, wet hair was blown dry, nails were cut, teeth brushed, and bowel movements recorded by Matron, who carried Milk of

Magnesia in her pocket for anyone needing a dose. At Caux we'd never have dreamt of undressing or discussing toilet habits in front of others, but I adapted quickly to the casual nakedness and openness, and enjoyed the kerfuffle.

After the bedtime commotion we'd have our hour of reading. If Mip was putting us to bed she'd first walk between the dorms singing a simple hymn, often *Jesus loves me, this I know, for the Bible tells me so*, and our small, high-pitched voices would resound through the upstairs rooms as we sang along. Most of us knelt over our beds to say quick private prayers before slipping between the sheets to read. Prayers were optional but most of us said them out of habit. For me prayers were a comforting link to another world, and every night I'd pray, 'Dear Jesus, thank you for today, and please be with Mummy, Daddy, Patrick, Granny and Grandad and keep them safe. And all my friends everywhere. Amen.' It didn't occur to me to pray for anything more specific.

Instead of a hymn, Matron would usually leave us to read with the warning, 'I'll be up and on the warpath if I hear any noise!' But through the wide-open dormitory doors sounds only travelled the other way. It was her TV and her distant laughter with Barbara that destroyed the peace. A little whispering went on, but generally we loved that time with our books.

The relentless routine helped me acclimatise. An occasional twinge of homesickness caught me off guard when hearing that sad music, or feeling the silky Liberty fabric of the Sunday dress Mummy had made me. But I cheered myself with the thought of more holidays like we'd had at Easter. Boarders here went home at the end of each term, so I presumed I could join my parents somewhere. I started to relax into a life that seemed simpler and freer than my last school, unaware that my parents had other plans for themselves. The dream holidays weren't going to happen because they'd soon be going to the other side of the world, and this time they wouldn't be back for two years.

16

Not the Hills of Home

Britain 1961

'We're needed in Brazil,' Mummy told me during my first school holiday from Pippins. 'Do you remember those Brazilians who came to Caux? The ones in the film? Well, it's a really important time for their country and they need our support. We'll be back before long, and we'll write you loads of letters.'

I knew the film she meant. It was called *Men of Brazil* and it was about dockworkers in Rio de Janeiro who'd applied Caux ideas when the port was in crisis. They'd sorted out the fighting – real fighting with knives and guns – between rival unions, and they'd made life better for the dockers and their families. I hadn't followed the politics, nor understood how a mother and father got married at the end when they already had children. But I knew the actors in the film were playing themselves and had helped write their story, so it must have been true.

While it wasn't hard to imagine Mummy and Daddy with these dockers in Rio, the news was disappointing. I'd returned to London on the school train excited to see my parents again. Now I tried to be optimistic, hoping they wouldn't be away long. After all, they seemed very busy in England. They often had people for meals at the Croydon house where we were staying, and their meetings in London were only a short train ride away. Sometimes I went with them into town if Granny and Grandad were busy.

One meeting I attended with Mummy was in the drawing room of 45 Berkeley Square. It was memorable because I'd never seen men cry before, apart from in movies. Mummy had already told me a secret on the train to Victoria. 'I'm afraid we've heard something very sad,' she'd said. 'It'll be announced at the meeting, so I wanted to warn you. Uncle Frank died last night.' She looked at me anxiously, but I wasn't sad or surprised. I knew he was, reportedly, extraordinary and much loved. But to me he'd always looked old and unwell, and I barely knew him. I was more shaken by the gasps of disbelief and raw grief at the meeting when the news was announced. 'Oh my *God*!' one of my father's friends cried out dramatically, bending forward over his knees and burying his face in his hands. I'd never seen such emotion expressed at these gatherings. Yet afterwards nothing much seemed to change. The work went on. And Mummy and Daddy were still off to Brazil. If anything, Uncle Frank's death had made them more intent on going.

It was only very gradually, over the next few school

terms, that I began to realise the 'visit' to Brazil was growing longer and longer. My parents' letters never even hinted at a return date, or plans to be in Caux. They never ended with 'look forward to seeing you soon'. It became easier to try not to think about it too much.

Throughout their absence I returned to Granny and Grandad at Chichester Road at the start of most holidays. Mummy had told me they would be my 'guardians' and that was comforting. I loved my grandparents. They were kind and generous with their hugs. With Granny I baked rock buns and sewed, while Grandad had me polishing brass, winding his chiming clocks, and testing the 'army assault course' he'd built in the garden. I liked his outdoor challenges, but was becoming increasingly afraid of heights. 'Come on, my dear,' Grandad would say. 'I can remember you running along that plank quite happily when you were very little!' But sadly for him that physical confidence had gone, and now I preferred the swing seats he'd built for adults, or croquet on the lawn.

We also played board games and watched TV together. I loved seeing weekday programmes we missed at school, like *Blue Peter*, *Crackerjack* and *Animal Magic*. Grandad's favourite programme was *All Our Yesterdays*, which I'd sit through with him because I'd watch anything. But its news footage of the 1930s and '40s was grainy and the commentary hard to follow. *Tonight* with Cliff Michelmore was easier, but I preferred *Hancock's Half Hour*, and the *Dick Van Dyk Show*. Better still were the cop shows *Z Cars*, *No Hiding Place*, *Maigret* and *The Third Man*, and quiz shows like *Double Your Money* or *What's My Line?*

My TV viewing, though extensive, was firmly supervised. Granny and Grandad were old-school. I had to change from shorts into trousers or a skirt in the evenings. And although bedtime was later than at school, I could sense Grandad's watchfulness during adult programmes. Some were out of bounds, including David Frost's *That Was The Week That Was*, the comedy series *Steptoe and Sons,* and anything involving comedian Benny Hill. These were considered too disrespectful, too rude, or simply too 'cor blimey'. 'I don't think we want any of this!' Grandad would say firmly, lunging for the TV's OFF switch at any prolonged kissing, suggestive jokes or mockery of the church or armed forces.

Despite the homely comforts, I was aware of the gaps here. I missed my parents, and I missed my brother. Patrick appeared occasionally, but his main base was our aunt and uncle's house in Worcestershire, and I accepted that I was too young and girly to join the older boys there. When Patrick did come to Croydon the household felt more complete. It didn't matter that he teased me, and called me 'Podge'. He could do no wrong as he was my clever big brother, and I liked seeing what he was reading and hearing his stories about school or Whitbourne.

Before his visits Granny used to stock up on baked beans, Nesquik chocolate milk, fresh oranges and Marmite, as he was particular about food and these were his favourites. One holiday when I knew he was coming, I asked Granny to buy a drink called Creamola Foam, a sweet fizzy drink made by dissolving crystals in water. It had taken Pippins by storm when someone brought in a tin of it from home and shared it out one teatime. I couldn't wait to tell Patrick about this cool discovery.

Granny mixed two foaming glasses of Creamola, but to my dismay he took a sip, grimaced and almost threw up. 'That's terrible!' he spluttered. 'Disgusting stuff!' I could see he wasn't joking, and I was so acutely disappointed and embarrassed at my failure to impress him that I changed the subject abruptly, as if nothing had happened. I didn't know what to say. We were so unused to each other, and I'd put him on such a pedestal, that I couldn't see the funny side of it, tease him, or even assert my own opinion. Granny quietly removed our glasses, and I never drank Creamola Foam again.

Another event I couldn't handle was the death of the 'school rabbit' while he was in my care for the holidays. My own hamster had made his escape early in my first term, before we'd had time to bond, so I'd been pet-less when entrusted with this ageing brown rabbit called Faun. Unusually, Faun's care was shared, as he'd been left at Pippins by a former pupil. The fact that he was unfriendly and had a sharp nip on him didn't put me off. I was proud to be in charge.

At Chichester Road Faun's cage was kept on a lower lawn, where I fed him and let him out every day. One morning Mrs Clarke, an upstairs neighbour, knocked at the back door. Mrs Clarke grew vegetables at the bottom of the garden, and had enjoyed slipping Faun an occasional carrot. Granny spoke with her in hushed tones before coming to find me, looking serious. 'I'm so sorry, darling, but Faun's dead,' she announced. 'He's lying peacefully in his cage, and Mrs Clarke doesn't think he suffered, so we mustn't be too sad. He was an old boy, and he probably had a heart attack.'

I felt sick and speechless. I'd been entrusted with Faun and he'd died. The shame of it! What on earth would we tell the school? I couldn't get my head round it. Granny tried to hug me, but I backed away, withdrawing from all engagement in the matter. By blocking it out perhaps the horror would go away. 'Do you want to see him?' Granny asked. 'NO!' I exclaimed sharply, adding a quick, 'No thank you,' as I didn't mean to be rude. Behind me I heard Patrick say quietly, 'I don't blame you,' and I felt understood.

I never referred to it again, nor was it mentioned. Granny and Mrs Clark must have quietly disposed of Faun and his cage. Even back at school the whole incident somehow melted away, apart from a brief word from Mip. 'I'm sorry you had to deal with Faun's passing,' she said with kindness. I nodded grimly and she went on, 'Perhaps you can help me with Gillie,' referring to her Lakeland terrier. 'I know she really likes you!' This was unlikely, as Gillie generally ignored us girls, but I now made a point of patting her and holding her lead on weekend walks. I was relieved to be forgiven and appointed Mip's dog minder, even if it didn't amount to much. Nobody else mentioned Faun. He obviously wasn't as important as I'd thought.

Yet I still felt ashamed. Granny had quickly dropped the subject, but her sorrowful face the day Faun was found dead still haunted me. I'd seen her sitting in the kitchen writing to Mummy. She'd stopped for a moment to watch me, with a faraway look in her eyes. I'd smiled, and unusually she hadn't smiled back. I had a horrible sense that the event was being relayed all the way to Brazil, and was making everyone sad.

I would have been willing to spend all my holidays with my grandparents, but I never spent the whole time with them. Mummy didn't want to overburden her parents, and she liked me to have the company of children. Perhaps she also preferred me to be among her MRA friends, now that my grandparents had little involvement with the movement.

Whatever the reason, I was packed off to a variety of places. I was always pleased to visit the Pelham Burns family in Sussex again, and hang out with Amelia. Mary PB was elsewhere these days, and now it was Amelia's mother Pamela who'd ferry us to the cinema or a neighbour's swimming pool. One summer Amelia and I were dispatched together to the Isle of Wight, to a farm belonging to friends of our parents. It was a picturesque coastal spot next to mudflats that flooded at high tide, and we were given tasks that included getting up at 6.30 to feed the calves and move them to pasture. Another time I stayed with a girl called Mary at her aunts' house in Sandbanks, Dorset. We spent happy hours on the beach, playing with the aunts' tortoise, and devouring adventure stories from the Book-Lovers' Library at Boots the Chemist.

Most of these parentless holidays created reasonably happy memories. But one longer trip to Scotland left me feeling wretched. 'You'll have a great time, you're so lucky!' my parents had written to me beforehand. And at that point a month in the Highlands with a crowd of other children sounded like pure Enid Blyton fun.

For this adventure I was put in the care of Molly, whom I'd known briefly at Caux. On the train journey from London to Glasgow, Scotland started to feel a long way away and Molly was welcome company. I barely knew her, but she was a link to a life I knew, while the family we'd be staying with were strangers.

We spent one night with this family in Glasgow, and my initial impression as I headed wearily to bed was of a large, noisy household. The following morning we jammed into two large cars, with countless bags, hampers, coats, boots and pets. The loud exchanges between family members continued, with some singing and a few heated arguments. I was happy to be ignored. I wasn't sure who everyone was and it was easier to switch off and watch the hills and lochs from the car window as we sped past them.

A deep ache grew in my stomach as we travelled further and further from familiar people and places. The glorious scenery, which as an adult I'd find inspiring, made me profoundly sad. This, I realised, was *Scottish Soldier* territory. These were the very highland hills the soldier pined for when he was dying in a foreign land. But now I was the one who'd 'wandered far away' and longed for different hills. Whenever I heard the song, or even the sound of pipes playing a lament, the yearning tugged inside me. I couldn't have said what or where I longed for exactly, but I'd have to fight back tears. And yet, even as the song saddened me, I found some comfort in hearing it too, because it showed someone else knew this pain. Someone understood.

Since Molly was a Caux person, I'd assumed this family would be Caux people too. But I realised they probably weren't. This wasn't like an outing at Caux, where grown-ups made sure everyone was happy. Wedged in the back of the car I felt invisible. This felt like a funfair ride you wanted to get off but couldn't, so you just hung on tight. Molly was preoccupied helping the parents with practicalities, and not the ally I'd expected.

After several hours including toilet stops and a crossing on the Ballachulish ferry, we reached a remote farmhouse. I was given a room with three other children, one of them a tomboyish girl. We were roughly the same age, but had little in common. At first I tried to blend in. I was used to boarding school banter and a teasing brother. But I quickly realised I didn't fit. I withdrew, observing the others and taking myself off to read whenever possible. My books took me away to boarding school capers, Dalmatian dogs in London parks, budding ballerinas touring Europe, and camping holidays. They swept me off to places I'd rather be.

It wasn't all bad, of course. I enjoyed the pets and the chatty youngest daughter, who asked me funny questions and also lived in a world of her own. But the girl my age and I never gelled as companions. One night she staged an ambush with her older siblings when I went up to bed. Perhaps they intended it as an ice breaker, but instead of play-fighting back as I'd have done at school, I stifled my surprise, ignored their flying pillows, and fled to my bunk. I chose not to be a good sport. Curled up fully-clothed under my blankets, I was a silent martyr while they poked and battered me to get a response. I knew I was spoiling their fun and scotching any chance of making friends, but I'd given up. All I wanted was to get back to school.

Initially the Scottish children's mother had been kind to me, but gradually I sensed her change. On a picnic I mentioned the midges, and she snapped at me, 'You do nothing but moan!' I was shocked. I hadn't realised what a pain I was being, and was embarrassed to be told off in front of Molly for not being cheerful, as we had to be at Caux. Unable to handle the awkwardness, I retreated further into my shell, feeling a terrible failure. I was counting the days until I could leave, and sadly I knew the others were too.

My return to Pippins for the autumn term came as a huge relief. Granny and Grandad's home was also safe, but sometimes it made me more conscious of my missing family and that made me lonely. On the school train to Axminster I clearly wasn't the only one pleased to be back among friends. Even those with settled homes were learning to cope with separation from loved ones, and having this in common drew us closer.

Without personal phones, broadband and instant messaging, our detachment from home was total. Expensive, poor-quality international calls were for dire emergencies only. So term-time contact with our parents was limited to a weekly exchange of letters, and occasional visits from parents who lived close enough. Even if we wanted to tell our family something immediately, we simply couldn't, so we stopped expecting to.

From my first moments at Pippins, during my tour of the gardens, I'd realised that some of the other 'Pips' lived abroad and, like me, were used to moving around. The girls appeared very English, but seemed to have come here from all over the world. I'd listened with interest on that first day to snatches of conversation. 'I had a rather strict Universal Aunt on the flight,' one girl had said while we were stroking guinea pigs in the pets' corner. 'But she did have a good supply of sweets!' 'Yah, they're usually pretty good,' another girl responded. 'We didn't have one this time, as Daddy's friend was going to London on the same plane – so I had to tag along with him. He was very dull – and had no sweets at all – hopeless really!'

'What IS a Universal Aunt?' I'd asked cautiously, but nobody sniggered at my ignorance. 'They're pretend aunts who go on planes with children if your parents can't go,' someone said. 'They get paid for it. My parents are in Tanganyika and they use them quite a bit.' Others had stories about their own journeys here. One had come from Borneo, and two sisters lived in Malaya. A tall girl called Daphne had flown in from Aden. I found this deeply reassuring. The girls knew about life in distant places. Scattered families were normal. So maybe it wouldn't be a big deal to admit I'd been at school in Switzerland and didn't have a home address.

I didn't yet know that many boarding schools like Pippins existed because the civil servants, administrators and military running the British Empire had wanted their children educated back here in the home country. But I knew my own grandfathers had both served in the army in India, and I soon found out that one girl's father worked in the wildlife parks of East Africa, another dad managed a Malaysian rubber plantation, and several others were with the Colonial Office or armed services. It sometimes felt like that big world map hanging over us in the classroom was the backdrop not just to our lessons but also to our lives.

If my enjoyment of Pippins came partly from empathy with the other girls, it was enhanced by at last becoming a successful pet owner. After the unfortunate Faun débacle, Jane and Aunt Elisabeth presented me with a beautiful young rabbit, as cuddly, calm and characterful as Faun had been hostile, wild and dull. I adored him. Snowy white with pink eyes, he had distinctive dark brown ears with a matching nose. I called him Smudge, and from the way he nestled in on my chest, or lolloped across the grass when I called him, I was certain the adoration was mutual.

The pets' enclosure was a favourite place to hang out, for day children and boarders alike. Even if you were alone, or didn't have your own furry animal, you could watch them, and feed them grass and dandelion leaves through their chicken wire. But having my very own bunny to care for was even better. We all took pet care seriously and needed little adult intervention. We fed the animals, cleaned their cages and gave them daily runs, taking our time. It was common knowledge gleaned from our peers that we shouldn't let the rabbits out on the grass together, for fear of fights or mating, and we were proud of maintaining a peaceful and tidy pets' corner.

Reading also eased me into boarding school life and we had plenty of time for it. There were bookshelves on the upstairs landing, and I also borrowed from Jane and swapped with other girls. We lapped up animal books, from *101 Dalmatians* to the true wildlife tales of Gerald Durrell and Joy Adamson. But probably the most-thumbed pages were the adventure stories by Noel Streatfield and Enid Blyton. These generally centred on English boarding-school children we could identify with, and there seemed to be an almost endless supply of them. The prolific Enid Blyton wrote lengthy series, my favourite being the Adventure series: *The Island of Adventure, The Castle of Adventure, The Valley..., The Sea..., The Mountain..., The Ship..., The Circus...* and, finally, *The River of Adventure*. Then there were the Famous Five books, 21 in all, and if these were exhausted there were dozens of others written by Noel Streatfield, including *Ballet Shoes* and *Curtain Up*.

Caught up in these books, I couldn't feel alone or bored. Many of their characters had unusual domestic arrangements, so it was easy to imagine them being personal friends. In *Ballet Shoes* three orphaned sisters are adopted by an elderly palaeontology professor during his world travels. He sends them home to be raised by his orphaned great-niece and her childhood nanny. Meanwhile in Blyton's Adventure series, Jack and his sister Lucie-Ann are orphans, while Phillip and his sister Dinah have a widowed mother. Given that my real friend Jane had a widowed mother, and my own parents were travelling the world, it was heartening to read about children thriving and leading lives of adventure despite their circumstances.

The Streatfield books had the added glamour of being about children attending ballet and stage schools, and they fuelled our interest in drama and dance. Like most of my classmates I loved our dance classes and school plays, and in my first term I was thrilled to be a dancing and singing ferret in *The Wind in the Willows*.

Another attraction of the Blyton adventures was the way children are left to their own devices in the holidays. The parents of the Famous Five happily let their youngsters go off unsupervised, hiking, camping and solving mysteries, while they themselves are working or taking holidays elsewhere. It didn't seem to matter that the oldest is only 12 and the youngest ten years old; it was the Five who would always take the lead in tracking down spies, smugglers and robbers, scenarios that we would re-enact in the Pippins gardens, our very own adult-free zone.

Enid Blyton also wrote whole series of books set in girls' schools, including *Mallory Towers*, *The Naughtiest Girl in the School* and the tales of *The Twins at St Clare's*. They feature schoolgirl clashes, new girls guarding secrets, and crises involving bullies or unfair staff. These may have been less easy to identify with, but the stories were also about midnight feasts, jolly pranks and loyal friendships, and once again, grown-ups played a secondary role. Having lived for years in a largely adult environment, the child-centred culture of these books, and of Pippins, felt liberating, even if our own adventures were tame by comparison.

One conscious attempt to introduce some Blyton-style fun at Pippins was sadly unsuccessful. 'We need to have a midnight feast!' I said to Jane one day. 'Could you bring us in some food?' It was a cheeky request, given that Jane was a day girl and couldn't participate, but she was happy to help. 'Would sandwiches be OK?' she offered. 'Some Marmite, some honey? With Twiglets?' And sure enough, she was back at school next day with some delicious sandwiches, carefully cut and wrapped. Very excited, we smuggled the goods upstairs and hid them in my clothes drawer.

The whole dorm eagerly anticipated the feast, but over successive nights not one of us managed to wake up around midnight. Without an alarm clock, we all slept soundly through until morning. So to our great disappointment the feast never happened. Weeks later I found the sandwiches in my drawer, the bread furry with mould. Matron must have spotted the brown paper package, but nothing had been said.

Like books, music also brought us escape, comfort and fun. Cold weather and drizzle were no deterrent to playing in the garden. But heavy rain or snow would bring us into the Common Room, and there we'd read, play games, or teach each other pop songs we'd picked up. I learnt all the words of *Tell Laura I Love Her*, *Que Sera Sera*, and *Would You Like To Swing on a Star?* from other girls. It never occurred to me to teach them the songs I knew. *The Polar Bear Song*, and *Normal Living* by the Colwell Brothers, would need explaining.

I have happy memories of dancing and singing to our old wind-up gramophone. Even at the start of the 1960s this was an old-fashioned device, but it was fun turning its handle and lowering the needle onto its 78 rpm records. These were mostly classical music or big band dance, with a few songs like *Lay Down Your Arms and Surrender to Mine*, and we made the most of them, careering around the room until we were breathless, and singing along with anything that had words. A favourite song was *This Ole House*, the fifties hit by Rosemary Clooney, and we'd try to copy the deep bass backing voices:

> *Ain't a-gonna need this house no longer*
> *Ain't a-gonna need this house no more...*

As we tried to swing and jive to these records, it was a classical piano piece that inspired us to leap about the most ecstatically. Liszt's *Hungarian Rhapsody No. Two* had us polka-ing dramatically to its crashing chords and increasingly fast tempo. *Dee DUM-dee-DAH! Dee DUM-dee-DAH! Dee DUM-dee-DAH! Dee DUM-dee-DAH!* If *A Scottish Soldier* and the *Coronation Street* theme evoked sorrow and longing, this was happy music in which we lost ourselves, trance-like and exhilarated. Enjoying dance and music for the sheer enjoyment of it was new for me. So was turning up the music to its highest volume while we shrieked and bumped into furniture. I hadn't let off steam like this before, and as the Liszt grew louder and faster I imagined I was taking flight, breaking free from life's burdens and disappointments.

17
Brazil 1961–63

Chérie and Bill were dazzled by Brazil. This vast country throbbed with energy and excitement. They loved the hectic, noisy streets of Rio, São Paulo and Recife, where mundane human dramas unfolded all around them, and their letters home were full of anecdotes. Bill described the exaggerated shoulder shrugs and eye rolls of the taxi drivers during their frequent squabbles with pedestrians and other cars. He also enjoyed the deafening roar that arose suddenly across an entire city whenever the national or local football team scored. Bill's accounts were illustrated with expressive stick figure cartoons sketched in ink on the thin sheets of his airmail writing paper.

Most stimulating of all for them was the way many Brazilians were taking to the ideas of MRA. Amid the country's startling excesses of wealth and poverty, intensified by political extremism and institutional corruption, they found individuals, from army generals to shanty dwellers, working together to effect community change. MRA teams were active in some of the docks and *favelas*, and practical models of a collaborative new society were emerging in places generally characterised by conflict. To see the practical advance of their work on this scale inspired them, and encouraged their wholehearted engagement. Chérie soon picked up fluent Portuguese, while Bill learnt enough phrases to get by with the wide range of people they encountered.

The couple had arrived in Brazil in the wake of one of MRA's biggest campaign tours, which had now moved on to other Latin American countries. The tour centred on the play called *The Tiger*, written by Japanese students who'd already performed their show in Europe and North America. Frank Buchman had urged the students to accept invitations to South America, and they'd arrived there as one part of a 150-strong mission from 28 countries. 'The show was almost a pageant', writes Ronald Mann, who with his wife Mary had joined the tour from Europe. 'And it was drawing crowds of 10,000 or more, so it had to move out of the theatres into the football stadiums'. In the north-western city of Manaus 90,000 turned out one evening to see it, and the tour extended even to remote parts of the country with the help of Brazilian air force planes.

The packed arenas can be seen online in an MRA documentary film of the tour called *A Tidal Wave of Hope*. Its opening newsreel-style commentary excitedly proclaims, 'The masses of South America have responded to the ideology of Moral Re-Armament, which is outbidding the materialism of Left and Right, and turning the tide for freedom in the entire hemisphere.' It quotes the

Uruguay daily paper *El Pais*, which called the campaign 'the greatest ideological offensive this continent has ever known'.

The novelty of a live, large-scale international spectacle drew the crowds. But the high level of interest, and the military terms used in the media coverage, can also be attributed to the Cold War, which was now at its height. In Europe the Berlin Wall was under construction, a physical marker of the world's ideological divide, and South Americans were also aware of being at the heart of this battle of ideas. *A Tidal Wave of Hope* notes that 'the Moral Re-Armament ideological offensive opened in Latin America on May 1st 1961, the very day Kruschev predicted he would take over the continent in the next two years, and Castro declared that Cuba would be the first soviet socialist republic of South America'. The Russian and Cuban challenge provoked the far-right to resist, and the MRA team determined to demonstrate a 'third way' beyond political extremism.

When he'd visited Latin America in 1931 during the Depression, Frank Buchman had been shocked by the opulence and exploitative practices of the wealthy classes. He'd seen this as 'preparing the soil for Communism, the most organised and effective leadership abroad today'. In the intervening years the fight against fascism had taken precedence, but Buchman had never stopped wanting to offer ideas that would pre-empt the spread of totalitarianism of any sort.

Buchman never lived to see the outcome of *The Tiger* campaign that he'd helped instigate. On 7th August 1961, while the mission was in progress and Chérie and Bill were still in London, Buchman had died in Germany. While not unexpected, his death still came as a shock to his team worldwide. The *Tidal Wave* film shows a packed football stadium standing silent in his memory before a performance of *The Tiger*, before the tour continued as planned. Across the world full-timers continued to support campaigns wherever they were felt to be needed, and Bill and Chérie joined those heading for South America. They'd reached Brazil in the autumn of 1961, ready to prepare for an MRA assembly in Petropolis in December. The conference would be the final stop of the seven-month Latin American *Tiger* tour.

'Life's full of surprises here', Bill wrote to Judi. 'It's not unknown for overworked or striking postmen to fling their mailbag over a fence and go home early!' Beside his scrawly writing he'd drawn a jokey sketch of a postman fast asleep, having tossed away his letters. While most of Bill and Chérie's regular letters from Brazil seemed to get through, few now survive, and there is no official record of the couple's time in South America. But it's possible to form a picture of their life there from photos and from other people's accounts. Of particular interest is a memoir written by their colleague Ronald Mann, who, having travelled with *The Tiger* in several South American countries, then returned to Brazil and worked alongside Bill and Chérie.

Like these two couples, many of the full-timers in Brazil at this time came from Britain and other parts of Europe. Most had arrived with little knowledge of the country or its culture, but were eager to learn. At the heart of the MRA work were local Brazilian teams already applying the ideas in situations around them. These included the Rio dockworkers whose experiences had been portrayed in the film *Men of Brazil* in 1959. This had been shot in and around the port of Rio, and it opens with the words: 'A battle of ideas is raging for control of the ports of the world. In Rio de Janeiro in 1953 two unions, one official and the other unofficial, fought for leadership of the port'. The film goes on to reveal how a change of heart among workers of both unions reopened a port at standstill, and transformed working relationships. The events had intrigued and brought on board a number of industrial, political and military leaders.

Similar transformations were starting to take place in the port of Recife, several city *favela* shanty towns, and various rural communities. The role of the incoming full-timers was to support the local teams, most of whom were in full-time occupations and couldn't be constantly campaigning 'on the road'. Bill and Chérie and their colleagues saw themselves as serving them, not directing or leading. They believed they were called to support a country in need. They were also acutely aware of Europe's historic power struggles in the region, and the devastating legacy of the slave trade and colonialism. The clock couldn't be put back, but the repercussions were still obvious in Brazil's divided society. They hoped their service could in some way help make amends.

Ronald Mann sums up their work in Brazil as 'a combination of reaching the country as a whole, meeting the leadership, and working alongside the dockers and *favela* dwellers. We would go to these *favelas*, slum dwellings built on the hills outside Rio where three million people lived, and at the invitation of the *favela* leaders set up a massive screen on some level ground to project the film *Men of Brazil'*. The shanty homes were largely populated by people flocking to the city for work. In the absence of affordable homes, they'd been forced to make their own shelters with whatever materials they could get hold of. There were few amenities, open sewage channels ran between the shacks, and when it rained the land was prone to flooding and disastrous landslides.

The European full-timers marvelled at the inventive home-making that went on inside these small, crowded hovels. 'People are so warm and welcoming despite their hardships', Chérie wrote in her letters home. 'And you wouldn't believe how many families have large televisions despite the cramped space! Their wages won't cover the cost of a flat or house, but they use what they have to create a few home comforts'.

One of Chérie's friends was Elsa Vogel, a younger French woman who initially went to Brazil for two years, married an MRA team colleague and ended up staying in Latin America for much of the next forty years. Elsa has written that 'walking through those *favelas* was like finding a little piece of heaven on earth'. She wasn't referring to the physical conditions or the poverty, of course, but the powerful community spirit of people there, with whom she formed lasting friendships.

The Rio port workers helped inspire some *favelados*

to make improvements to their lives. In one instance a group of shanty-dwellers went to see the state governor with a vision of how they themselves could address the housing problem. They proposed that, with state funding and materials, they could manage and carry out the building work themselves. The proposal was accepted and after a couple of years, Elsa writes, 'nearly half a million *favela* people were rehoused in decent houses or flats in the suburbs of Rio'. At the opening of one housing project Elsa recalls a community leader explaining that their achievement meant more than finally having a decent place of their own. The project had given them back their dignity.

After *The Tiger* campaign, the Brazilian team decided to make use of another new MRA resource, the film version of *The Crowning Experience* musical. A goal was set to reach a million people a week with the film, through live audiences and media coverage. To this end eight copies of the film were ordered from America, all expertly dubbed into Portuguese, and the star of the movie, the singer Muriel Smith, agreed to tour Brazil to publicise the film and reinforce its message. Sure enough, Smith's charm and her exceptional voice, combined with the film's topical theme of racial justice, attracted huge audiences.

Shortly before the tour was due to start, Ronald was staying at the home of a Colonel Pessoa. The full-timers often stayed with local supporters as they travelled the country. This particular host was an air force officer, who was frequently seconded to government to help manage special projects. The Colonel arranged for Muriel Smith and the film reels to be transported free of charge from America to Brazil on the national airline VARIG. He also made it his business to ensure there was an invitation committee of prominent national figures to welcome Miss Smith to his country.

Brazil was a federal democratic republic at this time, but the military, who later ran the country by dictatorship after a 1964 coup, were permanently in the wings. 'I had gradually understood', Ronald writes, 'that the military in Brazil regarded themselves as the country's guardians, ready to step into the political arena when things became too desperate. As they were regarded as being both patriotic and relatively free from corruption, they were also often called in by business leaders to handle diverse tasks – even to the running of steel plants'. Another military man involved in MRA at this time was General Hugo Bethlem, who had facilitated the invitation of *The Tiger* mission to Brazil. He was later to travel extensively with MRA, and his children attended Caux School to make this possible.

Bill and Chérie wrote home about their adventures with Muriel Smith in Brazil, and sent a photo showing Bill stepping out of a small six-seater plane with the singer in a rural area of the country. According to Ronald they made 'a very extensive tour of the country, with interviews and recitals on TV, and free commercials about *The Crowning Experience* several times a day'. Billboard spaces were donated in big cities, enabling them to display 20,000 film posters across Rio de Janeiro, and 30,000 in São Paulo.

One highlight of the tour for Ronald was a big dinner reception held to mark the film's opening in Rio.

It was laid on by the legendary self-made media mogul Fransisco de Assis Chateaubriand, known as Chatô for short, and nicknamed 'the Brazilian Citizen Cane'. Bill often mentioned him in his letters. Known for his political deals, presidential kingmaking, womanising and gangster associates, Chateaubriand seems an unlikely MRA recruit. But MRA workers never gave up on the idea that people can change. And in the meantime, Chatô gave the MRA work in Brazil his public support.

In 1960 a serious stroke left the energetic press tycoon confined to a wheelchair and communicating only through a specially adapted typewriter. Unable to attend the *Crowning Experience* dinner himself, he instructed one of his regional newspaper editors to host it and ensure that an array of significant local figures came along.

The event opened, according to Ronald, in an atmosphere charged with cynicism. The hosting editor introduced Muriel Smith, seated beside him, in a markedly sneering tone, and Ronald, who was tucked away at a side table, felt alarmed: 'I wondered what on earth Muriel would do and prayed hard for her'. As a seasoned stage star well before she joined forces with MRA, she was used to being treated as such. But as often happened, apparently, Miss Smith rose to the occasion. 'She was a great perfectionist', Ronald writes, 'and would normally never sing without being accompanied by a top-level pianist. But in that atmosphere she just stood up and sang without any accompaniment, in that incredibly beautiful voice of hers, an old spiritual *Were You There?* She then simply and naturally told of her life, and the change that had come to it. It cut through the cynicism like a searchlight on a dark night. At the end the editor apologised to Muriel for the way in which he had introduced the evening'.

Wherever she went in Brazil, the singer had the same extraordinary knack for both enchanting and challenging people. The shady practices of one state governor were so well-known that he'd been elected on the slogan *I may steal, but I get things done!* After a private viewing of *The Crowning Experience* for this Governor and his associates at his palace, Miss Smith came straight out with the question to them, 'How are you going to cure corruption in the state?' The question gave rise to an unexpectedly lengthy and profound discussion.

Simultaneous campaigns were underway in various parts of Central and South America, but Chérie and Bill stayed in Brazil, apart from one visit by Bill to Argentina. The tour with Muriel Smith was followed by another by a group of radical Peruvian students who'd been inspired by meeting the young Japanese in *The Tiger*. The Peruvians had come to agree that changing their political regime alone wouldn't bring lasting change. The idea of tackling corruption by starting with themselves seemed worth a try. Based on their experiences, the Peruvians wrote *El Condor*, a play about rival factions in their university, set against the wider political scene in Peru.

First shown at the Petropolis conference in December 1961, *El Condor* took to the road to promote MRA's ideas around Brazil. Local students and trade unionists took leave from their work to join them, while other fellow travellers included a São Paulo industrialist and some army generals, demonstrating that people could work together across the usual socio-economic divides of the country. One focus of the tour was the north-east of Brazil, where farm workers and students were striking and calling for revolution. Another was the port of Recife, known for its corruption and inept management. Later the tour extended to Europe and North America.

For a few weeks during the *El Condor* tour of Brazil, Bill and Chérie looked after the family of one of the travelling generals so that his wife could join him on the journey. They moved into the couple's house, and while live-in staff managed most household tasks, Chérie focused her attention on the four or five delightful children who called her their 'little English *mamãe*'.

Living with the Brazilian family made Chérie think all the more about her children in England. The distance between them felt enormous, and phone links were impossibly costly. At one point Chérie tried to encourage a flow of letters between her Brazilian charges and her own children, and the young Brazilians eagerly took up the idea. Chérie carefully translated their Portuguese messages, line by line, above their writing on each sheet of paper. But the notes didn't seem to draw much response from the English side of the exchange, and the pen-pal project was soon abandoned.

In the latter half of 1962 the pull towards Europe felt ever stronger for Chérie. But the successful tours had generated new opportunities for MRA all over Latin America, and the momentum kept the team pressing on relentlessly. Chérie found it difficult to share her family concerns with her colleagues, or even with Bill. They felt needed here, and didn't want to let their Brazilian friends down.

That October Chérie's dilemma became worse, when the Cold War suddenly moved beyond mere rivalry between nations towards the possibility of global catastrophe. The Cuban Missile Crisis involved a tense 13-day military stand-off between Russia and America when Russia decided to install nuclear weapons in Cuba. For two tense weeks the world stood on the brink of a possible nuclear war. All eyes were on Central America. In fact the fear of physical conflict subsided, and a settlement was reached between the two superpowers. But over that fortnight the prospect of an apocalyptic World War III felt real. The American Defence Secretary Robert Macnamara admitted later, 'I thought I might never see another Saturday night', and the Soviet Army Chief of Operations revealed that 'nuclear catastrophe was hanging by a thread… we weren't counting days or hours, but minutes'. The image of President Kennedy poised to fight off missile shipments as they crossed the Atlantic from Russia to Cuba had terrified people across all ideological divides.

Chérie felt increasingly torn. On the one hand helping prevent a third world war was exactly what the MRA team had signed up for. On the other, Chérie felt estranged from her children at a time of great uncertainty, when they could be vulnerable. The prospect of war brought back memories of her own family separations during the Second World War, when her younger brother had been with her in England, her parents in the Middle

East and her older brother in Asia. They'd received very little information about each other, and eventually, after six long years, they'd been reunited. But nuclear warfare was an even more horrifying prospect than conventional conflict. Being in a different hemisphere from her children was harrowing for Chérie during those fraught, critical weeks.

Yet even once the international crisis eased, Chérie was reluctant to raise the topic of her return to England. Looking around at team meetings in São Paulo, Recife or Rio, Chérie saw other European parents in the same position as her own. She knew that while she hadn't seen her children for over a year, others had been away from their youngsters for even longer. She told herself it was selfish to even mention the possibility of leaving. It would also seem she was putting her family and her happiness before this continent's vast problems. Encouraged by Bill, Chérie always returned to their core belief: God knows best, and following the Right Path means good outcomes for all concerned, including the loved ones back home.

It seems that some MRA parents comforted themselves with the belief that the heartbreak of family separation was only experienced by themselves, the parents, not by the children. It's unlikely Chérie entirely bought into this theory, since she hadn't enjoyed boarding school herself. But it's clear she did find solace in the idea that her children were in better schools than her own, in beautiful environments, and they were also in friendly, loving hands during the holidays. So to some extent she went along with one MRA father's view that, if children were well-occupied and with good companions, they barely noticed their parents' absence. It was the parents who felt the pain.

However, in time some of these parents came to regret their long absences. One was Ronald Mann, who, in his account of his 18 months in Brazil, refers to his return to Europe to rejoin his wife Mary and son John. Mary had been with Ronald in Brazil for the first nine months, while four-year-old John had been looked after by friends at her parents' home. She had then returned to Europe to start John at Caux School, and stayed on with him in Switzerland until her husband came back. 'It was only later,' Ronald writes, 'that I realised that I had got so engrossed in the fascinating campaign in Brazil and that this was too long a time to leave a boy between the ages of four and six. I didn't realise how much a boy needed his father at this point'.

In the end it was unexpected factors arising in Britain that made Chérie and Bill decide to make return plans. Firstly, the news reached them that Chérie's father Roy had suffered a heart attack and was recovering in hospital. 'We need to take life more slowly now', her mother Dulcie had written, 'and this means moving out, and into our own, smaller place'. They could no longer carry the responsibility of managing the Croydon property and providing regular holiday care for the grandchildren.

At the same time, it appeared that Judi may be having problems at school. Chérie had been dismayed to receive a letter from the headmistress of Pippins, apparently urging her to return to England. 'I am concerned about your daughter,' the head had written. 'We've generally found her hardworking and co-operative, but her behaviour has become unsettled. She's young for her year, but I think starting her at senior school next autumn will be good for her, and you will need to make a choice of school soon. Above all, and forgive my candour, I believe Judi would benefit hugely from seeing more of her parents and having an anchored home life'.

Bill hadn't been too worried by the letter. To him it sounded vague, and he considered it part of a headteacher's job to write such things. After all, Judi's own letters were full of cheerful school news. 'Unsettled' probably just meant 'spirited'. There must have been some misunderstanding, and they shouldn't leap to conclusions. But Chérie was troubled and mystified. She and Bill had followed their guidance faithfully, and she'd believed their children were being well cared for. Judi had always been a happy, easy child. What could possibly have gone wrong?

If the letter was a shock and a rebuke to Chérie, it also came as something of a relief, if she was honest. Because it was the sign she needed, the clincher to force them into a decision. She'd dithered, but now, in December 1962, she was certain that she must get back to England as soon as possible. Bill agreed, but he would stay on longer and join her sometime the following year.

18

The Jolliest School of All

Devon 1962

I was starting to enjoy the cosy isolation of Pippins. We were tucked away in our own private zone for young girls who, like me, had other lives but didn't think about them much. Here it was unremarkable that my parents were far away in Brazil, and nobody minded what they did. This was a comfort, as I was sure no one here would understand about Caux and 'normal living'. The very words 'MRA' or 'moral re-armament' seemed to make people look awkward, so they made me awkward too.

Caux School hadn't particularly helped with this, as MRA grown-ups would never describe what they did in one simple way. 'We're changing the world, starting with ourselves', they might say. Or, 'we're building the peace', or 'MRA's a way of life'. These statements invited more questions, and before long they'd be onto 'living by absolute standards' and 'listening to your inner voice'. It seemed there was no easy answer. The polar bear song at Caux said MRA was *a very simple secret*. Secret maybe, I thought, for those who hadn't heard of it or didn't understand. But not so very simple to explain.

Pleased as I was to receive my parents' regular letters, I didn't form much idea of what they were doing in Brazil. Not in a way I could pass on. They'd refer to their friends and events, but often they focused on their experiences of the country itself and the things I'd enjoy if I were there. Sometimes their comments made them seem even more distant. 'You can reach the top of the Sugar Loaf Mountain in a cable car! You'll love doing that one day!' one letter enthused, enclosing a postcard of the sheer rock. I wondered if they'd forgotten my terror of heights, or perhaps they'd never known about it in the first place.

The closest I came to imagining their daily life was when Mummy wrote about moving in with a family to look after the children while their parents travelled. A picture formed in my mind of my mother making the children eggs for breakfast, helping with homework and reading them stories, but I tried to push these thoughts away. It was kind of those Brazilians kids to write to me a couple of times. Mummy had translated their notes and enclosed them with her own letters. But when they told me how much they loved 'our little English mama' I didn't like it at all. She was MY English mama, surely? I didn't want to think about it.

The only people who asked me about Brazil were my schoolfriends' parents on days out. I quickly learnt to say 'I don't know' if they wanted to know Mummy and Daddy's occupation. The other girls probably knew little about their parents' activities either, but at least words like 'doctor', 'army' or 'bank manager' were quickly recognised and stopped further queries. It seemed that 'I don't know' served the same purpose.

The home lives of day girls – and boarders living locally – were a little more exposed, as sometimes they invited a friend home at weekends. I'd always enjoyed visits to Flint Cottage with Jane, and gradually I went to other homes too, like Roma's, where her mum kept racehorses and big poodles, and Tessa's, whose dad ran a doctor's surgery. In my second year at Pippins a new girl called Liz arrived who became a best friend, and I spent one half-term with her family in Cornwall.

Being together at all hours, it was hardly surprising that boarders became close. Two or three years of sharing dorms, baths, toilets, classrooms and playtime, week in week out, meant zero privacy, and chumminess was the only way to survive. Life was even more communal and hemmed in than at Caux, where we'd only shared a room with one other, and had frequently interacted with the wider adult community around us.

One Sunday my grandparents took me out to the beach at Budleigh Salterton. Granny was greatly taken with the way my fellow Pips welcomed me back at the end of the day. 'What utterly delightful girls!' she'd often remark, long after her visit. 'They just flocked around you when we walked in, asking about your day out. So kind and caring! They weren't going to let you feel any back-to-school blues!'

Even when I started occasionally contradicting Granny on principle, I couldn't disagree with her on this. We looked out for each other without even realising it, instinctively regarding other girls on days out as chicks missing from the nest. And Granny had spotted this.

In fact, outings didn't always make for the best weekends. The return could be upsetting, reminding us of family just when we were getting used to being apart. Mummy had once come to see me before she went away to Brazil. I'd loved taking a bus with her to the beach at Lyme Regis, just the two of us. But then, at the thought of going back, a weight crushed me inside, almost like a tummy ache. That parting had been painful. I'd waved her off from my dormitory window, oblivious of missing tea, sobbing as she walked away. It was worse than the first time she'd left me there.

The other downside to 'going out' meant you missed the weekend fun. On Saturdays we wore our own informal clothes. We weren't into fashion, we just liked the comfort of trousers and clothes you could get dirty. On Saturday mornings we had tasks: letter-writing and a little prep, but after that there was plenty of free time. After lunch, with our weekend sweets, there'd be an expedition, often involving a picnic tea. A favourite summer destination was the beach at Lyme Regis, but there were others. 'The Log' was a riverbank where a large pipe crossed the water: perfect for sliding over. We'd also 'go up Sector', a long lane heading out of Axminster into the countryside, or up to 'the Beacon', probably at Shute Hill, one of Devon's 89 historic sites where bonfires were lit to warn the county of sea invaders.

On the longer outings we never took a bus. Instead, Mip would drive us part of the way in her Morris Traveller estate car. Since we couldn't all fit in at once she'd take us in staggered shifts, cramming seven or eight girls at a time into the Morris. In the early sixties, car seatbelts weren't even standard, let alone compulsory, and our favourite place in the car was in the rear, where up to three of us could squash in behind the double doors, looking out at the amused drivers behind. Once we were seated, Mip would 'leap-frog' us along the route, setting down one carload to start walking while she returned for another. The walkers would proceed along the road, unsupervised and with no rendezvous point – nor phone contact in those days – until Mip's car reappeared. It was an eccentric form of school transport even then, but we loved it and no one came to harm.

On bad-weather Saturdays we might have indoor entertainment. One day we roller skated in the Hut, and Miss Ray showed old films. Another time we were taken to see Miss Ray and Miss Tonge performing in their village pantomime at Kilmington. It was a rare pleasure seeing our teachers let their hair down in their raucous roles, and Miss Ray had taught us the singalong songs by heart so that we could join in loudly with *Oh Mr Porter, what shall I do? I wanted to go to Birmingham, and they've taken me on to Crewe!* And *When you come to the end of a lollipop… PLOP goes your heart!*

Occasionally some of us spent a Saturday at Shute, a senior girls' school near Axminster where Mip had once taught, and where most of us were expected to go after

Pippins. Shute School was located in a four-storey 18th-century house, surrounded by spacious parkland where girls could keep their own ponies. In one wing was a small theatre, complete with footlights and tip-up seats, where we attended school productions of Gilbert and Sullivan. The scaled-up size of Shute was daunting, and the seniors appeared to be young adults already, chatting away about strange things like 'pashes', brassières and suspender belts. Eventually I learnt that a 'pash' on an older girl meant she was special to you. You did small acts of kindness for her, like laying out her dressing gown at bedtime or bringing her sweets. I presumed it was like being a fag at Patrick's school, where prefects made younger boys do chores for them. The visits to Shute were interesting, but we were always happy to return to our own small school where we were the big kids.

Saturday nights were the best part of the Pippins week, because we were invariably allowed into Mip's comfy sitting room in our pyjamas to binge-watch television. Mip would wander in and out, or settle in an armchair smoking, while we sat on her carpet transfixed by the black-and-white screen. We'd watch American cowboy adventures on *Bonanza* or *Rawhide*, followed by *Juke Box Jury* when celebrities judged which new pop records would be a Hit or a Miss in the charts. In 1961, when I first watched the programme, the Beatles and Rolling Stones had yet to take the world by storm, yet *Juke Box Jury* still seemed excitingly modern, and we'd wiggle around on the carpet to the music. Occasionally we saw *Thank Your Lucky Stars*, ITV's livelier pop show that had bands playing in the studio, and a teenager called Janice, who'd vote on new songs and was famous for saying 'I'll give it five' in her Brummie accent. But those enticing glimpses of ITV and its commercial breaks were rare. The BBC was the default channel for children according to Mip, and she controlled the switches.

After the pop music there was a gentle cop show, *Dixon of Dock Green*, and when PC Dixon gave his regular summing up and his final 'Night all!' it was usually time for bed. If Mip was distracted we sometimes caught the 'Wakey, wa-a-a-a-akey!' cry at the start of *The Billy Cotton Band Show* and watched a few minutes of leggy dancing girls in high heels and fancy hair-dos. But after the pop shows that seemed old-fashioned, something grannies might watch, and no one pleaded to stay up.

Sundays were more formal than Saturdays, as we wore our best dresses and walked in a crocodile to St Mary's Church in the town centre. The morning service was brief, and the references to God reminded me of Caux. I'd never attended a church regularly before, and came to enjoy the peaceful routine of the hymns, psalm, prayers and brief sermon. Afterwards we returned to school to change into casual wear for free time interrupted only by meals and the afternoon walk.

The Sunday outing, led by Matron or a teacher, was nothing like as popular as our Saturday expeditions. The walk usually felt too long, with no particular destination, no lift in Mip's car and no picnic. The only good thing about it was the return to Pippins, where a doughnut or cake often awaited us with our tea, followed by more TV in Mip's sitting room. The BBC ran classic drama serials on Sunday afternoons, including Dickens's *Oliver Twist* and *The Old Curiosity Shop*, and R. D. Blackmore's *Lorna Doone*. Another teatime favourite was a serial called *Stranger on the Shore*, and its sequel *Stranger in the City*, following the sad story of a shy French teenager who becomes lonely and led astray when she comes to Brighton to learn English. We'd happily watch anything, from wildlife programmes to *Captain Pugwash* cartoons, but our viewing was often curtailed by friends returning from weekends out, or Matron hustling us upstairs. Sunday bedtimes came too early, with Matron intent on getting us tucked up in bed, our clean uniforms draped on the chairs beside us, all set for Monday.

When I eventually resumed my diary during my first year at Pippins, its brief notes were becoming more assertive. I was no longer the nervous newbie trying to fit in, but an old hand, enjoying my friendships. By my second year there were signs I was pushing back a little against school authority and the world of my parents.

'What about MRA?' Jane asked me suddenly one day when we were chatting in the garden. Years later Jane thinks there may have been 'talk about smoking, or some other activity I would have disapproved of'. By her own admission she was more rule-abiding than me. I wasn't actually far behind her, but I liked to *appear* to be a rebel. The topic inspiring Jane's query may have been smoking, but it could equally have been revenge on a strict teacher, or running away, or an outrageous prank. I wouldn't have dared do any of these things in practice, but I enjoyed imagining the possibilities.

In fact, I did once puff on a cigarette, while staying at a day girl friend's house. In a field beyond their garden her brother had produced a cigarette and lit it for a group of children to try out. It was solemnly handed round, and without exception we coughed, spluttered and agreed it was disgusting. The next day someone spotted a newspaper headline linking smoking with possible death from cancer. It was a new thought at a time when smoking took place everywhere, including in dining rooms, offices and even TV studios. Even in non-smoking homes, like my grandparents', ashtrays for visitors were standard. So the news that cigarettes might be deadly terrified us. *Might that one furtive experiment kill us?* we wondered. I'm probably not the only person in that group who never touched a cigarette again.

Whatever it was that inspired Jane's 'What about MRA?' challenge, I reacted sharply. 'What about Mer-aar?' I snapped back defiantly, trying to form the dreaded letters M – R – A into a feasible word that wouldn't arouse our friends' interest. I also wanted to make it plain I wasn't interested. Jane was reminding me of the world I'd come from. But linking Caux's 'normal living' to life here seemed impossible, and I preferred not to think about it. Nothing more was said, and poor Jane no doubt felt rebuffed.

I was surprised at Jane's nudge, as her family didn't talk much about MRA. Aunt Elisabeth and her mother and her aunt were upright and conventional, but they were also easygoing with us girls. I wasn't aware of any talk of rules, quiet times or meetings when I was at Flint Cottage. And while it was true that Jane's mum had withdrawn Jane from our dance class because Miss De Vos introduced the new Twist craze into a routine for the school play, she never tried to stop *me* doing it. I knew from Jane that Aunt Elisabeth also considered the Beatles song *Roll Over Beethoven* an insult to classical composers, but again this didn't impinge on me. At school Mip's rules applied, and I was happily hooked on our weekend fixes of *Juke Box Jury*, which offered plenty of Chuck Berry, Beatles and twist music.

For all our interest in the growing sixties' pop culture, we were innocent and unsavvy by modern standards. We knew very little about rock 'n' roll, and less still about sex and drugs. 'Do you want to know where babies come from?' a friend called Amanda asked me in break one day. 'They get born after mothers and fathers marry, don't they?' I replied. We'd watched TV programmes showing animals born in the wild and they seemed to come out of the mother's rear end somehow. I imagined human babies did the same, but hadn't thought much about it. 'No, I mean how babies get *made*,' Amanda persisted. She demonstrated with her hands and fingers. 'If that's the man,' she said, waving a finger, 'and that's the woman, then one goes into the other!'

I didn't have much idea what she was talking about, having little knowledge of male or female anatomy, but I had no reason to doubt her, given that her parents lived on a wildlife park and knew the *Born Free* Adamsons. I'd never discussed the subject with an adult, and it wasn't something covered in school. My blank indifference must have disappointed Amanda, who ran off to find a more responsive audience. I consulted my new friend Liz. She didn't seem any more clued-up or interested than I was, even though I was sure she knew more than me about bodies. Once she'd told us in the dorm that when she was sore 'down there', pointing vaguely towards her tummy, her mother had smoothed on some cream. 'Eugghh!!!' we'd all protested. 'That's a bit personal!' 'No it's not!' Liz had retorted. 'She says that's what Mummies are for!' And I'd suppressed a flash of envy at the thought that she could be so familiar with her mother.

One special bond between Liz and me was our rabbits. Liz had arrived at the school with a big albino rabbit called Minnie, a beautiful match for my handsome boy Smudge. We knew enough about animal reproduction, at least, to know that a female and a male could easily produce baby rabbits if they were left together, so we decided to let them meet. The details of what the pair might do remained a mystery to us, despite Amanda's best efforts. We simply knew that rabbits inevitably reproduced if they weren't kept apart.

Sadly our efforts appeared to fail. We lowered Smudge into Minnie's cage, whereupon, after a brief sniff, he leapt on his new friend in what looked like a brutal attack. 'Quick, get him out!' Liz shrieked. 'He's murdering her!' I lifted a flailing Smudge from the cage and he hopped off around Pets' Corner. Minnie checked her food bowl, apparently unperturbed. No damage done. They just hadn't liked each other. We went back to keeping the rabbits apart, and forgot all about it.

On Tuesdays and Fridays after school I had piano lessons with Mrs Wilson in the common room. In the middle of playing a piece one day we heard urgent knocking on the door, and Liz burst in, wearing the blue overalls we wore in the garden. 'It's HAPPENED!' she announced dramatically. 'Minnie's had babies! I just found them when I went to clean her cage!' Mrs Wilson was swept up in the excitement, the piano was abandoned, and we all hurried over to Pets' Corner. Sure enough, there in the sleeping area of Minnie's cage, we could see – was it two? three? no, four! – pink, wormlike creatures wriggling in the hay. Within weeks they had grown into perfect mini versions of their furry parents: two all-white like Minnie, two with Smudge's exact markings. They brought much delight to the school until, at three months old, they were separated and found new owners before they multiplied again.

Learning about life through our pets and television was a slow process, and we had little interest yet in fashion, make-up or boys. But it felt adventurous to occasionally do things we knew the teachers wouldn't like. Probably our most daring activity was to chat to some state school kids across a fence that ran past one of our garden camps. I wrote in my diary *Meet boys again. The drip throws stones.* The encounters amounted to little. The other children couldn't get into our grounds, we couldn't climb out, and nobody tried either option. But having this secret from the staff and just talking about 'meeting boys' or 'the drip' seemed daring and cool in itself.

By my last year I'd moved on from Enid Blyton. My 1963 diary has a packed *Books Read* page, and where Blyton had once dominated, the list includes 13 books by Angela Brazil, with titles like *A Fourth Form Friendship* and *Jill's Jolliest School*. These term-time adventures of confident, self-reliant schoolgirls a few years older than myself made the Famous Five feel childish. The new stories were tougher, and probed the girls feelings and relationships. There are schoolgirl gangs, routine meanness, jealousies, and devious lies to win friends, although misunderstandings or bruising experiences are always resolved by the end of the story. It didn't matter to me that this prolific author had been writing in a distant, pre-war age. I was gripped.

Once again, Angela Brazil's girls were easy to identify with, having unconventional family circumstances, and challenges they had to meet without adult help. In *Nesta's New School*, Nesta is abandoned in a Swiss boarding school, very near Caux as it happens. When she's suddenly orphaned, she discovers that she was in fact adopted, and has a family in England. In other stories girls are routinely left with uncles, aunts or random guardians, or spend the holidays with teachers or schoolfriends. This felt familiar.

The books also touched on aspects of boarding school I hadn't thought about. 'These places toughen you up,' Daddy used to say. 'They make you strong and independent.' I hadn't heard anyone question this assumption before, but Angela Brazil characters sometimes hinted that this independence came at a price. In *A Fourth Form Friendship* there's a reference to Aldred and her big brother being 'in a sense, visitors at home' once they become boarders. Their father and aunt start treating them differently. They don't have to help around the house as much, and special outings to museums were arranged that hadn't been part of their holidays before.

The theme is developed in *The Jolliest School of All*, set in a school near Naples. A pupil called Lorna admits to her teacher Mrs Clark that she's dreading the holidays with her reclusive father. Mrs Clark tells Lorna, 'I sometimes think that girls brought up at boarding school are apt to lose the right sense of value of their own relations. Their companions and games fill their lives, and they go back for the holidays almost like visitors in their own homes. When they leave school they're dissatisfied and restless, because they've never been accustomed to suit themselves to the ways of the household, and have no niche into which they can fit. The old round of "camaraderie" is over, and they have been trained for nothing but community life.' Mrs Clark urges Lorna to go and make friends with her father 'and he'll begin to realise that he wants you'.

Lorna's sense of rejection and her view of school as a safe haven felt authentic, although I didn't consciously interpret this as my experience at the time. I didn't doubt I was loved. Yet I often felt like a visitor with my grandparents, and, for a long while after their return, with my parents. I wasn't used to them, and didn't know where I fitted in their lives. Staying among my community of boarders had become more comfortable.

However, back then the Angela Brazil stories were simply absorbing page-turners, and immersing myself in them didn't knowingly help me reflect on my own tangled emotions. Nor did they help me understand my confusingly mixed reactions when I heard that Mummy was finally coming back to England.

19

The Big Freeze

Devon 1963

We knew little about national or world events at Pippins, having no access to papers or television news. This must have occurred to Mip, as one day she announced that every other teatime she'd 'invite' a famous living person to join us, and we'd have to find out in advance who they are. All this meant was that she'd give us a notable name, and we'd consult each other or a teacher or the encyclopedia as to their significance. Over tea Mip would then ask us what we knew about them, and tell us more. The 'guests' were almost all white and male, and they included President John Kennedy, the cosmonaut Yuri Gagarin, Mao Tse Tung, General Franco and Pablo Picasso. One I knew straight off was our own Prime Minister Harold Macmillan, whom I'd once seen at Victoria Station.

Despite the absence of news, we knew all about one

national event, which impinged on our lives enough to disrupt the school routines. This was the Big Freeze, one of the coldest winters ever recorded in Britain. It started in the run-up to Christmas 1962 with a series of bitterly cold days, and by Boxing Day snow had covered the country and stayed put. Blizzards swept across Wales and the south-west of England, causing 20-foot snowdrifts. Roads and rail lines were blocked, farms and villages cut off and powerlines came down. As rivers, lakes and even the sea iced over, we heard that helicopters were dropping food parcels, and ferrying emergency patients to hospital.

While branch lines stayed closed British Railways kept the mainline services running from London to the South West. On Thursday 17th January 1963 I wrote in my diary: *Pack and leave for Waterloo. Leave for school. The rest of the school's not coming, except for the train people, till Tuesday. What fun we will have. (Not that I don't like the others.)*

About ten of us arrived that evening at Axminster Station, and teachers had to navigate icy roads narrowed by high banks of snow as they drove us to the school. For a few days we enjoyed an adventure worthy of our school story books. Classes were abandoned and we had the run of the building. Mip borrowed sledges and skis for use in the garden or at Trinity Hill, a short drive away. On our first Saturday I recorded that Miss Young walked us *down town* to the shops, an unheard-of treat, where *I bought dominos and a book. Then we went sledging.* Even after classes officially restarted the following week nothing was quite normal, and it took another seven days for all the day pupils and remaining boarders to gradually return. We had extra time to look after the pets and donkeys, we still played in the snow in lesson times, and we watched more TV even on weekdays.

The excitement gradually faded as the snow went on and on. This wasn't like Caux winters, which people were prepared for. Pippins had central heating, but most British homes, including the house in Croydon, depended on open or electric fires. On TV we watched people round the country struggling with frozen pipes, power cuts, and problems accessing food and fuel. We started to wish the cold spell would stop.

On Wednesday 6th February I wrote *V. bad weather. Snow, snow, snow. No daygirls came but one. Stopped snowing in the afternoon. Went for a walk amongst the rivers of melting snow.* Then the following day: *Went to do the pets. Rain. Thaw. HOORAY. We haven't had rain since last year.* But the respite was brief. By 9th February it was back: *Snow again. Beastly beastly.* The severe cold continued, and that Sunday we were even allowed to watch a service on TV instead of walking to St Mary's Church.

By mid-February we were over the worst in Axminster. My last mention of snow is on 14th February. *Had two Valentine cards. It thawed a lot and there are only a few patches of snow.* The thaw brought widespread flooding in Devon, and over the school wall we watched water streaming down the pavements towards the town. A few days later the main roads across Dartmoor reopened, but it wasn't until early March that troops relieved one farm cut off by snowdrifts for 66 days. On 5th March Britain had its first frost-free day since Boxing Day, and the Big Freeze was officially over.

School quickly returned to its familiar patterns, and my year started gearing up to the impending changes ahead. Most girls already knew what senior school they'd be going to in the autumn, but I hadn't a clue and preferred to avoid the subject. It made me feel unusual again. I was also slightly on edge because, amid all the excitement of the Big Freeze, Mummy had arrived back in London.

Back in December, when we'd heard she'd be back after Christmas, I'd been ecstatic, but when it came to our actual reunion I felt a little flat. I wasn't used to having her around, and I privately worried about what lay ahead. My diary record of her return is matter-of-fact: *January 1 1963: Mummy came home yesterday, and today we went shopping with her. I wrote Christmas thank you letters in the afternoon and watched TV.*

On my parents' return I'd hoped we might live as a family somewhere. But Daddy had stayed on in Brazil 'for a little longer', six months as it turned out, and it didn't happen. We were still at my grandparents' home, where Mummy and I shared a guest bedroom. The holiday still felt like I was biding time before returning to Pippins, an increasingly attractive prospect after watching TV images of Devon submerged in snowdrifts.

My relations with both Mummy and Granny were different now. The little chats and hugs I'd shared with Granny weren't the same when they were both around, while Mummy felt like a stranger, or a special visitor who might be off again soon. We hadn't spoken for well over a year, and I felt shy opening up to her.

Mummy's reappearance also returned me to the world of MRA. On her second day back, she took me to London to see the musical *Space Is So Startling* at the Westminster Theatre. The show was about the American and Russian 'space race', and it was in the middle of a public run. Among the cast, theatre staff and audience were many faces I recognised, and I even came across Marion and Angela, who I hadn't seen since Caux School. Marion, I learnt, was now at a boarding school in Scotland, and she was here because her father Matt was in the show. He had a memorable role as a Russian diplomat who takes off his shoe and bangs it in a furious rant, to make a point. It was a reference to the Soviet President Kruschev who'd famously done the same thing at a recent UN Assembly, and the theatre audience roared with laughter.

A couple of days later Mummy took Patrick and me to Oxford for a week, to the home of her friends Garth and Margot. I'd met their daughter Mary when I'd once holidayed with her and her aunts in Dorset, and her brother Geoffrey was Patrick's age. Their house was a cosier version of the Charles Street houses, with visitors, meetings and conversations about 'the work'. Mary and I helped lay tables, dry dishes and entertain guests. It wouldn't have occurred to us not to play our part. We accepted that our parents' work was important, and complying made life easier. We also had plenty of time to play in the snow and have fun, and my diary mentions board games and a puppet show, with trips to the cinema and a pantomime.

The weather crisis and unusually exciting start of term rapidly drew my attention away from Mummy's return and back to that parent-free world at Pippins, where family contact was largely reduced to weekly letters. Even with Mummy in the same country, my parents felt as distant as ever once I was back at school.

However, on the Saturday of the February half-term my diary notes that *Mummy took me out after lunch. I took Barbara out too. We played games at the Cedar Hotel.* The next day, Sunday, *Mummy took just me out to the Cedar Hotel, and Jane and Aunt Liz had lunch with us.* On the Monday *Mummy visited Shute School. I stayed in bed all day with a cold.* Evidently thought was being given to some senior school options.

The diary pages for my four-week Easter holidays are left blank, but resume on 23 April when, *After an early lunch, Mum took me to the Waterloo Station cinema before setting off for Pippins.* My only memory from that holiday in Croydon is of one brief and stilted conversation with my mother. I was slowly waking up one morning and Mummy was sitting up in the twin bed beside me with her cup of tea and notebook, having her morning quiet time.

Shockingly, out of the blue, she asked me, 'Do you know about how we have babies?' 'No!' I snapped, worried she might tell me. I knew by now that the topic was a minefield, better left alone. I wasn't even curious, I just wanted her to change the subject. She persevered. 'Well it's something you should know about, now you're growing older.' So while I lay staring up at the Victorian ceiling rose above me, she gave me a short account of male and female eggs producing embryos, and a brief introduction to periods. 'Don't you have any questions?' she asked. 'You can ask me anything you like.' 'No, it's OK,' I said. And to my relief the subject was dropped. She resumed her quiet time, and we were soon getting up for breakfast as if nothing had happened.

In my final summer term at Pippins Mummy visited me twice. The first occasion was at half-term, when we both stayed with Aunt Elisabeth and Jane.

Friday 7 June: I went to Jane's house and Mummy came and joined us in the afternoon.

Saturday 8 June: Jane and I hosed each other after lunch. Shopped in Chard before lunch.

Sunday 9 June: At 8.31 we listened to Patrick's Bromsgrove school choir on the wireless.

Monday 10 June: Went to Charmouth. Mummy, Jane and I swam. Very cold in the sea. Had picnic lunch and saw butterfly exhibition.

Tuesday 11 June: Mummy went back in the morning. Smudge and I back to school at 6pm.

The other visit was a day trip she made from London to see me in the school play, Maeterlinck's *The Bluebird* at Kilmington Village Hall. I don't know if this Friday visit was so brief because of her other commitments or mine. It's quite possible that I'd pushed my own agenda for that weekend, and since the term was ending soon I was indulged. Whatever the reason, my diary records that no sooner had I greeted my mother after the play than I was off to spend the weekend with my friend Liz in Cornwall. I suspect Liz and I had long planned it. She was my best friend among the boarders, and we felt almost related through our rabbits.

It was not until several years later that Mummy told me she'd returned early from Brazil because Mip had concerns about my conduct. It surprised me, as I didn't see myself as a problem child, and believed I'd blended in quite well. Yet, with hindsight, the signs of my unpredictable behaviour are there. My diary makes a number of references to my being 'in trouble' at school, and I remember surprising myself with a few angry outbursts directed at a teacher and even my beloved granny.

Once in the holidays I'd gone with Granny to a neighbour's flat to practise on her piano. Usually Granny just sat and listened to me play, but that day she gently suggested that a passage could be played more quietly. A fury flared up in me that surprised us both, and I fumed back at her, 'I don't need a horrible old grandmother breathing down my neck and telling me what to do!' I was immediately shocked at myself. I loved Granny dearly, and had never spoken like that before. Hopefully I'd picked up enough from my Caux schooling to apologise profusely, but I suspect the incident was simply dropped by both of us. Dear Granny was generous and forgiving, and it didn't seem to wreck our closeness. But she must have been as horrified as I was.

At school there was another unexpected explosion, this time with Matron. My father would later refer to it proudly as the famous time I 'led a school strike', and I'd cringe at his version of it, especially as, like many childhood 'memories' we never actually shared, he wasn't there to witness what really happened.

It happened on a Sunday in the summer of 1962, when Mummy was still in Brazil. Matron had taken us on a long, dull walk along a country lane bordered by tall hedgerows, which blocked any views that might have given us a sense of progress. We begged to go back to school, but Matron insisted we walk on further before retracing our steps. I suggested to a small group of fellow grumblers that we should simply stop walking and 'go on strike'. A few girls proceeded with Matron, while most of us sat down on the grass verge. When she finally reappeared Matron looked cross, and told us we deserved 'six of the best'. She marched us briskly back to school, where she took me aside and gave me a sharp telling-off.

Something in me snapped, and instead of taking it on the chin and apologising, I was defiant. Again, my angry words seemed to have a life of their own. 'You make life a misery!' I shouted. 'I hate this place, it's horrible! I wish I was anywhere but here!' Once more I shocked myself. If someone else had spoken these words I'd have considered them foolish and obviously asking for trouble. What was more, I hadn't even meant what I said. I liked the school.

But I didn't know how to backtrack now, and Matron was furious. Normally we'd be sent to see Mip, and a punishment might entail going early to bed or missing sweets or TV. But Mip was out that afternoon, so Matron and Big Barbara decided to lock me in the attic.

It was miserable and scary under the roof. The attic had two dark rooms reached by stairs that rose steeply from behind a door on a rear landing. One room had a bed for Big Barbara when she stayed overnight. Otherwise this floor was mainly a storage area, full of school trunks and out of bounds for pupils. A small window was too high to open or look through and I was cut off, with no idea how long I'd be kept up there once the key had turned in the landing door. For all I knew I'd be there all night, without books, food or water. A numb detachment overtook me and I couldn't cry. My boarding school armour-plating must have been in place, and it was like watching someone else's story unfold. The Caux lessons about quiet times and apologies might have offered an exit route, but it didn't even occur to me to try them.

In the event, I didn't spend the night in the attic. Shortly after the bedtime baths could be heard running on the floor below, Mip must have returned. Because the next thing I heard was Big Barbara unlocking the door at the bottom of the stairs and yelling, 'Mip wants you in her room. Now!'

'So Matron tells me you were rude and disobedient, and you said you want to leave the school. Is that right?' the exchange with Mip began. 'Yes,' I mumbled miserably. 'Well, I'm very sorry to hear that. You'll have to apologise to Matron. And I think you'd better write to your parents and tell them you want to leave, don't you think?' the Head continued calmly. 'Yes, Mip,' I concurred, wondering how to get out of that.

She escorted me into an empty classroom, and gave me a blank airletter form. 'Sit here and write to your parents. And knock on my door when you've finished.' I sat at a desk, weeping now, and I dashed off a letter to my parents as requested. Except… I didn't say I wanted to leave the school. I knew I couldn't ask that. It wasn't up to me. They had important things on their minds. And in any case, I didn't want to leave. Where else would I go? This was my safe place. So I simply wrote that I was unhappy, and in trouble. I drew a picture showing everyone else as angels using spears to prod me, represented by a small devil. I didn't like what I'd got into, but I had no idea how to extricate myself from it. Filling the sheet with sad thoughts, I took it back to Mip.

The headmistress scanned the letter vaguely, put it on her mantelpiece and, to my surprise, gave me a big hug. Then she walked with me to find Matron and apologise, which I duly did. 'OK, all done,' said Mip. 'Go to bed now, and let's have no more of this.'

My friends asked me in awe what had happened, and the bedtime routine continued as usual. But after my bath Mip called me down to her room again. 'Are you feeling a bit better about all this?' she asked. 'Yes, Mip,' I said, fully chastened. 'You didn't mean this nonsense about wanting to leave, did you?' she went on. 'No, Mip,' I replied. 'So we'll just tear this up, shall we?' Mip reached for my airletter as

I nodded, and she ripped the paper to shreds, but I felt a flicker of regret that my parents would never read it. 'You didn't mean any of this, did you?' she said, flashing a warm smile, not waiting for a reply. With a quick peck on my cheek, she directed me to the door, and the whole bewildering episode was over.

Nonetheless I was left with a slight aftertaste of shame, and a reputation as a rebel among the staff. Matron never forgave me and was prone to making sarcastic comments about me being 'exempt from school rules'. I was determined things wouldn't spiral out of control again, but my 1963 diary refers to several minor scrapes.

> *Matron put me off TV.*
> *Get blown up by Rocket for not knowing what today was. (Ascension Day apparently)*
> *Go to bed early as I had a friendly fight in the dormy.*
> *I have to do the washing up with Prue, because I caught giggle-itis from Sarah.*
> *Get caught talking to the boys.*

In the final term I even fell out with Mrs Wilson, my favourite teacher. On 16th May 1963, I wrote *Had a horrible piano lesson, and I have begun to dislike my piano lessons*, although later entries showed the situation did improve: *Piano lesson was a good one. Mrs Wilson is in a good mood.*

My final week at Pippins must have been an emotional rollercoaster.

Tuesday 16 July: Got in hot water with Mip for making a racket after lights out.

Wednesday 17 July: In trouble all day. One of my worst days at Pippins, and I am dying to leave this prison. (Beside this I've drawn a small picture of a prisoner behind bars.)

Thursday 18 July: We packed this morning. Had a beastly music lesson. ('Beastly' is later crossed out and replaced by 'nice'. Maybe it was only 'beastly' because it was the last lesson.)

Friday 19 July: Say goodbye to Mrs Wilson my piano teacher. Very homesick for her. Clean out my desk. Report reading. Luckily she doesn't read out my conduct!

Saturday 20 July: Go raspberry picking at a fruit farm in Musbury and picnic by a river.

Sunday 21 July: Some boarders broke up today. Raspberries for lunch. Boiling weather.

Monday 22 July: Everyone goes home except the train people. We play about.

Tuesday 23 July: Get up early to catch the train to Waterloo. I LEAVE PIPPINS! And glad I am too, as I never really liked it there. (Beside this I've added 'I did really'.)

Wednesday 24 July: See Daddy for the first time in nearly 2 years.

On the train back to London I wondered if I'd recognise my father when I saw him. At Waterloo the guard kept shouting 'All change!' and it seemed directed at us school leavers, for whom nothing would ever be the same again. It felt strange stepping out of the carriage and away from my friends. We'd shared every minute of each day and night, and now we were to be scattered between different schools around the country, never to meet again. Mummy had told me I was down for the weirdly-named Winceby House School in Sussex, which didn't take pets, so even my beloved Smudge had been despatched to a new Devon home.

It was also 'all change' at the house in Croydon. Granny and Grandad had moved to the New Forest for a quieter life, and Mummy and Daddy had taken over their bedroom. I was happy to have a room to myself again, and the dining room was now a bedroom for Patrick, leaving another spare for guests. Without my grandparents, the heavy Victorian décor they'd left behind seemed even more dated, far removed from Liz's modern, stylish house in Cornwall, and even living in a flat felt strange. I noticed a new bustle in the place. The phone in the hall rang frequently, guests came more often and watching TV in peace was less easy. We were back in the world of Charles Street and Caux.

I'd easily recognised Daddy when I first saw him, hugging him happily. But back at the house there was a mild tension in the air as we got used to being together again. My parents fired questions at me about school and tried to discuss my school report, but I didn't see the point of talking about any of it. They didn't know people at Pippins and couldn't understand. I recalled that time at Caux when Dot had urged me to identify and fix my mysterious 'problem', and I dreaded further quiet times. I still hadn't got the hang of them, and adults always had the final say, whatever one said.

Fortunately distractions arose and Pippins post-mortems were forgotten. Within days of my return Daddy drove me and Mummy to the Midlands for Patrick's school Commemoration Day. We all dressed up, and Mummy had bought me a small straw hat, while she wore a veiled hairband matching her gloves and bag. Bromsgrove School was indeed more formal, and far bigger, than Pippins and even Shute. I watched in awe as young men, including my 15-year-old brother, strode around in blazers and boaters. Was this what senior school would be like?

Saturday 27 July: After prizegiving we had a picnic lunch. We watched some cricket. And at 9.30pm there was a superb tattoo.

Sunday 28 July: After a night at Whitbourne M and D and I set off again for Bromsgrove, went to the Chapel there, and had picnic lunch. Arrived home late having had a puncture.

It was a memorable weekend, but my hopes of spending more time together as a family were soon dashed. That Saturday diary entry had a line added: *PS On 27th July MRA Assembly started*, and this wasn't the normal summer conference at Caux. It was a simultaneous London version, at the Caxton Hall in Westminster, running through August. Daddy may have returned, but his work continued pretty seamlessly.

Then we also lost Patrick. We'd left him at school, as for some reason his term lasted two more days. But almost immediately after his return to London, my brother was packed off to America for five weeks with a group of British teenagers who'd been invited to an MRA youth conference.

Most of that August I spent to-ing and fro-ing to central London with Mummy, as life revolved round the assembly in Westminster that Daddy was helping to run. Usually I sat at the back of meetings discreetly reading a book, or I helped in the kitchens of the conference building. Sometimes I attended matinées of an MRA play called *Through The Garden Wall*, which was showing nearby at the Westminster Theatre. A constant flow of delegates stayed with us in Croydon.

It was all a little like being back at Caux, except that, between conference activities, there were some excellent outings. One day some Scottish houseguests took me and their daughter to Battersea Funfair and on a tour of Parliament. Another day Mummy arranged a boat trip to the Tower of London. On Mummy's birthday we had a picnic by Cleopatra's Needle on the Embankment and watched a Cinerama movie called *The Wonderful World of the Brothers Grimm*, rated *EXCELLENT* in my diary. Best of all, after one morning at the Caxton Hall, Mummy and Daddy took me to see *The Sound of Music* at the Palace Theatre. It was blissful to be watching this big Broadway and West End hit musical together, just the three of us.

An expedition was made to Barkers department store in Kensington High Street to buy my new school uniform. Mummy told me I'd enjoy Winceby House, as it had its own beach and came highly-recommended by friends. At Barkers I was kitted out with navy gym tunics, white blouses, a blazer, hat, and stripy tie. The thought of wearing these cumbersome clothes for real gave me the collywobbles, but the famous Derry & Toms roof garden café, next door to Barkers, was an excellent distraction, and a milkshake helped me push away my worries for now.

Occasionally one parent had to work in Croydon and I could amuse myself in the flat. Apart from reading, piano and TV, I had two special projects. One was a scrapbook of news cuttings about the Great Train Robbery, which took place on 8th August and caught my imagination. Another was writing my own Angela Brazil-style story, entitled *New Girl at St Catherine's*, which I typed and crudely bound into a book. I loved these days, but even here I couldn't always escape the adult agenda. One day in late August my diary records: *After lunch I went with Mummy to collect signatures for the People's Declaration. Out of 30 homes 10 signed.* This referred to a petition calling for a halt to the country's tide of 'atheism, decadence and corruption'. We made friends with several neighbours as a result of calling door-to-door, but I always let Mummy do the talking.

In early September I recorded: *Great excitement, P. came home from America.* I was even more pleased when Daddy drove Mummy, Patrick and me – all four of us in one car! – to visit Granny and Grandad in Hampshire. It was like a real family holiday, although Daddy only stayed one night. For a few days we went to the beach, walked among wild ponies, consumed cream teas and collected fresh fish from the quay at Mudeford. In the evening we played Pit and Racing Demon. I wished we could stay forever.

My father's absence was acceptable, as I knew by now that he didn't 'do' relaxation for its own sake. He was a driven man, and holidays, like retirement, were to him time-wasting notions. 'A Caux conference is the best holiday!' he'd still say if time off was suggested, or, 'Those meetings in Paris were the perfect break.' Seeing friends or pursuing leisure activities required a clear purpose, beyond simply enjoying oneself.

There was one exception. Rugby. And if a good match was on it was suddenly acceptable for him to sit glued to the television. Daddy had played rugby for his college and London Wasps and it was a passion. Yet even with sport he'd feel compelled to point out the life lessons it taught. 'Now *that* showed perfect, selfless teamwork!' he'd exclaim. 'This man shows true leadership!' Or he'd complain, 'They're simply not playing to win. We all have to play to win!' Apart from this, and a few other significant sports events, the only TV he watched was news and current affairs. He saw little point in comedy or quizzes, and would watch a drama or topical review purely in order to keep up with the Westminster Theatre's culture war. Instead he read voraciously – history and global politics, never fiction – and made long phone calls.

Just occasionally we'd coax Daddy into playing a game. But mysteriously Daddy's 'play to win' philosophy didn't extend to board games, least of all to a favourite called *Careers*. Its very name seemed to touch a raw nerve, and he'd refuse to suspend his principles in order to play well. *Careers* requires players to set themselves personal life goals at the start, by allotting a total of 60 points between three areas: Money, Fame or Happiness. 'Just as in real life, each player has his own idea of what success really means', the rulebook states. However, the winner is the first to achieve their 60 target points, so a little pragmatism is essential when setting your goals.

'I'll go for 60 points of Happiness,' Daddy would invariably announce. 'No, no, no!' everyone else would insist. 'You can't win if you don't *share out* your 60 points. Going round the board you'll pick up points in all three areas. So you *have* to spread your goals more evenly. For example: 20 Money points, 20 Fame and 20 Happiness.' But EVERY time Daddy refused to aim for Money or Fame as a life goal, and inevitably he'd lose badly. The game was simply not designed for extremely idealistic people.

Still, I soon forgave Daddy all his quirks when the holidays ended abruptly, and it hit me that I might not see him again for... how long this time? They'd never intended to go to Brazil for so long. Where would they go next? I braced myself for disappointment.

Once again my diary entries stop suddenly at the end of that 1963 summer holiday. I was about to embark on a different life in a strange place with unfamiliar people. All traces of life as a junior were cast behind me, and the diary had to go. The prospect of senior school was alarming. What would I say to all these big girls? How could I explain I'd spent most of my holidays at an assembly?

I thought perhaps my sketchy knowledge of pop music might help. It was mostly gleaned from *Pick of the Pops* on the BBC's Light Programme and *Juke Box Jury*, but at least I knew Freddie and the Dreamers from The Searchers, and could sing along to the new Beatles single *She Loves You*. So that was a start. Discarding my comics, I leafed through the fashion and problem pages of Granny's *Woman's Journal* and Mummy's *Womens' Own*, knowing that the talk at Winceby was unlikely to be about ideology or the Cold War.

Setting off on the school train from Victoria Station, I still didn't feel in any way prepared. Desperately I thought about God's pocket and prayed fervent silent prayers that everything would be alright. As I sat in the railway carriage alongside other tongue-tied new girls, a pop song went round in my head in time with the swaying train. It was the soothing harmonies of a pop duo called The Caravelles. Life was uncertain and sad and these singers seemed to feel the pain of it too.

When you leave me, my golden rainbow disappears
And you leave me a broken heart that's full of tears
These ain't rainbows in my eyes, why should I lie?
You don't have to be a bay-ay-aby to cry.

20

Britain 1963

Chérie's homecoming was not how she'd pictured it would be. For one thing, Britain had nearly been brought to a standstill by one of its coldest-ever winters. Her flight to London had narrowly avoided cancellation, and an air stewardess had told passengers that even the Trafalgar Square fountains and River Thames were frozen over. Chérie had shivered on the bus carrying her on gritted roads into central London. Having grown up in India she loved a hot climate, and she knew the chill of the draughty rooms at Chichester Road would be a shock after a Brazilian summer.

All the same, the reunion with her family was an exciting, warming distraction from her private struggle with the cold, and Chérie basked in almost overwhelming gratitude at seeing her children and parents again. Her awareness that nothing in life can be taken for granted had been heightened during her flight, when she'd sat next to a woman perspiring both from anxiety and the thick tweed suit she had on. 'I had to wear this outfit,' the nervous traveller explained to Chérie. 'The last time I flew out from Rio my plane crashed off the runway into the sea. You remember? That Panair flight last August? My son was with me, and he swam round searching for me, knowing I couldn't swim! Amazingly most of us survived, as you know. And it was this same suit that kept me afloat and saved my life!' Chérie told this story to her family at their first meal together. 'What with the weather here and this woman's experience, you can imagine… I spent much of the flight praying for a safe arrival!'

Time seemed to have played tricks in Chérie's absence. In Brazil the months had flashed by, but the changes she now noticed made her absence appear much longer. Her parents had slowed down, while her children had grown up. Patrick, who'd be 16 later that year, was a young man with a deep voice who'd started shaving. Judi, at ten, was taller, slimmer and had grown her hair. They seemed quiet after the exuberant Brazilian children she'd been with, and while clearly happy to see her, she sensed some holding back. Chérie wanted to find out so much, and talk about her own experiences, but she saw it would take time. 'Everyone has to get used to being together again,' Dulcie reassured her in private. 'You and your brothers were like this when we returned from India – reserved and over-polite! But believe me, these two couldn't wait to see you.'

Chérie was sharing a room with Judi and looked forward to mother-daughter chats, but these proved difficult. 'There aren't any problems,' Judi would insist when her mother tried to discuss school. 'I've got lovely friends and it's really nice there! The teachers and matrons can be mean, but that's school, isn't it?' Dulcie encouraged Chérie not to take Mip's letter or Judi's school reports to heart. 'After all, nothing major happened. Maybe when they say "easily distracted" in class she's simply finding the lessons dull? She's with a charming bunch of girls, and she loves going back after the holidays, so things can't be too bad!'

The topic of school was dropped, but Chérie was still determined to talk to her daughter about 'women's matters', now that she was ten. She'd seen Judi listening to pop songs and reading her grandmother's Agatha Christie and Mary Stewart novels instead of the favourite Enid Blytons Chérie remembered. Yet when she tried to chat about sex and menstruation, Judi seemed to freeze. Chérie persisted briefly, but an occasional 'yep' or 'hmm' response to a question was the only sign her daughter was listening at all. Chérie cut short her explanations, deciding the school might do it better anyway.

Communication was best in the evenings, when they sat around the fire and companionably watched television. Chérie liked to keep up with the news, although the poor coverage of South America disappointed her. But she also enjoyed shows like *Dixon of Dock Green* and *Double Your Money* – easy family viewing. 'We're not so sure about some of the newer programmes,' her father Roy warned her. 'We've been steering the children away from some of them. Better to play a game instead.'

Chérie watched the 'newer programmes' when Judi was back at school and reported back to Bill on the changes she observed in British culture. 'Most TV is harmless fun, but there's a noticeable increase in swear words and innuendo. And there's a very popular "review" (songs and sketches) on Saturdays called *That Was The Week That Was*. Its sole purpose is to satirise and debunk the establishment and positive values. I saw one where they were mocking the military, the church and even Monty! They follow every new trend going, and one programme ended with the entire cast and technical team doing the Twist! That's the latest dance craze: a kind of solo jive. It can be done quite gracefully – Judi tries it out to the radio – but it can also be very suggestive.'

From her British colleagues Chérie soon heard that the 'debunking' approach of *That Was The Week That Was* was sweeping popular culture and the arts. In the context of the Cold War, the MRA team feared it was playing into hostile hands. They knew that since Lenin's time the Russians had discreetly supported liberalisation and decadence in the West. These were tendencies Russia didn't want in its own country, but considered more effective tools than conventional warfare when it came to undermining capitalism in Europe and the United States.

Satirical and racy new plays were of course not instigated by the Soviet machine, but MRA teams saw them serving its purpose by undermining morality and the shared values that support democracy. They had little doubt that communist strategy had for years been exploiting political and industrial division. Now they believed Britain's cultural life had become a new battleground.

In response to the perceived threat, the MRA team in London had decided back in 1961 to develop its work at the Westminster Theatre. Chair of the Theatre's Trustees, Kenneth Belden, wrote of 'an assault today upon the mentality of our country by influences which are hostile to its best interests and which could undermine the character of the nation'. The trustees wanted to make the Westminster 'more and more a centre for constructive drama that would not merely expose the follies of mankind, but give people new courage and purpose, and a new will to tackle the problems of the contemporary world'. Until this point the Westminster Theatre had presented MRA shows periodically, and other production companies had rented it in between. From now on, MRA would have continuous runs of its own, 'in a more sustained attempt to bring a new trend into the theatre and a new thinking to the public'. Many plays subsequently produced were written by Peter Howard, the writer who led the MRA work worldwide after Frank Buchman's death.

On Chérie's second day back in Britain she and her children braved the cold weather and went into central London to see Howard's new musical *Space Is So Startling* at the Westminster Theatre. The show took a satirical look at the superpowers' current 'space race'. Despite its weighty themes it offered catchy songs and light relief in scenes featuring two protest groups, the 'twisters' and the 'squatters'. The twisters were partygoers, who sang and danced to promote freedom and escapism:

Why worry? (twist, twist, twist, twist) *Just exist!*
(twist, twist, twist, twist)
If you're feeling low (twist, twist, twist, twist) *you*
can do the twist!
And even if, in a year or two, someone drops a bomb
on you
You won't feel it on the scene, and think of the fun
you will have in between!

Meanwhile the squatters believed problems called for confrontation and protest:

It would help a lot (a lot!) if the world would learn
to squat!
Problems fade and seem such rot, if everyone would
learn to squat…

MRA plays always ended with some kind of pointer to a 'third way' solution, and by the final scene the protests have been replaced by a new song: 'What we need is an end to "anti": anti-this and anti-that'. Meanwhile, the wise and magical Mr Nod, who's been observing Planet Earth's capers throughout, concludes, 'Nations are full of hate and fear nowadays, but the new world will be built by new men who won't be bought by dollars or bullied by tyrants.' The final song urges:

The world can be one family where all men learn
to share
Enough for need but not for greed, as nations learn
to care.

Back among her London colleagues, Chérie was looking for a plan for the remaining school holidays so that she could give her parents a break. So when Margot, her friend from the Hays Mews and land girl days, invited her to bring the children to her home in Oxford, Chérie jumped at the offer. Margot and her husband Garth's house was a busy MRA centre, and their children Geoffrey and Mary were close in age to Patrick and Judi. The youngsters would be company for each other, while Chérie caught up further with the UK team. The week included skiing for the boys, sledging for the girls, and a tour of the Oxford colleges, a timely opportunity since both boys would be applying for university soon.

Chérie admired Margot's bustling household and had flashes of unease, which she knew Bill would dismiss. Nobody here mentioned her absence from her family, but Chérie knew it had been too long. Her children had become distant. At no point did she question her calling, but she felt it was time for some reassessment. The thought of the Croydon house becoming her and Bill's new base seemed a possibility. Chérie felt in limbo without Bill, but once he returned in the summer they could discuss it properly.

The new school term was approaching when the three returned to Croydon, but the snow caused last-minute delays. A phone call from Judi's school announced that boarders travelling by train would now travel two days later, while other pupils would arrive a week later than planned. 'I can't wait to get there and be in the advance guard!' Judi exclaimed. 'It'll be like one of those school stories! We'll be cut off by snow, with no teachers, surviving on Mars bars and icicles!'

Chérie was disappointed at her daughter's impatience to leave, but quickly decided it was a blessing. Whatever had happened the previous term couldn't have been too bad. After seeing Judi off at the station, Chérie told her parents, 'She was so happy getting on that train with her friends. She can't be as troubled as the headmistress thinks.'

With both children back at school, Chérie gave more attention to her parents' move to Hampshire. She also rediscovered the pleasures of gardening and dressmaking, interests she'd had no time for in recent years. She frequently went into central London, where the Charles Street houses were busy with activity geared to filling seats at the Westminster Theatre. Pre-theatre receptions were laid on for coachloads of theatregoers rallied from around the country, and Chérie helped cook for these. The hope was for the plays to reach as many people as possible, spreading ideas that would reinforce MRA's work in industry, education and international relations.

Meanwhile Chérie searched for a senior school for Judi. When the weather allowed it, she visited Shute School in Devon, the choice of many Pippins parents. But it didn't feel 'right'. She didn't know any Shute parents, and didn't want to impose further on Elisabeth, whose daughter Jane was moving to a day school some distance away.

Over the next months, two friends recommended their own daughters' school in Sussex, and Chérie liked the sound of Winceby House, with its sea views and proximity to London. Winceby seemed to lack academic rigour but at least it wouldn't be a stretch after Pippins. Chérie hadn't had direct contact with Judi's teachers since Caux, but she considered her daughter an all-rounder, less interested in study than her scholarly brother. She was proud of Judi's piano-playing and her national and county-level essay-writing awards, and felt sure she'd enjoy Winceby's music and ambitious school plays.

In early summer Chérie's parents moved to the New Forest, and Bill flew back from São Paulo. Chérie was pleased he'd made it in time for Judi's summer holidays and Patrick's school Commemoration Day, while Bill had his sights set on supporting MRA's London Assembly in August. He teased Chérie for turning soft after her months with her parents and children, but occasionally she won some concessions.

A typical exchange would have run:

Chérie: Surely you deserve a bit of a breather?

Bill: And why would I need a holiday? Our work keeps us in top form!

Chérie: Spend a bit of time with the children then. Patrick will be off to America soon.

Bill: I see plenty of the children. We went to Bromsgrove. Judi's here all holidays. They're a wonderful gift! But we can't take our eye off the ball. And we need to see what to take on next…

Chérie: Well, I'm booking a musical to take Judi to. And I've promised my parents I'll take the children to see them when Patrick's back. Can't we all go, before we scatter again?

Bill: The Assembly debrief will be on – a crucial chance to agree on strategy. It's a testing time, with Frank gone.

There could be factions arising if we're not careful, or opportunities missed. Don't look so disappointed! Maybe we can take a few days…

Even Bill must have had mixed feelings when Patrick went to the United States so soon after his own return from Brazil. But he saw the trip as an important chance for his boy to see the world with other teenagers, mostly sons and daughters of British full-timers. They'd all be leaving school soon, with decisions to make about their futures, and they'd been invited to spend a month at a youth conference at Mackinac Island. With any luck there'd be a new injection of young people into the MRA team.

The summer sped past too quickly for Chérie, and it didn't feel long before Patrick was back at school and Judi was starting at Winceby House. But she was happy living with Bill in Croydon. In between their London commutes and entertaining, she thoroughly enjoyed the novelty of their shared maintenance tasks around the building. They'd taken over her parent's painting, fixing, gardening and seeing to the needs of tenants, and she almost let herself dare think of the Croydon house as 'our own home'. On the other hand, staying put wasn't generally an option in the life they'd taken on. She still wanted to be ready to go anywhere they might be needed.

There were a number of options as to what she and Bill might do next. In the old days they'd have consulted Frank Buchman about it, and now it was Peter Howard and others close to Buchman who steered MRA's global strategy and workforce. Full-timers were often invited to take up a specific task, but they could initiate alternative plans if they were agreed with others and matched the main blueprint.

To many London colleagues the most pressing needs lay in Britain. MRA was experiencing a fierce backlash to its Westminster Theatre plays, and to its books, petitions and full-page press advertisements. Many people saw Western society's shift towards increased permissiveness, free expression, and a new focus on self-fulfilment and individuality as entirely positive. Amid the cultural changes, critics perceived MRA to be promoting outdated wartime values such as public service, self-sacrifice and moral fibre. As society grew steadily more liberal and secular, MRA resisted, fearing that a slide into self-obsession and moral collapse would ultimately foster extremism and a collapse of democracy.

Not surprisingly, the movement became pigeonholed as backward-looking, ultra-conservative and anti-communist. While some MRA supporters may have accepted and deserved these labels, many mainstream full-timers like Bill and Chérie were dismayed that their work should be seen in the same light as reactionary groups like the Clean-Up TV Campaign, which was an offshoot from their work, or, decades later, the Moral Majority, which wasn't. They saw themselves not as conservative stick-in-the-muds, but radicals, presenting a fresh approach to pre-empt the authoritarian solutions of Nazism or communism. In any case, the British MRA team had been publicly attacked since the 1930s and media hostility came as no surprise. Many saw it as a sign of making headway, and it spurred them on.

Ronald and Mary, Bill and Chérie's colleagues in Brazil, were among the many who committed themselves to the ongoing Westminster Theatre campaigns in Britain. But Bill and Chérie realised their hearts lay elsewhere. They had always been drawn to the wider global scene, and to the 'second track' diplomatic efforts that went on quietly behind the scenes in crisis areas. The couple had a growing certainty that they should again pick up their work in the Middle East, where they had long-standing friendships. Even in Brazil, Bill had stayed closely informed about the region and its challenges.

Few of Bill's friends in Britain shared his interest, and doubts were raised by some of MRA's leadership about his timing. For many westerners, the critical geopolitical significance of the Middle East only came into focus later, in the early 1970s, when the Arab countries started to use their natural resource of oil as a weapon in global politics. But Bill and a group of his colleagues had long seen the crisis growing. They'd also been concerned about the deep wounds left to fester in that region from colonial times, wounds that the West appeared to ignore despite the pain and division they still caused.

Five years earlier, Bill had attempted to fight his corner in a similar way. Amid rising tension in the Middle East, he had written urgently to Frank Buchman in America, suggesting that MRA intervention was imperative. It was June 1958. Bill's letter reports on post-Suez developments in the Arab world, citing intelligence he'd received from a

British cabinet minister, Foreign Office officials and senior oil company officials. He outlines the crisis in the Lebanon, Arab fear of Israel, tensions in the Yemen and Aden and expanding Soviet influence across the Arab world. With Moscow making every effort to woo President Nasser in Egypt, Bill strongly recommends that a group of European politicians versed in the ideas of MRA should visit Nasser immediately. He urges Buchman's team to 'open the door, as Frank did to the Germans in 1947', and concludes, 'We have had none of our forces in Egypt since August '56, and I think it would be necessary for a small reconnaissance to be made at once'.

The letter, now filed in the Oxford Group archives, doesn't appear to have provoked any response. It had arrived when the 83-year-old Buchman was bed-bound and weak. Buchman's biographer Garth Lean writes of this time: 'Buchman still originated many fruitful initiatives, and was effective and compassionate as ever when meeting people face to face. But it was impossible for him to know the personal situation of his many hundreds of whole-time colleagues throughout the world, and mistakes regarding them became more frequent'. Bill missed the direct contact he once had with Buchman, and it would have been disappointing to have his insights and urgent suggestions ignored.

Some of Bill's colleagues shared his frustration, in particular his American friend Harry Almond, who'd also been pushing for greater focus on the Middle East crisis. In his memoir Harry recalls one point in the late 1950s when all the Arab state leaders were due to meet in Cairo. Harry and Bill's good friend Dr Abdel Khalek Hassouna, the Secretary-General of the Arab League, had requested that an MRA team meet with them. Harry had checked with Buchman's inner circle, intending to respond positively to the invitation and at least travel to Cairo himself. 'But I was rebuffed by senior colleagues in MRA over the plan', he writes. 'Hurt and bitter at those who I believed had spread false information about the proposed trip, I cancelled it and retreated'.

In time Harry came to forgive them, and even to convince himself that maybe his proposal for 'a Middle East action' then was wrong. They were trained to be team players, and generally accepted that their own 'guidance' may not be accepted as such by others. Harry found another way to serve MRA, in America. The conference centre at Mackinac Island was expanding in 1959, with the construction of a film studio for MRA films. Extra transport was needed to ship building materials from the Michigan mainland to the Island in Lake Huron. So for a couple of years Harry became the skipper of a large industrial barge operating the route 12 hours a day all year round, even when the lake iced over.

Bill must have been making a similar mental adjustment at this time, when he went with Chérie to Brazil. They left soon after Buchman's death, no doubt aware the MRA work could splinter and fall apart if full-timers didn't rally round key campaigns like those in Latin America. It's also possible that those in leadership positions were steering Bill away from the Middle East, as they'd done with Harry.

Whatever the past pressures and disappointments, Bill with Chérie and Harry with his wife Beverley all returned to offering their services in the Middle East in late 1963. And this time they won through regardless of diverging opinions among their peers. Harry writes of dark nights at the helm of his boat on Lake Huron wondering 'Was this icebreaking really what I was meant to do with my life? I began to think that I must take up again my original calling to the Middle East and its relations with America.' Like Bill he'd kept up with events and friends in the region. Then, in 1963, quite unexpectedly, he found himself formally invited by a former Lebanese President to move with his family to Beirut and establish a regional MRA base there.

Harry and Beverley's decision to accept this invitation coincided with Bill and Chérie's return to London from Brazil, and must have been a key factor in the British couple's own renewed dedication to the Middle East. Their many friends across the Levant, Gulf and North Africa welcomed the four of them back along with several other Europeans who joined the new initiative. The team included Marcel and Théri Grandy in Cyprus, British academic Dr Charis Waddy, writer Mary Rowlatt, and an Arabic-speaking British teacher, Peter Everington.

Together they devoted themselves to help strengthen the deteriorating links between the Middle East and the West, and support the local MRA teams in the region. For Bill this was a continuum of the commitment he'd made during the war, to help build the peace. He was more certain than ever that MRA could help pre-empt catastrophe by bringing people and nations together for the common good. In 1942, as a soldier sitting in his tank turret in Egypt, he'd written of his desire to join 'an expeditionary force with a life-long goal' and, twenty years on, he was still determined to see it through.

While Harry and Beverley relocated with their two school-age daughters to Beirut, Bill and Chérie decided to stay on at their South London home, and join their colleagues across the Middle East when needed. Much of their work would be done in London and in Caux, so Croydon was as good a base as any. The children could stay in the school holidays and there was further space for guests or helpers if they needed to travel.

Another benefit of their house was the income raised from its flats, although this didn't cover their expenses, and without a salary, Bill and Chérie still considered they lived on 'faith and prayer'. The idea of trusting in God's provision was real to them. One night they prayed for the use of a car, and the following day they received a phone call from a doctor in Derbyshire who supported MRA. He'd no doubt heard of Bill's transport needs and offered him the use of an Austin Cambridge no longer needed by his surgery's car fleet. The doctor even insisted on paying the car's ongoing tax and insurance costs.

Such incidents happened regularly, and were celebrated as Divine generosity. Another gift paid for Judi's school fees. A magnanimous friend called Oliver, wanting to support Bill and Chérie in their new work, offered to cover Judi's private education. He was her godfather and had barely met her at the time, but for her remaining school days he kept a close avuncular eye on her. 'Protecting your investment,' Bill would tease his friend gratefully when he treated Judi, as a teenager, to yet another West End meal at Simpson's in the Strand or Gennaro's, or a debate in Parliament where he had a pass to the Press Gallery.

Just as their arrangements were falling neatly into place, some surprise news reached Chérie and Bill in the spring of 1964. As far as they'd known the children were content, and Judi was doing well in her senior school. She'd already made a good friend and had stayed with the girl's family in Hampshire during the first school holidays. Their daughter had maybe seemed a little quiet and wrapped up in her reading when she returned, but she'd apparently gone back to school quite happily.

So Chérie was taken aback to receive a phone call from Judi's new headteacher saying that regretfully all was not well at school. Even within the friendly confines of Junior House, she said, 'Your daughter just isn't settling down.' Chérie was lost for words for a moment, and struck by an uncomfortable sense of déjà vu. She was reminded of the words of Judi's previous headteacher. Now it was the Winceby head advising Chérie that in certain lessons her daughter was stirring up trouble, and those teachers found her difficult.

It was hard for Chérie to take in. She considered both her children bright and well-behaved. The girl playing up in class didn't sound like her own amenable daughter. Even Dot John at Caux, though wary of an independent streak, had never called her a troublemaker. Then the news got worse. 'I'm afraid there has also been a case of her biting another girl,' the head went on, 'and of bullying someone else. I'm afraid, Mrs Conner, we really can't have this, least of all in Junior House, where we want the younger children to feel happy and secure.'

Biting. Bullying. *Could this be true?* Chérie wondered. And if so, how could she, as a mother, not have seen this erratic behaviour coming? And what was the head leading up to? Was her daughter about to be expelled? 'Oh it hasn't come to that yet, Mrs Conner,' the headmistress assured her. 'Your daughter is well-liked, and more intelligent than she lets on. And personally I've always found her very polite and pleasant. But it's only right that you should know about these incidents, and that I should issue a warning. Your daughter has to learn there are boundaries that can't be crossed.'

Chérie replaced the phone receiver in a daze. Her daughter knew all about boundaries. She'd been taught all her life to live by standards of love and unselfishness, so how could she possibly be violent towards other girls? What on earth would make any normal, happy girl bite or torment someone?

In her search for answers new insights came to her. The last months had been hectic, full of meetings and consultations on their new plans. Boarding school was a huge convenience. But Chérie realised how few conversations she'd had with her daughter, not only about school but life in general. When Judi's last headmistress, more than a year ago, had urged her parents to give the girl more time, and 'an anchored home life', she'd responded quickly, returning from Brazil. But back in Britain life had become busy. They perhaps hadn't made space for their family to get to know each other again, or put down roots. Perhaps for their children nothing much had changed at all.

Bill disapproved of Chérie's hand-wringing, and took the head's warning in his stride, just as he'd done when 'that letter' had arrived in Brazil, and again when they read Judi's final school report at Pippins. 'It's not too serious,' he reasoned now. 'She's allowed to be a little wayward at her age. Maybe she was standing up for herself. In any case, we'll seek guidance on the right steps to take. We've been guided towards this Middle East initiative, and the children will be provided for too. In abundance.'

He looked at Chérie, loving her motherly concern despite himself. She made him think of his own mother, who'd forever worried over her own cherished children. This extraordinary maternal heart-power has its place, he thought. But in a battle one has to stay tough and focused on the target at all costs, not waver at every challenge.

This time Chérie was already certain what they had to do. There was an obvious way forward. It should have been clear to us much sooner, she thought. But how on earth would they persuade their happy, independent daughter to agree to it, when she was obviously so content with her new friends and her school life as it was?

21

Sure of a Big Surprise

Bexhill-on-Sea

'Take it from me, your new school will be nothing like prep school,' Patrick warned me in a rare confidence before I became a senior. We'd spent little time together over the past seven years and couldn't be considered close, but we were protective of each other.

'How?' I asked, eager for advice even if it was discouraging. 'Well, prep schools are small and friendly, and a quirky head can make it quite fun. But senior school's another matter. Everything's bigger, and the language and rules are different. Just don't be surprised by how homesick you'll get.' In the weeks to come I was grateful for the warning. During frequent sobs in a toilet cubicle I'd think of Patrick's words and take comfort. Homesickness was a rite of passage boarders went through. It wasn't just me.

Winceby House, the new 'home from home', was a three-storey brick building overlooking playing fields to one side and the choppy grey waters of the English Channel to another. The school and grounds are now long gone, replaced by modern housing, but the memory of arriving at this bleak, windblown site still makes me shiver. I couldn't imagine ever being able to find my way round all its connecting wings, staircases and nooks. Pippins had kept elements of its small country house origins, but this place was a full-blown institution.

As for the senior girls, they seemed older and more worldly-wise than my Angela Brazil book characters. This was the early 1960s after all, and the big girls' chat was nothing like the banter at The Manor House School. Instead of talk about winning awards, solving mysteries or protecting the school honour, they spoke of boyfriends, The Beatles and Mary Quant. Cool words included *mod*, *square*, *fags*, *with-it*. *Having a gas* or *a blast* was a good thing. *A bummer of a time* wasn't. They also talked about apparently glamorous people I'd barely heard of, like Christine Keeler or Profumo or April Ashley.

The thought of being stranded here for years made me nauseous and tight-chested at times, as well as tearful. Being reasonably close to London and having my parents in the same country didn't help much. They could fly away at any time, and I might not even know. Without the friendships built up at Pippins I felt more remote from family than ever. I threw myself back into my boarding school persona, trying hard to fit in. This took different forms, sometimes exhibiting bluff and bluster, sometimes withdrawing into the shadows. Survival was all, and disassociating myself from my parents' world seemed essential. Any discovery of how different we were could be ruinous.

It seems strange that I never discussed the challenges of boarding with anyone, apart from that one brief exchange with my brother. But my capacity to face and voice my fears was limited. My parents were still unfamiliar, and there were no obvious others to talk to. In any case, I knew boarding school was a non-negotiable part of life's training: the place where you learn to put up with things. I'd once heard Peter Howard describe how his own daughter had begged to be taken away from a boarding school she hated. His response had stuck in my head. 'Anne,' he'd told her, 'if I take you out of school now, you'll be running away from things for the rest of your life!' So back she went. I knew my parents would take the same line, so there was no point even raising the subject.

At bedtime I continued to pray for the wellbeing of family and friends, as well as my own. But I never prayed to be rescued, partly as I couldn't visualise what that might look like, and partly because I knew I didn't deserve a miracle. Spiritual gifts were for impossibly good people – they had to be earned. Since my time at Caux I'd assumed that even parental love was conditional, and presumably I wasn't doing enough of the right things to be loved or wanted. Still, I kept up my brief nightly prayers, and sometimes took solace from those lines I'd memorised years before about God's Pocket.

If you have a kind of worry, you need not worry at all
'Cos you know you're in God's pocket, where you
cannot have a fall.

Being part of a whole new cohort of 20 or more girls boosted my spirits a little. We were all starting at once and I was no longer the sole newcomer arriving mid-year, as I'd been at previous schools. Seeing other tear-stained faces was reassuring, and we were all lodged together in Junior House, which was set apart from the main school building across the playing fields and looked a bit like a private house from the outside.

What was more, the matron of Junior House, Miss Kortright, known as Fifi, was friendlier than Matron at Pippins. A stocky woman with a short, severe haircut and a Labrador called George, she had a firm manner yet seemed to be on our side most of the time. She certainly worked tirelessly on our behalf. With her assistant Sue, she got us up in the mornings, fed us and dispatched us to school, and welcomed us back after class. She was also our hockey teacher and our Girl Guide leader. With each role her outfit changed: white lab coat, shirt and tie as matron, baggy shorts and sweater for games, and full Guide kit when we had to wear ours.

At first the weekdays spent over at the main school seemed to drag, and our return to Junior House was a relief. Then as the weeks progressed and we knew what to expect, school activities became less daunting. I never liked filing into assembly every morning, as the buxom Miss Bourne thumped out the *Washington Post* march on the piano. The senior girls watched us coming in last, and the smirks of some made me self-conscious. But the classwork was undemanding, and once I recognised this I relaxed a little.

Another private worry was quickly sorted out. I knew two girls here were family friends, with links to my other world. Given that I never spoke about that life I wondered if they'd give me away. But it wasn't a problem. One of them, a year or two older than me, had been at Caux School and we'd briefly shared a bedroom in Mountain House. But after exchanging furtive smiles when we first passed in a corridor we completely ignored each other. Presumably she didn't want any mention of Caux either.

The other girl, Geraldine, was more relaxed, actively seeking me out during hockey and announcing enthusiastically, 'I know your brother!' At 15 or 16 she seemed way older than me, and I glowed with pride at being treated as a pal by such a cool and attractive senior. My friends and I were even more impressed when we learnt Gerry was a popular rebel, who cheerfully risked being gated by smoking and making unauthorised trips into town. I was confident she wouldn't blow my cover, as she evidently belonged to more worlds than I did. I even owe my enjoyment of hockey to Gerry, as our banter and stick-clashing on the pitch made me throw myself into the game with unusual enthusiasm.

Before long I had a best friend in my own year. Libs had the same sense of mischief and fun, complete with infectious giggle, that I'd enjoyed with Marion at Caux. A good chuckle with Libs took the pain out of certain episodes that might otherwise have escalated into minor disasters. One was my repeated failure at Guides to light a campfire using only two matches, a skill required to achieve our Second Class Firelighters' Badge. My two matches always fizzled out immediately on the damp firewood we'd gathered from the beach, while all the other girls managed it. My frustration might have spiralled into angry or tearful outbursts if I hadn't seen the funny side with Libs.

Our friendship helped me stave off many a wobbly moment. We picked up on each other's down moments and had a way of comforting each other by pulling faces. Libs puffed out her mouth and nostrils to look like a sad hippo, while 'my face' involved rolling my lower lip like a tube at the side of my mouth, to make a character Libs named Tusk. If one of us felt sad we'd make our face and sigh deeply, eliciting a hug from the other and an empathetic 'Ahh… Hippo!' or 'Ahh… Tusk!'. To us it was an amusing ritual. The idea we were using a wacky persona to express emotion in that buttoned-up environment wouldn't have crossed our minds.

I liked the other girls too, and came to enjoy the fun of the common room and the dorm I shared with Libs and five others. We'd chat about pop, fashion and how to be 'with it', even though we didn't wear stylish clothes or cosmetics ourselves. A teen magazine called *Jackie* started up in our second term, and if anyone had a copy we'd pore over its advice, teen romance stories and pop star pin-ups. The problem pages were as innocent as we were, and sex wasn't discussed either in the magazine or among the girls.

In one issue of *Jackie* we learnt how to grow long hair quickly, something we yearned to try on our short school cuts. Apparently if we rubbed salt into our scalps and slept by a dish of water then our dehydrated locks would lengthen as they stretched towards the water. We gullible 11-year-olds decided to have a go, using salt and bowls smuggled up from the supper table. The experiment never took off, as Fifi quickly spotted the strange objects on our chairs and demanded an explanation. 'It'll never work, you chumps!' she laughed. 'It must be an April Fool trick! Now, clear it all away before you get soaked!'

Fifi was our link with the outside world. One morning she woke us up with the shocking news that John Kennedy, the American President, had been shot dead. We were appalled that this could happen to the handsome world leader, and when, for years to come, people asked the famous question, 'Where were *you* when you heard…' I'd remember Fifi's solemn face and our gasps of dismay.

Another morning Fifi brought less dramatic news when she opened the dormitory door. She'd be taking me and another girl down the road to sit an exam at a local school. It was the first I'd heard of this, and it seemed odd. Why me? The other school was a state school, and the two of us stood out in our severe navy tunics, ties and hats. None of the other children spoke to us. We were escorted to desks in a hall with dozens of others, and sat what later turned out to have been the 11-Plus exam. I didn't know what this was and had never seen a test paper like it. But I had a go, and thought no more of it.

Before long, when I discovered I'd failed the exam, this

small, almost forgotten event suddenly became a matter of deep significance and shame to me. I'd always passed exams before, and it was galling to find that this particular test seemed to be a crucial gauge of how bright you were. People would ask 'Did you pass your 11-Plus?' in the way they might ask about your age or your hobbies. I tried not to show what a loser I felt, but I determinedly lost interest in classwork, preferring to pass notes and doodle than follow the teacher. Two or three years passed before I discovered, to my surprise, that I could do well in exams after all, and I began to re-engage with lessons.

I never discovered why my parents wanted me to sit the 11-Plus. Presumably they were keeping some options open, as a pass gave one entry into a state grammar school. It must have been clear Winceby offered little in the way of scholastic challenge, and a history of Winceby House describes this period as the school's 'years of decline' before closing down. Suffice to say, my favourite lesson became sewing with Miss Barr, mainly because it never actually felt like a lesson at all.

Miss Barr's stately portliness and wobbly chins reminded me of the opera singer Madame Castafiore in the *Tintin* series, and while the class sewed she would read us books. To my surprise, friends asked her to read out my own mystery story *New Girl at St Catherine's*, which I'd written the previous holidays and brought to school. I was proud to have this narrated by Miss Barr with the same dramatic fervour she'd applied to *Susannah of the Mounties* in the weeks before.

Living in a separate building meant we juniors didn't

have to learn all the school's routines straight away. But we soon learnt about order marks, given by teachers for minor offences like inattention or lateness. The penalties for order marks, imposed by prefects, were never too onerous. When I first presented myself to Deborah, my Head of House, I found her surprisingly friendly and matter-of-fact. Instead of lecturing me on letting down the House, as Angela Brazil's sixth-formers might have, she simply told me to write out fifty times 'I shall not talk in class'. Another time she gave me a piece from *Hamlet* to memorise, and I enjoyed learning Gertrude's beautiful speech about Ophelia:

> *There is a willow grows aslant a brook,*
> *That shows his hoar leaves in the glassy stream…*

and so on.

Once or twice in that first term Mummy and Daddy took me out for the day, and we'd drive along the coast to Pevensey or Eastbourne. They picked me up in their 'faith and prayer' car, and I'd sit in the passenger seat, with Daddy driving and Mummy in the back with the picnic. She always brought a large thermos pot of her delicious Marmite-flavoured beef stew, and since it was usually raining or blowing a gale we'd eat in the car, parked by the sea or overlooking the countryside.

I loved seeing my parents, despite blanking them from my thoughts at school, and I relished their undivided attention. For the duration of their visit I'd immerse myself in their company and their news. School would be blocked out completely, and I'd brush away my parents' questions. Once as we walked on a beach we spotted an older Wincebian approaching, and I was gripped by embarrassment and dread. She offered a friendly greeting as we passed in our matching uniforms, but I ignored her entirely, fearing my parents would engage her in conversation.

Sometimes Daddy drove onto a deserted country lane and let me lean across to take full charge of the steering wheel while he operated the pedals. The fun of pretending I was driving made me laugh with abandon, and it was like the old days together in Charles Street, when we'd listened to songs on my parents' radio. It was also how I'd felt when dancing mindlessly in the Pippins common room. There was a freedom in those moments when a weight lifted and I didn't worry about anything.

When it was time to be dropped back at Winceby the spell broke and my mood plummeted. I'd thought I was used to goodbyes but I wasn't, and that same aching melancholy continued to haunt me in adult life when I faced station and airport partings, or even the return from a weekend away.

Back at school I'd block the happy memories of the day out, and resist comparing notes with friends who'd been with their own families. It wasn't their lunches at expensive hotels that bothered me, because I much preferred Mummy's stew. More jarring by far were the extravagant shows of affection some girls exchanged with their parents when returning to Junior House. These were the girls who began their letters home *Darling, most belovedest Mummy and Daddy*. I told myself it was a sign of weakness, unnatural even, to be so clingy. In truth I longed for that closeness, and I'd learnt to belittle it. I'd determined to be unsentimental and independent, the sure way to cope with life's disappointments. And if I couldn't avoid tears I'd shed them privately, because crying also showed weakness.

My birthday came and went in my first term, without any embarrassing revelations. But a couple of other events brought my two worlds perilously close, just when I thought I was successfully keeping them apart. One day my piano teacher Miss Bourne announced that in a couple of weeks' time I'd be playing a piece in a music festival at the De La Warr Pavilion in Bexhill. I wasn't too thrown by this, although it was the first and last time I played a piano solo at such a grand venue. More concerning was the news a little later that my godfather Oliver, whom I'd then barely met, would be coming from London to hear me play, and he'd be taking me out to tea. My parents weren't coming, and I was used to others standing in, but I wondered what my friends would make of this irregularity.

As it turned out, none of my classmates were playing at the festival, and it was just Miss Bourne and myself who drove to the Pavilion in her car. 'Make sure your godfather includes Miss Bourne in the tea party,' Fifi had insisted while checking my hair and uniform beforehand. I'd nodded, but knew very well that I'd do my best to keep the two adults firmly apart.

Uncle Oliver was waiting in the foyer, a dignified, middle-aged man in a dark suit and coat, carrying a hat and umbrella. Over tea he regaled me with tales of his world travels with Uncle Frank and Uncle Peter Howard, and of escorting people at Parliament and the Palace. I was transported back to Caux and best behaviour, sitting up straight, listening attentively, ready for a pep talk or a quiet time. But there was no extra agenda, and when Miss Bourne came to collect me I regretted not eating more of the dainty cakes and sandwiches. The meeting of the two worlds had, after all, gone smoothly and I could have relaxed and had more fun.

As the first school holidays approached I was invited to visit Libs at her home, and again I became guarded. I was thrilled at the invitation itself. But would there be awkward questions? And what if she then stayed with me, and saw how we lived? Nevertheless, I did go home with Libs, and found the relaxed 'normality' of her life a delight. I revelled in the easy banter between Libs, her brother and their genial parents, as comfortable as friends would be in each other's company. Their house in Hampshire was wonderfully ordinary, and her father's job in the Navy comprehensible.

Then it came: 'What does your father do?' The question I always dreaded, fired by Libs's mother. 'I don't know,' I replied as usual, hoping that would close the topic. 'Of COURSE you know!' she persisted, beaming at me warmly as if I was joking. 'Well no, not really,' I stuttered. 'Well, I kind of do… but I can't explain it properly.' She must have sensed my discomfort as she quickly moved on, no doubt making a mental note to consult Fifi or my mother about it when she had the chance.

When it came to the return visit of Libs to the flat in Croydon, I bit the bullet, hoping for the best, and it was a happy week despite my fears. When Libs was dropped off I was painfully aware of how strange our shabby ground floor flat in a Victorian house must seem. But my parents managed to behave quite normally. Daddy was out a lot, and Mummy left us to chat and play and watch TV. What a relief!

Best of all, Mummy took us to see a matinee of the West End musical *Oliver!* Libs and I hung over the dress circle rail, excitedly examining the orchestra pit below as the musicians tuned up. We gave them names and pretended, in loud voices, that they were our friends. 'Ooh, Stanley looks a bit tired today, on the double bass.' 'And there's Lavinia!' 'And Tim's on time for once!' The musicians were, of course, complete strangers but we fantasised that other theatregoers would think we were in showbiz too. It made us feel glamorous, until we finally laughed at our own silliness and settled down to enjoy the show.

By contrast, I went into tongue-tied mode a few nights later when Daddy took us to a play at the Westminster Theatre. I dreaded going to the Theatre or the Charles Street houses with a schoolfriend in tow. My parents had to bring MRA into everything. If there wasn't a play or public meeting on there would probably have been a book or Colwell Brothers record to offer. It seemed far too difficult to explain to Libs our link to this theatre, so I didn't. Maybe she'd think we went to the theatre a lot for fun. And at least the two of us were being dropped off on our own, which felt quite grown-up. My parents didn't need to go as they'd seen the production before with other guests, so we'd be meeting Daddy in the foyer afterwards.

The play was called *The Hurricane*, set on a remote farmstead in an African country struggling for independence. Unlike at the New Theatre the other night, where I'd only pretended to know people, here I actually did know many of those on stage as well as some in the auditorium. But this time I kept my head down, determined not to catch anyone's eye, as I didn't want to have to explain the place to Libs and open the full can of worms. For her part, Libs seemed pleased to be going to any London production, and she took the play in her stride despite its serious themes.

I managed to avoid an encounter inside the theatre, but was less successful as we left. We were walking out into the street and past the stage door, when one of the principals of the cast, Phyllis Konstam, swept out onto the pavement. She was still heavily made-up, and, drawing up her fur collar against the cold, she exuded the full glamour of a West End star. In fact, 'Aunt Phyll' *was* a star, who had played in several Hitchcock movies, but she was also a friend of my parents. She and her famous tennis-player husband Bunny Austin had worked with MRA for many years, and their son John was a good friend of Patrick's.

I tried not to notice her, but she spotted my father. 'Oh, hello Bill,' she said casually, adding, 'Hello you two!' to us girls. 'Packed audience tonight!' Daddy called back, steering us towards his parked car, while Phyll walked away up the street. It was the brief exchange of friends who meet frequently, with no hint of surprise in their voices, no need for prolonged chat on a chilly night.

'Gosh!' said Libs, looking astonished. 'She KNOWS you! For REAL! The lead actress! She called your dad "Bill"!' 'Oh yes,' I said vaguely, 'Patrick's friendly with her son.' 'Wow… how come you didn't say that before?' Libs's question hung in the air a moment or two. 'I didn't really know…' I mumbled, tailing off as we tumbled into the car. Daddy was preoccupied unlocking doors, wiping windows and warming up the car, and somehow I managed to divert the topic onto something else.

I wonder now how poor Libs put up with my evasions and secrecy. I didn't want to keep things from her, but I felt trapped. *Be yourself, be yourself, how simple life can be*, the Colwell Brothers used to sing at Caux. That's easy for people who know who they are, I always thought. But I wasn't sure that I did. I was in a tangle.

Apart from having different identities in different places, I was starting to glimpse the emergence of yet another side of myself that I didn't like at all. Just when I thought I was getting the hang of senior school and had a chance of fitting in, something mortifying happened. I bit someone. And not just any someone. It was my school 'godmother' Gilly, whom I liked and who had been very kind to me when I started at Winceby. There I was, trying not to attract attention to myself, and I bit her!

The trigger to the incident was trivial. Some of us were playing a game in the Junior House common room, and Gilly jokingly told my opponents what cards I was holding. It seemed utterly unfair and in a flash of fury I sank my teeth into her hand. I knew at once this was a terrible idea. It was plain wrong, it shocked my friends, and suddenly I was the focus of curiosity for everyone in the room.

Luckily, Gilly wasn't hurt and viewed the attack with cheerful amazement rather than rage. 'Oh my gosh! What HAVE you done to me, you beastly little tiger?!' But light indents of my teeth showed on her skin, and she took pleasure in showing everyone. Then inevitably someone told Fifi, who strutted in and snapped, 'Now this has got to STOP!' as if I'd long been in the habit of biting people. I was stunned and chastened, and I like to think I apologised to Gilly, but I don't remember. It's possible I clammed up in shock. She was, in any case, forgiving, and the incident came to be seen as a bit of a joke.

The biting did stop. But I continued to act impulsively in ways that left me both regretful and puzzled, as they so obviously asked for trouble. Most typical were the wisecracks in class. Some of the teachers struggled to hold our attention, and I started enjoying offering cheeky ripostes that made my friends laugh.

One afternoon we were walking with Fifi to a hockey field a short distance from the school site. It suddenly struck me that our curved hockey sticks were perfect for tripping people up. 'Look at this!' I said to someone next to me as we followed behind Fifi, and I hooked my stick round in front of one of the matron's ankles. I didn't intend to actually bring her down, nor did I. I saw it as a bit of fun. But Fifi spotted the wandering stick end hovering by her foot, and she struck out firmly. 'Don't you DARE fool around like that. Do you really want to go round hurting people?'

Well no, I truly didn't, and the words stung me. But I did want to be fearless and cool. Above all I wanted to get through boarding school, and appearing bold or amusing seemed one way to do it. When Mummy told me later that she'd also heard I'd bullied another girl, I was horrified. Not me. I was no bully. I was afraid of being bullied, so surely I couldn't be one myself? But then I thought back to a quarrel I'd had with a friend. I couldn't recall why we argued, but I knew I'd said something spiteful to gain the upper hand, and I could picture that girl's hurt eyes, under her long fringe, filling up with tears. It was awful to face the fact that I HAD caused her distress while I was so busy asserting myself to evade my own pain. That made me a bully.

Nothing further was said about these incidents at school, and I convinced myself things were going better. Then, towards the end of my second term, my parents drove down to Bexhill to take me out for lunch. As usual Mummy brought her delicious stew, and the weather was wet and windy. We found a good parking spot looking across fields to the sea, and we ate our picnic in the car. But this time I was in for a surprise.

I'd moved to the back seat with Mummy, and we'd been talking about the stormy weather, Fifi's cooking and school radiators. Then, out of the blue, as we started tucking in to our bowls of stew, an unexpected question came from Daddy in front. 'How would you feel about leaving Winceby?'

I was speechless for a few moments. The question was so surprising I couldn't grasp what it meant, and thoughts raced through my mind. Was this a joke? A game? Some kind of test? I looked at Daddy's eyes in the rear-view mirror, to gauge how serious he was, and they looked steady, sincere and kind. Beside me Mummy was watching my reaction intently. I set down my bowl of stew to give this my fullest attention.

The question seemed crazy. I hadn't been at the school long. I was just getting into it. We'd bought the uniform. I had a best friend. Something must have happened. Were they going away again? Or had I been expelled? The school must have told them about the biting and the order marks. But I just COULDN'T start out all over again at another school. Not another boarding school. Not another change. So soon! And what on earth would I tell Libs and the others?

'But… how?…. no… why?' I stuttered, finally finding my voice. 'What do you mean? How CAN I?' In a gentle, matter-of-fact way Mummy explained, 'We just wondered what you'd feel about leaving Winceby and going to day school? A day school in South London. You could come back and live with us at Chichester Road.'

Still the thoughts tumbled around my head. Leave and go to day school? That seemed unthinkable. No one I knew in my parents' world was given this option. You had to stick at things and come out stronger. You couldn't take the easy way out. 'You mean… leave Winceby AND stop boarding?' I checked, still not sure I'd got it. 'Live with you in the flat? All the time?' I had to be dreaming.

'Yes, exactly that,' Mummy said, looking at me anxiously. 'Day school. Look, we know how much you love boarding and how much fun you have with your friends, but there are all sorts of reasons why this might be a good thing to do. You might really enjoy it. We're going to base in London more, and you'd come back to the flat every night. We can be together a bit more.' She paused, then added apprehensively, 'What do you think?'

My incredulity suddenly gave way to a spontaneous surge of excitement. Lunch was forgotten. Doubts swept aside. I was actually being given the chance to run away, and I hadn't realised how badly I wanted this. The prospect of stepping clean away from all the cover-ups, the homesickness, the packing and unpacking and general uncertainty now came as a breath-taking release. And we'd actually live together! I didn't 'love boarding'. It was simply something I'd had to do, and I'd never dared dream of any alternative.

'Of course I'd like it!' I cried out, finally convinced this wasn't a hoax. I wanted to fling my arms round my parents' necks, but such shows of affection didn't come naturally. 'Yes, I really, really would!' I stressed. 'More than anything! But what does it mean? Can I go right now?' 'No, no, you can't go now,' Mummy smiled. 'You have to finish the term, and then the summer term. The school needs a full term's notice.' 'But I can't do that!' I said, slumping right back in my seat in dismay. This prospect of family life might melt away if we waited. Things would change again, and I'd never get out. 'I can't stay at Winceby that long!' I pleaded. 'It would be terrible. I'd be in No Man's Land. Trapped. I wouldn't belong anywhere at all. And my friends wouldn't understand either...'

My escape from Winceby seemed a matter of desperate

urgency now, even though I had no practical idea of what I was walking towards. There was no crystal ball to preview the realities of being a teenager at a suburban day school, and of living with parents who'd been such strangers. The dreaded question 'What does your father do?' would follow me wherever I went, even to day school, and there would still be different worlds to span. Even the realm of day school would be a startling change from the boarding culture I'd been used to. But at this moment all I wanted was the chance to be somewhere lasting, where I fitted.

As for my parents, they were clearly delighted at my enthusiasm, and made no suggestion of a quiet time to reflect, or a discussion of any pros and cons. There wasn't even any interrogation about my order marks. Presumably my wholehearted buy-in came as a relief to them as they'd made their decision already.

I returned to Junior House that afternoon in high spirits, but I kept my secret to myself. I'd promised not to mention anything until the headmistress had been notified, although silence about home arrangements was instinctive to me anyway. And miraculously, the question of staying on through the summer never arose again. Perhaps my parents had heard my desperation, and the school was pleased to release me early. In any case, the term of notice was waived, and I had only a couple more weeks to wait. I'd be going home, and for the first time ever that phrase seemed to really mean something. Something significant.

At the very end of term I told my best friend Libs that my parents had stopped travelling and I'd be switching to day school. I knew they hadn't actually stopped travelling, but it was easier to keep it simple. The news was very abrupt and tears were shed. We swore to keep in touch, but we didn't, and I missed her very much. As it happened, all my friends would be moving on only two years later, when the school closed for good. Winceby House was to join the many minor boarding schools that closed in the 1960s as the demand for places declined.

On my last night as a boarder a handful of us remained in Junior House after those girls collected by car, including dearest Libs, had gone home. The rest of us were taking the school train to London the next day, and to compensate for our delayed holiday, Fifi had a termly ritual known as The Guzz. Each of us could request anything we liked for our final supper, and then she'd take us to the cinema in town. Fifi laughed when I requested scrambled eggs on toast for my Guzz meal, humble comfort food that Granny and Mummy cooked to soft perfection. The movie we saw that night was the 1957 wartime epic *Bridge on the River Kwai* and we returned to our dorms joyfully whistling the *Colonel Bogey* march, like the brave prisoners of war we'd seen fighting for freedom.

As our train jogged towards Victoria Station the next day I daydreamed about creamy eggs and Marmitey stew, *Blue Peter*, *Pick of the Pops*, *Jackie* magazine, a bedroom of my own, maybe a pet. Slowly I was daring to let the truth sink in. A space had been set aside for me. A special place that was not just for passing through. In the carriage the whistling and singing of *Colonel Bogey* started up again and I joined in jubilantly. Because I too had been liberated and I was heading to a safe haven.

Afterword

Chérie and Bill continued to be MRA advocates and mediators in the Middle East for more than 30 years. During that time Bill became a confidant of political leaders in many parts of that region as well as in Europe. The couple based in their house in Croydon for a further six years before moving to live in central London. They maintained their lifelong commitment to Moral Re-Armament. Bill died aged 82 in 1997, and Chérie at 94 in 2011.

Judi continued her education at a South London day school while living with her parents in Croydon. She graduated in modern history at St Hugh's College Oxford, and became a journalist and BBC Television producer. She has a Master's in global mass communications and has worked as a media consultant, coach and leadership trainer in several countries. She married BBC journalist Kevin Geary, they have two sons, and they live in Norfolk and London.

Moral Re-Armament (MRA) was re-named Initiatives of Change (IofC) in 2001, and rebranded for a new era 'to promote trust, ethical leadership and sustainable living'. Two offshoots of the movement are Alcoholics Anonymous and the Twelve Steps, whose programmes are based on MRA's key principles. Written archives of the Oxford Group/MRA are held by the Bodleian Library at Oxford University, and online archives can be found on www.foranewworld.org and www.vimeo.com (IofC & For a New World Archives pages).

Sources

PUBLICATIONS

Harry Almond, *An American In The Middle East*, Caux Books 2009

David Belden, *The Origins and Development of the Oxford Group (Moral Rearmament)*, doctoral thesis Oxford University 1976

Kenneth Belden, *The Story of the Westminster Theatre*, Westminster Productions, London 1965

Kenneth Belden, *The Hour of the Helicopter*, Linden Hall 1992

Angela Brazil, *The Jolliest School of All* 1922

Angela Brazil, *A Fourth Form Friendship* 1911

Graham Britnell Green, *Winceby House School – A Very Special School*, YouByYou Books 2008

Frank Buchman, *Remaking the World*, Blandford Press 1958

Frank Buchman et al., *Ideology and Co-Existence*, MRA booklet 1959

W. L. M. Conner, *Builder of a Global Force* – compilation of Frank Buchman quotes, Grosvenor Books 1990

C. Day-Lewis, *The Buried Day*, Chatto & Windus 1960

Daniel Dommel, *Cyprus 1959–1960 – an Unfinished Story*, Caux Books 1998

Daniel Dommel, *Acteurs de Changement en Amérique Latine*, l'Harmattan 2002

Tom Driberg, *The Mystery of Moral Re-Armament*, Knopf 1964

Daphne Du Maurier, *Come Wind, Come Weather*, William Heinemann 1940

Edward Evans, *Gentleman's Relish*, Sapey Press 1993

Stephen Foot, *Life Began Yesterday*, Harper 1935

Eugene Ford, *Cold War Monks: Buddhism and America's Secret Strategy in Southeast Asia* Yale University Press 2017

Hannen and Cameron, *Where Do We Go From Here?* Blandford Press, London 1952

Agnes Hofmeyr, *Beyond Violence*, Grosvenor Books 1990

Leif Hovelsen, *Out of the Evil Night*, Blandford Press, 1959

Peter Howard, *Innocent Men*, Heinemann 1941

Peter Howard, *Fighters Ever,* Heinemann 1941

Peter Howard, *Ideas Have Legs*, Coward McCann 1946

Ole Bjørn Kraft, *World Journey – World Perspective* (World Mission and The Vanishing Island), Blandford Press, 1956

Garth Lean, *Frank Buchman: a life*, Constable 1985

Mary Lean & Elisabeth Peters, *Stories of the Caux School 1955–65*, Caux Books 2009

Philip Leon, *The Philosophy of Courage*, Blandford Press 1947

Archie Mackenzie and David Young, *The Worldwide Legacy of Frank Buchman*, Caux Books 2008

Ronald Mann, *Moving the Mountain*, Aldersgate Productions 1995

Morris Martin, *Always A Little Further: Four Lives of a Luckie Felowe*, Elm St Press 2001

Frank McGee, *A Song for the World,* Many Roads Publishing, California 2007

C. M. MacInnes, *Bristol at War 1962*

Archie Mackenzie, *Faith In Diplomacy,* Caux Books 2002

Brigadier A. Roy Oram, *An Army Doctor's Story*, Feedaread Publishing 2013

Jacqueline Piguet-Koechlin, *Germany 1948*, Caux Publications 2004

Irene Prestwich, *Irene Prestwich of Tirley Garth: A Personal Memoir*, Grosvenor Books 1971

The Rising Tide pictorial magazine, 1938

Cecil Rose, *When Man Listens*, Blandford Press 1956

A. J. Russell, *For Sinners Only*, Hodder & Stoughton 1932

Michel Sentis, *90 Jours De Ma Vie en été 1955,* 2011, Archives of the Canton of Vaud

Gillian Slovo, *Every Secret Thing: My Family, My Country*, Little, Brown 1997

Alderman T. H. J. Underdown, Lord Mayor of Bristol 1940–41, *Bristol Under Blitz* 1942

Elsa Vogel, *No More Bullets!* Archives of the Canton of Vaud, 2013

Virginia Wigan, *Hope Never Dies: the Grandy story*, Caux Books 2005

Jens J Wilhelmsen, *Eyewitness To The Impossible*, Caux Books 2016

Geoffrey Williamson, *Inside Buchmanism*, Watts & Co 1954

Anne Wolridge Gordon, *Peter Howard Life and Letters*, Hodder & Stoughton, 1969

LETTERS AND RECORDS

Correspondence between Frank Buchman and William Conner, Oxford Group Archives, Bodleian Library Oxford University

United Nations General Assembly New York, *Minutes, Agenda Item 5 of the Third Emergency Special Session 7th August 1958*

U.S. Congressional Record 1st August 1958 Report by Congressman Sheppard (California) on the MRA Statesmen's Mission

PERSONAL ACCOUNTS

J. M. Conner, personal diaries 1961, 1963

P. R. M. Conner, notes on Bromsgrove

William L. M. Conner, wartime memoir, unpublished

W. L. M. Conner, *From El Alamein to the Greater Jihad*, transcript of a talk given 18.10.1994

Revd Julian Thornton Duesbury, *A Visit to Caux*, 1960

Margaret E. Lancaster, *A World Away* Memories of 28 Wilton Crescent, July 1989

Matthew Manson, *Her Sparkle Will Add to Heaven's Light: Margaret Miller Manson 1913–1966*, memorial tribute 1966

FILMS

Freedom, 1957, MRA Productions available on www.foranewworld.info/material/films, copyright Initiatives of Change UK

The Crowning Experience, 1959, available www.foranewworld.info/material/films/the-crowning-experience, copyright Initiatives of Change USA

Men of Brazil/Homens do Brasil, 1959, copyright Initiatives of Change USA

Hoffnung, 1960, copyright Initiatives of Change USA

A Tidal Wave of Hope, Documentary1961, www.foranewworld.info/material/films, copyright Initiatives of Change USA

Chief Walking Buffalo, Documentary 1962, www.foranewworld.info/material/films, copyright Initiatives of Change Canada

PLAYS

The Forgotten Factor, Alan Thornhill, 1940

The Vanishing Island, Peter Howard and Cecil Broadhurst, MRA 1955

Pickle Hill, Peter Howard, 1960

Through The Garden Wall, Peter Howard, Blandford Press 1963

The Hurricane, Peter Howard and Alan Thornhill, Blandford Press 1960

Space Is So Startling, Peter Howard and Anthony Howard, 1963

Acknowledgements

I'm grateful to my family and friends who encouraged me to write this book. They include other alumni of Caux School and some who'd never heard of MRA and wanted to know more about its now little-known history.

My brother Patrick and friends of my parents, including Peter and Jean Everington and Elsa Vögel, helped me fill in some gaps. I also owe much to the memoirs of Harry Almond, Agnes Hofmeyr, Edward Evans, Ronald Mann, Jacqueline Piguet-Koechlin, Michel Sentis and others who lived and worked alongside Chérie and Bill. The research wouldn't have been possible without the archives of the Bodleian Library in Oxford and the *www.foranewworld.org* website. Many thanks to the hardworking archivists who've made this information, including videos and photos, publicly accessible.

I wish I could personally thank all my special schoolfriends for the big difference they made to my childhood. A few, including Amelia (then in Sussex), Marion (then at Caux School) and Jane (then in Somerset), I still see, and I hope I've shown them over the years how important their friendship has been! Others, such as Liz and Libs at my English boarding schools, I lost touch with almost immediately after leaving, so sadly I've never had the chance to reminisce with them, let alone explain myself and make amends for my secrecy.

Particular thanks go to Kevin Geary, Marion Porteous, Patrick Conner, Mary Lean, Virginia Gay and

Robert Saxton for their ideas, queries and support on the manuscript. Also to Louis, Jack, Rachel, Freya, Olive, Anna, Hari and Toby of the newest generations in Chérie and Bill's family. Their spirit and strength will doubtless carry them through the present and future wars of ideas.

ABOUT THE AUTHOR

Judi Conner has worked internationally as a BBC Television journalist, media consultant, coach and trainer. She lives in Norfolk and London.